Living Diaper to Diaper

The publisher and the University of California Press Foundation gratefully acknowledge the generous support of the Anne G. Lipow Endowment Fund in Social Justice and Human Rights.

Living Diaper to Diaper

THE HIDDEN CRISIS OF
POVERTY AND MOTHERHOOD

Jennifer Randles

UNIVERSITY OF CALIFORNIA PRESS

University of California Press
Oakland, California

Portions of this manuscript have been adapted, with permission, from the following previously published works:

Jennifer Randles, "Addressing Diaper Need as Racial Stratification Through Intersectional Family Justice." *Journal of Marriage and Family* 84, no. 5 (2022): 1408–1426.

Jennifer Randles, "Fixing a Leaky U.S. Social Safety Net: Diapers, Policy, and Low-Income Families." *Russell Sage Foundation Journal of the Social Sciences* 8, no. 5 (2022): 166–183.

Jennifer Randles, "'Willing To Do Anything for My Kids': Inventive Mothering, Diapers, and the Invisible Inequalities of Carework." *American Sociological Review* 86, no. 1 (2021): 35–59.

Jennifer Randles, "'Why Don't They Just Use Cloth?': Gender Policy Vacuums and the Inequalities of Diapering." *Gender & Society* 36, no. 2 (2022): 214–238.

Jennifer Randles and Jennifer Sherman, "Diaper Despair and Deflecting Inequalities." *Contexts* 22, no. 1 (2023): 12–17.

Library of Congress Cataloging-in-Publication Data

Names: Randles, Jennifer M., author.
Title: Living diaper to diaper : the hidden crisis of poverty and
    motherhood / Jennifer Randles.
Description: Oakland, California : University of California Press, [2026] |
    Includes bibliographical references and index.
Identifiers: LCCN 2025034120 (print) | LCCN 2025034121 (ebook) |
    ISBN 9780520401198 (cloth) | ISBN 9780520401204 (paperback) |
    ISBN 9780520401211 (ebook)
Subjects: LCSH: POVERTY—UNITED STATES. | LOW-INCOME MOTHERS—
    UNITED STATES. | DIAPERS—SOCIAL ASPECTS—UNITED STATES. | POOR
    FAMILIES—UNITED STATES.
Classification: LCC HC110.P6 R36 2026 (print) | LCC HC110.P6 (ebook)
LC record available at https://lccn.loc.gov/2025034120
LC ebook record available at https://lccn.loc.gov/2025034121

GPSR Authorized Representative: Easy Access System Europe,
Mustamäe tee 50, 10621 Tallinn, Estonia, gpsr.requests
@easproject.com

35 34 33 32 31 30 29 28 27 26
10 9 8 7 6 5 4 3 2 1

To Bridget, my beloved mother,
the one whose love and labor diapered me, and
Bridget, my daring daughter,
the one I was fortunate enough to diaper

Contents

List of Illustrations

Acknowledgments

To the parents who confided their diaper stories to me, thank you for teaching me what intensive mothering really looks like. Your inventiveness in the face of overwhelming challenges holds many lessons for us all about the true meaning of "good" mothering. Thank you for trusting me to relay your individual stories authentically, to put them in a larger social context, and to ensure that they live on in the pages of this book—and have impacts beyond them. I hope that I have done justice to these stories by expanding their reach, not just extracting their content, and that your voices bring visibility and understanding to a problem from which far too many families suffer.

To the diaper advocates who shared their valuable time and wisdom despite busy schedules running diaper banks, educating the public about diaper poverty and inequalities, and striving to meet a community need that few before them recognized, thank you for teaching me how a diaper is indeed more than a diaper. Your work is necessary and inspiring.

To the editorial team at the University of California Press, especially Naomi Schneider and Aline Dolinh, thank you for recognizing the value of the book, seeing it into print, and working with me to find just the right title. The research for and writing of this book were generously funded and supported by the American Sociological Association and National Science Foundation Fund for the Advancement of the Discipline and the College of Social Sciences at California State University, Fresno.

Thank you to my qualitative research writing group partners who read nearly every word of yet another book: Daisy Rooks, Jennifer Sherman, Jennifer Utrata, and Kerry Woodward. Your feedback, encouragement, and constant reminders that diapers are indeed sociological—and your brilliant advice about how to convince others of that—were invaluable. Without them I would not have gotten the project off the ground, and it certainly would never have resulted in this book.

Thank you to my generous friends, family members, and colleagues who engaged in ongoing conversations or provided helpful feedback that allowed me to hone ideas and make this book so much better than it would have been otherwise. I especially thank Amber Crowell, Tracy Randles Orrick, Sharon Brooks, Joya Misra, Jennifer Reich, and Sarah Halpern-Meekin.

To Elizabeth Lowham, thank you for encouraging me to bring every aspect of myself as a scholar to a new role during the two years I finished this book. I'm especially grateful for all the coffee, tea, and support that helped me get through the last long phase of seeing this book to fruition.

To Laurel Westbrook, thank you for helping me hatch so many of the ideas that infuse this book, putting up with all my diapers puns, and reeling in my alliteration when it got out of hand. Your friendship, encouragement, and love sustain me and my work in so many ways.

To others in my given and created family, thank you for the love, support, and constant questioning about when this book would finally be out. I knew you kept asking because you wanted to read it and that you really will when it is published.

To Christine Bailey and Bill Becker, you continue to inspire and convince me that I won the in-law lottery.

To Bridget and Bennie Randles, your enthusiasm for this project and this book meant the world to me. Mom, thank you for letting me interview you about your experience of diapering me, and for sharing in such vivid detail how you ran diaper pins through your hair. That story has become one of my favorite memories.

To Patsy Clement, I hope you can hold this book in your hands when it is published, knowing in your own way how your love and story of paper diapers inspired it.

To the late Dorothy Randles, who changed many of my paper diapers, I still miss you every day two decades after your passing and know you would have been this book's most avid reader. I am so fortunate for the group of mothers whose love, labor, and care wrap around me each day.

To Craig, you remain awesome—an awesome partner, an awesome co-parent, and an all-around awesome person with whom to travel this serendipitous life. I'm certain you changed more diapers than I did, and I'm so grateful for that and all it represents. Thank you for believing in this project from the beginning and seeing it through to the end. Mostly, thank you for truly loving me and embracing all that matters to me. I promise not to get too many new plants when this book comes out.

Finally, to Bridget, it has been a privilege to watch you grow up alongside this project. Its seeds were planted when you were still in diapers, and I wrote the final words of this book when you hit your double-digit era. Thank you for letting me share our diaper story and the insight it provided. I knew that I had chosen the right topic when you could articulate why this research mattered when you were three years old. You brilliantly said, "Some babies don't have diapers? But babies need diapers! That's not fair. All mommies, daddies, and babies should have diapers." I couldn't have said it better myself.

1. Introduction

INTERSECTING INEQUALITIES OF DIAPER DILEMMAS

"Everything I do is for her because I know how easy it would be for her to get taken from me," said Aisha when we met on a warm April afternoon in a fast-food restaurant parking lot.[1] She lifted the T-shirt from her torso to expose several fraying holes and stuck out her right foot to show me where the strap of her worn gray flip-flop was starting to detach from the sole. "You see, I wasn't lying. I told you I'm still wearing the same clothes and shoes as when I was pregnant. I have to buy the diapers instead. When you have a kid, there's no focusing on you. You have to take care of their needs, from changing the diaper to making sure they're not hungry. That takes a lot."

Aisha—twenty years old, Black, and a former foster youth—was a proud mother to eight-month-old Shannon. Paid for mostly through an emergency Section 8 housing voucher received by Aisha's boyfriend and Shannon's father, Cedrick, they all lived in a one-room, five-hundred-square-foot apartment with Cedrick's fifteen-year-old brother Travis. Aisha received $680 a month in cash aid and earned $350 more through her job sorting donations for a housing assistance organization. Because of his severe asthma and sleep apnea, Cedrick struggled to work. Instead, he cared for Shannon while Aisha worked, a necessary arrangement given that the cost of childcare for an infant would have far exceeded Aisha's

1

combined income and aid. Aisha and Cedrick would also have needed to provide about thirty-five disposable diapers per week while Shannon was in daycare. "It really brings [Cedrick] down that he can't provide more for his daughter," Aisha shared with me, "that I have to work because he can't. But because he takes care of her, we can stretch the diapers." Thankful that the housing voucher covered most of the rent, Aisha sighed nevertheless. "It's still hard because other bills have to be paid. We've still got to buy the diapers. Nothing else covers the diapers, not WIC, not food stamps."

That public programs didn't cover them was one reason Aisha worried more about getting Shannon's diapers than ensuring they had enough food. She could use her cash aid and income to pay for diapers, but the eighty-five dollars a month Aisha usually spent on two boxes of 120-count diapers took almost 10 percent of her combined aid and take-home pay. That didn't include wipes and the diaper cream needed to prevent diaper rash on Shannon's sensitive skin. "It's a huge dilemma for me," Aisha explained. "I need to save money, but if I don't buy the more expensive diapers, she breaks out and wakes up in the middle of the night. I've seen diaper rashes that bleed. I don't want her to go through that. I can just keep wearing these holey clothes and shoes until she's potty trained."

Aisha had tried other strategies to get diapers. She asked for help from her welfare case worker, only to be told, "You already get cash aid. Why is it so hard for you to get diapers?" Aisha responded, "When you have to pay the rent, your food stamps don't cover everything, and your household has other needs, balancing each month is hard. It's not that we don't want to get the diapers or just don't like spending money. We always run out of stuff. The last thing I want to do is run out of anything for her. Heaven help us if we run out of diapers." Yet Aisha frequently found herself scrounging for diaper money immediately after fastening Shannon's last clean diaper. "I can't tell you how many times I've had to go diaper shopping when she's literally wearing our last clean one or it's already full," she admitted. Without transportation to a nearby discount supermarket, Aisha often had to buy smaller three-count packs at the corner store that cost up to three dollars—nearly four times as much per diaper bought in bulk boxes. Neither welfare nor heaven were much help to Aisha in these situations.

Aisha got a little help from a local charity that gave out diapers every Wednesday. But that too presented challenges, as she told me:

They'll give you free diapers for your baby. It's just hard because you have to buy a bus pass, find transportation, get from work to downtown. They usually want you to bring the baby so they can verify that you have a kid, but having the baby on the bus is a hassle. It's a lot just to get what you need. I don't blame them. There are a lot of people that like to scam the system, but there are more people who really need the help. All that to get fifteen diapers, maybe twenty. That will last three days, less if she's sick.

Aisha received diapers at these weekly giveaways only twice. The time, money, and hassle weren't worth "free" diapers for a few days. She therefore had to devise other strategies to get diapers and diaper money. Aisha cleaned neighbors' houses, sold recyclable cans, and joined diaper borrow-and-swap groups with friends. She ate cheap foods like noodles, cereal, and tortillas for most meals. "I got to feel full for as little money as possible," Aisha told me. "I feel better as a parent when I know she has what she needs. It's a different hunger." Always needing the money for diapers instead, Aisha couldn't remember the last time she bought her own period products, underwear, or deodorant.

However, there was one strategy to which she wasn't willing to resort: cloth diapers. As a poor mother of color who lived with the constant fear of losing her daughter to the child welfare system (as her own mother had), Aisha couldn't risk using a type of diaper others might deem inappropriate. She explained:

> You really have to be careful with those. If you start walking in public with your kid, they might see it as a kid in rags. It's no longer back in the day when there were no normal disposable diapers. What if you went in front of a judge, and you had to say, "I didn't have diapers or diaper money, so I used cloth diapers"? If your kid pees in a cloth diaper, it could soak right through. I'm pretty sure they can take your kid based on what you believe, and if you believe cloth is better than Huggies, that's your right, but I wouldn't do it. . . . It's embarrassing to have to ask for diapers for your own kid because it comes with questions of whether you're taking care of her. The last thing we want in our lives is [Child Protective Services], especially when you've been in the foster care system.

Although cloth could be a stopgap option when disposables ran out, Aisha was afraid that anything but a "normal" diaper on Shannon could trigger suspicion of her fitness as a mother. Besides, Aisha didn't have the money to invest in a full set of cloth diapers, her apartment lacked washer and dryer hookups, and the nearby laundromat cost six dollars a load. The exigencies of poverty, racist stigma, and a weak social safety net intersected to make expensive disposables a necessity for Shannon. Providing enough diapers evoked something deeper for Aisha than making sure Shannon was clean and dry. It meant that she was a good mother "trying my hardest for my kid so she doesn't end up in the system. My baby may not be wearing name-brand diapers, but she has what she needs." Aisha still expressed regret. "I wish I could give her so much more. I'm sure a lot of people see parents like me struggling with diapers and think, 'Not my kid, not my problem.' They get to go home to their kids every day and not worry. Their kids don't want for diapers." That Shannon did was a daily dilemma Aisha worked hard to manage, often at the cost of her own needs and comfort.

Aisha's dilemma is not rare. Nearly half of American mothers of young children experience this problem called *diaper need*, not having enough diapers to keep their infants dry, comfortable, and healthy without sacrificing other essentials.[2] But as Aisha's story suggests, *needing* diapers wasn't the full extent of her diaper struggles. Much of her distress derived from the shame and lack of support connected to not having enough. Need is merely the state of requiring something. But within the broader context of social meanings and systems—such as hygiene norms, parenting ideologies, and gender, race, and class inequalities—the subjective experience of lacking necessities like diapers is fraught with unfairness and feelings of fault that the need itself doesn't fully capture. Aisha also struggled with what I call *diaper despair*, the emotional anguish, physical suffering, and social stigma associated with managing diaper need and indignity connected to it. Related but distinct, diaper need and diaper despair reflect our society's failure to adequately provide for families in need and then layer blame and shame on top. This dual distress is a deeply personal problem for struggling families like Aisha, Shannon, and Cedrick who don't have full access to the basic necessities required to stay fed, safe, and clean. It is also a uniquely American social problem that reflects how family life, inequality, and the US social safety net have changed in recent decades to undermine low-income parents' abilities to provide essentials for their youngest children.

Within the folds of a diaper is a profound sociological story of stratified access to basic human needs and public efforts—and failures—to address it. This book tells that story and the stories of mothers like Aisha who not only struggle to get enough diapers for their children but also experience more and more severe diaper despair due to intersecting inequalities of gender, race, and class. These stories teach us why we should all care about diapers, a necessity of early childcare that can so easily be taken for granted or seem inconsequential unless your baby doesn't have them.

NOT OUR KIDS, BUT STILL OUR PROBLEM: WHY WE SHOULD ALL CARE ABOUT DIAPER DESPAIR

My memories of diapering my own daughter are vague. Perhaps that's due to the mind's tendency to blur the less enjoyable aspects of parenting—in this case, dealing with the literal shit of childrearing. It's more likely that what I remember—and what I had the privilege to ignore or forget—reveals how inequalities shape the most minute aspects of parenting. I do vividly recall the excitement I felt when I had reason to buy a box of diapers. I was barely seven months' pregnant and eagerly preparing the nursery with a crib, rocking chair, closet of baby clothes, and changing table stocked with lotion, wipes, and stacks of diapers in three sizes. Family and friends recommended having a few different brands and sizes on hand before the baby was born in anticipation of any allergic reactions or a baby big enough to outgrow newborn and size 1 diapers within the first few weeks. Because I had the time, money, and car trunk space to spare, I waited to buy diapers when the store where I usually shopped ran a sale on diapers and offered gift cards if I spent $100 or more on baby supplies. With those discounts I paid about a dime a diaper. I drove them home, put some on the changing table, stuck the boxes in the closet, and didn't give the diapers another thought until I delivered my daughter two months later. Planning to return to work shortly after the birth, it never crossed my mind to use cloth. But I knew friends who did, and their families all looked like mine—two married, white parents with high-wage jobs that offered paid family leave and afforded homeownership with personal washers and dryers.

Until my daughter was potty trained when she was two-and-a-half years old, I kept a couple of boxes on hand at home, took a package to her daycare every other Monday morning, and packed several bags with enough diapers for two days. When my baby had diaper rash or diarrhea, I changed her more frequently to keep her delicate skin dry. If her diaper was still dry when I undressed her for bath time, I threw it away and put her in a fresh diaper after bathing. If a little poop or pee got on the new diaper while I was changing her, I tossed it and gave no thought to the occasional double diaper change. Once when I was at her pediatrician's office, I had forgotten to restock the diaper bag. A kind nurse gave me two diapers and the benefit of the doubt that my lack of diapers was a simple slip of the mind amid the sleep deprivation and haste of new parenthood. When out in public, my daughter had a droopy diaper more times than I could count. Yet I never once worried what others would think of me, my daughter, or my mothering abilities as I waited until it was convenient to change her.

Though this all may seem normal for many parents, these are diaper decisions made possible by privilege. I didn't make diaper choices. I *had* diaper choices. And no one called me a bad mom for any of them. The nearly half of mothers in the United States who struggle to get enough diapers for their babies don't have this same experience of diapering. They don't get the same opportunities to ignore or forget. Those who face diaper despair keep track of every diaper—where it is, how long it will last, and exactly how much time they have to get more before the last diaper becomes too full. They keep strict diaper budgets and running mental tallies of their limited diaper supplies, and they know who can be counted on among family and friends to help with diapers or diaper money in a pinch. Like Aisha, they go without their own food, clothes, and other necessities to buy their babies' diapers and yet still worry if they are good enough moms doing right by their children. When their infants have diaper rash or tummy troubles, it's more than an uncomfortable or sick baby; it's a crisis that requires more diapers. Previously worn, unsoiled diapers get put back on after bath time, and clean diapers marked with the accidental drop of poop or pee are never thrown away. Changing diapers wasn't my favorite part of early parenting, but I never had to expend much effort or energy to ensure I had enough to change.

With little money to buy them and no room to transport and store them, mothers facing diaper need cannot buy three boxes at once. Like

Aisha, they often buy only three single diapers at a time because that's all they can afford at a store they can access by foot or bus. They don't tend to use cloth diapers. But they know how to make diapers out of almost any cloth or paper item around the house—paper towels, toilet paper, wash rags, pillowcases, and more. If employed or in school, they sometimes miss work or class—and the pay and education that could help pull their families out of poverty—because they can't afford the disposable diapers almost all daycare centers and childcare providers require. More likely to be poor mothers of color, parents who experience diaper need and despair are not as easily given the benefit of the doubt when they are without diapers in the presence of professionals. They constantly worry about being in public where a diaper deemed too wet or dirty is an indelible sign of unfit parenting. My own daughter was still in diapers and not much older than Shannon when I met Aisha. In a devastating irony, as a white affluent mother who never worried about the watchful eyes of the child welfare system or where my next diaper would come from, I spent significantly less per diaper than Aisha. Beyond that, for me, diapering required none of the sacrifices that cost Aisha far more than diaper money itself.

My and Aisha's radically different experiences of diapering our daughters are not without consequence. They take a toll on children, parents, families, healthcare and educational systems, and so many other spheres of our society. Like Shannon, almost half of infants and toddlers in the United States live in poor or low-income families. In 2018, when I interviewed Aisha, a household of four people was considered "poor" according to government guidelines if they brought in $25,100 or less annually in combined income from work and welfare.[3] As the primary breadwinner in her household, Aisha received in welfare cash aid and earned from her job a total of $12,360 a year. The household's rent and food assistance were worth about as much but still didn't pull Aisha's family above the poverty threshold in California, one of the more generous states when it comes to safety net policies and government basic needs assistance. Sadly, this meant that Shannon was still part of the more than 20 percent of American children under three who live in poverty. Age is highly predictive of one's likelihood of being poor in the United States, such that individuals sixty-five and older have the lowest poverty rates and are only about half as likely as children to live in poverty. As infants grow to be toddlers, young children, preteens, and then teenagers, their poverty rates decline with every stage. In a particularly American twist on inequality and deprivation, the very youngest children in greatest need of diapers are the poorest.

Shannon, as a Black child growing up in the United States, had a two in five chance of being poor, nearly three times the likelihood of growing up in poverty as that of white children like my daughter Bridget. That Bridget always had enough diapers while Shannon often went without is not a coincidence. It is the result of persistent racial prejudices and a long history of institutionalized racism that deny basic needs like diapers to some children while others have access to more than they could ever use. Families raising the youngest children, especially children of color, struggle most to access basic needs, with serious and widespread consequences for infants' and toddlers' health and development. Parents facing diaper despair often must stretch diaper supplies, including using diapers that no longer fit, creating makeshift diapers, having children go diaper-free, reusing dried diapers, or leaving the same diaper on for days.[4] Ill-fitting diapers, using diapers made from nonbreathable materials, and infrequent diaper changes can increase children's risk for urinary tract infections, diaper dermatitis (or diaper rash), and yeast infections in the diaper area.[5] All three conditions are primary reasons children visit pediatricians and emergency rooms, and they can become severe enough for hospitalization. Infants without enough diapers can also experience sleep disruptions and developmental delays, such as later crawling or walking.[6]

Lest we are quick to judge and condemn parents who resort to diaper-stretching strategies, we should instead ask ourselves why we live in a society where leaving on a dirty diaper—or sacrificing other basic needs to afford clean ones—has become necessary for so many families. In a cultural context where babies are expected to wear diapers and parents are tasked with providing them as part of responsible caregiving, leaving a diaper on longer can be an act of parental love. A baby without a diaper, or worse still, a baby covered in their own urine or feces, invites stigma and shame. Ultimate judgment may be foisted upon the parent, but without a diaper there is no dignity, only disgrace, for a very young child. When faced with impossible choices, a parent may reasonably and affectionately choose a dirty diaper over no diaper at all.

A growing number of families make decisions rooted in diaper despair. Prior to the COVID-19 pandemic, research found that about one in three families with young children in the United States struggled to get enough diapers.[7] More recent research has found that diaper insecurity affects closer to half of families raising children younger than four years old.[8] Like material hardship in general, diaper need is closely associated with poverty, but it is neither universal among nor exclusive to poor families. When asked if they ever don't have enough diapers to change their children as often as they would like, most poor and low-income parents (about three in five) indicate on surveys that they experience diaper need.[9] Yet these numbers could reflect how surveys measure diaper need as much as its true prevalence. It's possible that parents are reluctant to answer yes to any question that implies they are not adequately caring for their children by changing diapers less often. Preferences for diaper-changing frequency also vary by children's age, degree of skin sensitivity, and type of diapers used. Nevertheless, the best research efforts to gauge the extent of diaper need indicate that most poor and low-income families struggle with some degree of diaper insecurity. Many families we might not expect to struggle also report diaper need. Although estimates vary across studies, about one in three middle-income families making more than $50,000 per year meet the criteria for diaper insecurity, as do about one in five high-income families bringing in $100,000 or more annually. Moreover, families with recent experiences of job loss and those whose economic situations had worsened over the past year were most likely to report that they changed their children less often than they would like, suggesting that diaper need is associated not only with low income but also with unstable income.[10] All told, diaper access seems to be particularly sensitive to financial stress and uncertainty.

We should all care about diaper despair, even if the children in our own lives never want for diapers, because it's a distinctive window onto many challenges facing families with young children in the United States. It points to controversies over who should have children, who is ultimately responsible for meeting their needs, and what we're all obligated to provide for our youngest society members. Diapers have become an issue of reproductive justice, which entails equal rights to have (or not have) children and to parent those children safely and humanely. As access to contraception and abortion rights in the United States have been limited in recent years, it becomes increasingly important to consider how stratified access to basic childcare needs like diapers reflect broader race, class, and gender inequalities related to who has self-determination over their reproductive choices. Those choices include not only the ability to determine if and when to become a parent but also access to and control over basic resources needed to parent in healthy and dignified ways.

As one of the largest sources of postconsumer waste, diapers raise important questions about childrearing's impacts on the environment.[11] If you have ever worn or used a disposable diaper, it is still sitting almost fully intact in a landfill, where it will continue to decompose for at least the next five hundred years. In 2018, 3.3 million tons of throwaway diapers used in the United States were landfilled, and manufacturing disposable diapers has an even greater environmental impact than their disposal.[12] Given the significant water and energy required to grow cotton for and continually wash and dry them, cloth diapers may not necessarily be a more environmentally friendly choice.[13] Carbon emissions created by disposable and reusable diapers are roughly equivalent, given typical laundry habits and appliance efficiency; cloth diapers are only "greener" if they are acquired secondhand (or used for subsequent children), washed in cool water in full loads, and fully line-dried.[14] So-called "ecofriendly" diapers made of more sustainably sourced materials—a third option—cost up to three times as much as standard disposables and are neither fully compostable nor biodegradable.[15] Ergo, all widely available, socially acceptable diapering options still take a significant toll on the planet.

Major childcare agencies that issue health safety guidelines recommend single-use disposable diapers to reduce fecal contamination in daycare settings.[16] Although using cloth diapers in childcare facilities is now legal in most states, many childcare providers still cannot or will not use cloth diapers. Care facilities that are willing and able to accommodate cloth diapers typically charge more for tuition, raising the price of what is already one of the most expensive costs of childrearing and making cloth diapering cost-prohibitive for even middle-class families. Fewer than three in five infants and toddlers in the United States are cared for exclusively by parents, in part because safety net policies increasingly force parents to work as a condition of receiving assistance. This means that most children in the United States spend a significant portion of their awake hours in the care of childcare providers who are often reluctant to use cloth diapers for reasons of safety, storage, and labor.[17]

At home, cloth diapering among financially strapped families tends to cost *more* than disposables. Families without in-home washers and dryers—or without homes—cannot easily get to public laundromats with bags of dirty diapers in tow. Nor can they readily afford the cost to wash and dry each load. It costs around two to four dollars to wash a load of laundry and two to three dollars to dry, totaling four to seven dollars per load. Assuming a family washes a load of diapers every other day, the costs to launder cloth diapers would be nearly the equivalent of the average monthly cost for disposables. That doesn't include any start-up costs for cloth diapers in different sizes or accessories, such as special bags to store soiled diapers. Even if they could access and afford public laundry facilities, parents know they would face stigma when washing urine- and feces-covered garments in shared spaces where they risk others' social disgust. Cleaning dirty diapers can be gross and unsanitary no matter where one washes them. But a key difference is that more affluent families can do this in the privacy of their own homes, where disgust is individualized not a public matter susceptible to social scorn and shame. In short, not buying disposables doesn't really save parents money or embarrassment when they must still buy, store, and clean cloth diapers.

The cloth conundrum isn't just about which diaper type is cheaper. The transition from universal cloth diapering to disposables also reflects changing gender dynamics of work and cultural understandings of "good" motherhood and proper childrearing. The rising popularity of single-use diapers coincided with the influx of American mothers into the paid labor force. From 1975 to 2019—when disposables became the dominant diaper type in the United States—the employment rate of mothers with children under three years old nearly doubled from 34.3 to 63.8 percent.[18] Although disposable diapers have always been a convenience commodity that helped mothers manage the dual demands of employment and unpaid childcare, advertising highlighted disposables as a product that allowed mothers to provide optimal maternal love and care.[19] Capitalizing on gendered norms of maternal domesticity, cloth diapers were discouraged through messages that soiled cloth diapers were unsanitary and

irritated infants' delicate skin, and hence "good" mothers chose disposables. Cloth diapering never regained popularity in the United States,
where more than 95 percent of infants now wear disposables most or all
the time.[20] Whether families opt for disposables isn't society's biggest
social and environmental diaper dilemma. It's that the capitalist labor
market, work and family policies, childcare infrastructure, and standards
of parenting practically demand disposability.

Collective diaper options and choices—and stratified access to those
choices—have wide and long-lasting consequences. Each American child
will use on average five thousand to six thousand diapers before they are
toilet trained.[21] In recent years more than 3.5 million babies have been
born annually in the United States, where nearly all infants wear disposable diapers and almost half live in low-income, poor, or deeply poor families.[22] That means a lot of trash (about twenty-one billion diapers landfilled each year) and a lot of diaper need and despair. People in one of the
richest and most technologically advanced countries, especially one that
purportedly supports families and values children, should be able to
resolve these personal and social diaper dilemmas. To do so, we must
learn to see a diaper as a multifaceted and complex social artifact, one that
simultaneously represents a feat of modern technology, a basic bodily
need for health and dignity, a conduit of parental care and love, a capitalist
commodity, and ultimately garbage. To address diaper despair, it is especially important to recognize diapers as a necessary public good.

A DIAPER-SHAPED HOLE IN THE US SOCIAL SAFETY NET

Urinating and defecating are biological requirements, but norms and
practices around how we contain, manage, and dispose of bodily waste—
and who is expected to pay for materials and do the work that requires—
are social and cultural. Diapering is thus not just a physical process but an
economic and political one shaped by inequalities and power dynamics
that structure who has access to diapers and the ramifications of lacking
them. Some of these ramifications are physical and psychological. Families
struggling with diaper need are also more likely to struggle with other
forms of deprivation such as food scarcity and housing insecurity.[23]

Parents' efforts to fill their diaper gaps can, as in Aisha's case, lead to skimping on other essentials. Diaper need is an adverse childhood experience linked to poverty and worse mental and physical health outcomes during both childhood and adulthood.[24] Mothers like Aisha who must manage diaper insecurity are more likely to experience depression and anxiety.[25] This risk is especially high when the postpartum period coincides with high diaper demand.[26]

Given diapers' central role in early childcare, parents often experience low parental self-efficacy—a feeling of having failed as a provider and caregiver—if they cannot get enough diapers. Beyond the work of managing limited diaper supplies, diaper insecurity is about managing the stigma, self-doubt, and social and economic fallout of lacking diapers. Although both mothers and fathers manage diaper need, women bear the brunt of diaper despair. Not only are women more likely to provide childcare in general, but they are also especially likely to do the bulk of care for young children, make the majority of household purchasing decisions, and perform most of the cognitive labor associated with anticipating and monitoring family members' needs.[27] In short, overall, mothers change, buy, and worry about diapers more than fathers. This gendered care labor is firmly rooted in taken-for-granted cultural norms in the United States dictating that young children wear diapers and that individual parents, primarily mothers, provide them as part of responsible childrearing. Expensive disposable diapers have become ubiquitous and near universal in the United States, just as growing low-wage work, rising childcare costs, and a fraying social safety net have made it more difficult for parents to access and afford them. Diaper need is a form of relative poverty that denies parents' and children's well-being, dignity, and full participation in a society where diapers have become a costly necessity of early childhood central to the social organization of caregiving in late capitalism.

Yet diaper need and diaper despair are neither happenstance nor inevitable. They are a result of deliberate economic and policy choices and abysmally low levels of public support for raising children, especially very young children. On its face the modern disposable diaper is a piece of absorbent layered polymer fabric affixed by side adhesive tabs. Within those layers is a continuously unfolding social history that reflects changing hygiene norms and demands of a capitalist economy rooted in an

individualistic two-parent nuclear family ethic. The history of diapering—
the diverse items fashioned into diapers, how and when diapers were
changed, and who did the hard labor of diapering and cleaning diapers—
is fundamentally a story of changing work and family dynamics deeply
fraught with gender, race, and class inequalities. Mothers and other
women caregivers and domestic workers in prior generations laboriously
washed diapers by hand as part of intensive and time-consuming near-
daily laundry. The physical, mental, and economic costs of diapering have
not disappeared as ever-more sophisticated diaper technologies have been
developed to help families manage the messier and laborious demands of
caring for infants and toddlers in a society that does exceedingly little to
offset expenses of raising young children.

These diaper dilemmas are experienced individually among parents like
Aisha whose daily lives are profoundly shaped by the strife and shame of
insufficient diapers. But those dilemmas are created by the social conditions of poverty, paltry safety nets, and public refusal to bear the collective
costs of raising the next generation. Childrearing is particularly expensive
in a country without universal public childcare, where the average cost of
full-time facility-based care for an infant is higher in most states than the
cost to attend a public university.[28] The ubiquitous use of disposable diapers in the United States is a direct result of the reality that affording diapers and the myriad other costs of childrearing requires most parents to
work outside the home for pay. Especially since mid-1990s welfare reform,
access to many safety net policies—including welfare cash aid, food stamps,
and tax credits—have increasingly required employment as a condition of
receiving assistance.[29] Ironically, despite the transition to a work-based
safety net, policies intended to cover childcare so that parents can work or
attend school, such as the Child Care Development Block Grant, are not
entitlements; only a fraction of eligible families receive assistance, and the
amount doesn't always cover families' full costs. As one of the very few
countries without universal paid family leave after the birth or adoption of
a child, many parents cannot afford to stay home with their children,
where using cloth can be a more feasible diapering option.

Diaper need and despair are consequences of this financial precarity
that characterizes so much of American parenting among those who cannot access living-wage employment or sufficient public support to meet

their children's basic needs. Some parents of young children cannot afford to work due to intermittent and inconsistent schedules and low wages that don't amount to much more than the costs of infant childcare. Most daycare facilities require that parents provide numerous disposable diapers per day, which can cause parents to miss work and therefore the money needed to buy diapers.[30] The $100 average monthly diaper bill would use 8 percent of a full-time, year-round worker's salary if they earned a $7.25 federal minimum wage. Childcare and diaper expenses are among the many reasons that parents with infants and toddlers face the highest caregiving costs. Younger children also tend to have younger parents with less education and more time before they reach their peak earning years.[31]

While these economic and political factors create a context ripe for diaper need, fiscal and safety net policies intended to help low-income and poor families do not generally recognize diapers as a *need*. As of 2025, diapers are not covered by the largest public direct assistance programs, including the Supplemental Nutrition Assistance Program (SNAP) and the Special Supplemental Nutrition Program for Women, Infants, and Children (WIC). Intended specifically for food items only, SNAP and WIC categorize diapers as "unallowable expenses," along with alcohol, pet food, soap, and other nonfood hygiene items like menstrual supplies.[32] Although states may use Child Care Development Funds (CCDF) for diapers, childcare centers receiving CCDF subsidies are not required to provide them. With few exceptions state Medicaid programs provide diapers only as a qualifying medical expense for children over a certain age (at least three years) medically diagnosed as incontinent.

The political invisibility of diapers has another costly consequence. Because diapers aren't recognized as a qualified medical expense for most children, they are still taxed in many states at rates ranging from 2.5 to 7.5 percent. This doesn't include additional county and municipal taxes, which combined mean that some parents who can barely afford diapers are paying over 10 percent more in taxes for a need that the government does not officially recognize their children have. This is akin to how many US states tax menstrual pads and tampons, along with diapers, as "nonessential" discretionary items. Research on menstrual politics has analyzed how the "tampon tax"—also considered part of the "pink tax" on menstruators, most of whom are women—reflects public taboos and stigma that directly increase the social and economic costs of having a uterus.[33] Both menstrual products and diapers touch on issues of marginalized identities related to gender, age, and poverty. It is therefore no coincidence that hygiene items associated with the bodily and care needs of children and women remain mostly outside the purview of policy and public support.

Those who manage corporeal products deemed *waste* are typically afforded the lowest social status.[34] Women primarily perform carework involving menstrual blood, feces, and urine—labor that demands social invisibility due to how "contaminated" bodily products transgress personal boundaries and dignity. Doing the dirty work of diapering is not only devalued. Socially speaking, it's disgusting, not talked about in polite company, nor appropriate for political deliberation, especially when those deliberating are typically white, affluent men who have never changed a diaper or faced diaper despair. Disgust characterizes diaper need as a sociopolitical issue in another important way. Political scientist Ange-Marie Hancock coined the phrase *politics of disgust* to refer to an "emotion-laden response to long-standing beliefs about single, poor African American mothers that has spread epidemiologically to all" recipients of public aid programs.[35] Calling attention to multiple meanings of *disgust*, Hancock highlighted how public opinion of mothers like Aisha marginalized by intersecting inequalities of race, class, and gender reflects an instinctive, deep aversion to the notion that poor mothers of color need public support to raise children. Looking at diaper need through this political lens of disgust reveals why public opinion about diaper insecurity not only reflects repugnance toward dealing with bodily waste but also profound disapproval provoked by a sense of being "disgusted" with those who are presumably too poor to have children.

Social and political disgust associated with the basest and most basic bodily needs like urination and defecation is not equitable. Disgust is racialized, gendered, and shaped by norms of class and age. Recall the last time you walked into a public restroom. Did you pay to use it? What about the toilet paper, soap, and hand towels you used to clean yourself before returning to work, school, or your public outing? Many of us take for granted having free access to certain hygiene items in public bathrooms, so much so that the idea of carrying our own toilet paper in social spaces would seem peculiar and suspect. But there are other hygiene items—

infant diapers, wipes, menstrual products, and incontinence supplies—
that are not typically normalized as publicly provided, despite how such
items are equally necessary for staying clean, being comfortable, and
avoiding socially stigmatizing smells and stains. To put a finer point on it,
why is public toilet paper free but diapers and tampons are not?

One key reason is that users of these items tend to be of certain ages and
genders. Keep in mind that diapers are not just for the very young. Diapers
and adult briefs that contain urine and fecal leaks are typically used by
those younger than five and older than sixty-five. Bodies inevitably age, our
urinary tracts and bowels weaken, and life experiences like childbirth,
gravity, and illnesses accumulate, making incontinence a daily part of life
for older adults. If you are reading this, you've likely worn your last infant
diaper but not the last diaper of your life. Estimates suggest that more than
half of us will need adult incontinence products at some point, with sales
of adult diapers on track to soon outpace infant diapers and every other
paper-based household product.[36] Given limited public support for caregiving of the young and prejudices toward the elderly, it isn't surprising
that we accept little social responsibility for providing these items.

Gender also shapes which hygiene items we recognize as necessary and
worthy of social support. Not only are women the primary demographic
for menstrual supply use, but due to pregnancy, childbirth, menopause,
greater susceptibility to urinary tract infections, and longer life expec-
tancy, women are more likely to experience incontinence and for a longer
portion of their lives. More than 60 percent of women in the United States
experience incontinence at some point, about double or triple the proportion of men who do.[37] Furthermore, women and girls of all ages are disproportionately responsible for the labor of diapering the young and managing incontinence among those of all ages. This means that women pay
more—monetarily but also in stress, stigma, and shame—when these
items are neither available nor affordable. They also pay opportunity costs
when lacking hygiene supplies prevents them from going to school, working, and participating in public life.

The one form of direct public assistance that can be used to purchase
hygiene items—Temporary Assistance for Needy Families (TANF) or cash
aid—is increasingly limited. Before mid-1990s welfare reform, nearly
three in four families in poverty received direct cash aid; now fewer than

one in five poor families do.[38] Time limits, sanctions, and work requirements passed as part of welfare reform legislation have undercut eligibility for unrestricted cash assistance, especially for poor mothers of color. Welfare reform also resulted in significantly greater state discretion over how federal TANF block grants could be spent. Consequently, states now spend only about one dollar for every five dollars received through TANF grants on direct basic assistance.[39] Benefit amounts have barely increased since the mid-1990s to offset inflation and increased living costs. In most states the value of TANF benefits has decreased by at least 20 percent during the past two decades.

However, the work-based safety net, particularly tax credits for low-wage parents, has become stronger. With the demise of welfare came the rise of the Earned Income Tax Credit (EITC) in 1993 followed by an expanded Child Tax Credit (CTC) in 1997. The goal of these tax credits was to raise full-time, year-round workers with dependent children above the poverty threshold. For many families, tax credits did just that. In 2018 the EITC was responsible for lifting more than three million children above the poverty line and lessening the severity of poverty for six million more. There was an even greater poverty-reducing effect of the EITC when combined with the CTC, which together lifted 5.5 million children out of poverty while making poverty less severe for 6.4 million additional children.[40] A key part of the contemporary social safety net, tax credits provide crucial wage supplements to poor and near-poor working families. Yet they were designed to support people with low-income not parents with no income, meaning that families most likely to struggle with diaper scarcity—those who make very little in earnings or nothing at all—have not benefited much from tax credits.[41]

At the same time, the inflation-adjusted cost of diapers has increased. In 2000 the average cost of disposable diapers per infant per year was $515, or about $970 in 2025 dollars.[42] Now the average cost of diapering one infant is closer to $1,200 per year, with diaper costs continuing to rise. In all fifty states, TANF benefits are insufficient to pay utilities and rent for a modest two-bedroom apartment, and no state benefit is above 60 percent of the poverty line, leaving little money for diapers.[43] The $100 average monthly diaper bill for one child would alone use 9 percent to 49 percent of the average state TANF benefit for a single-parent family of three.[44] The fraying cash aid social safety net has particularly stark consequences for families of color facing diaper need. Because poverty rates for Black and Latine households are more than double the poverty rates for white households in the United States, young children of color are significantly more likely to live in families that struggle to access diapers.[45] The proportion of federal and state welfare funding that goes directly to families as cash aid has dwindled in all states and for families of all racial backgrounds in recent decades. Yet states with larger populations of Black and Latine children spend even less on direct cash aid.[46] This move away from basic support was not surprising considering welfare policy reform goals to promote "personal responsibility" and economic "self-sufficiency." Cash aid is no longer an entitlement if one meets government definitions of poverty or as a means for accessing necessities for survival, safety, and self-respect but rather a "benefit" one must earn through making appropriate work and family choices. The confluence of these changes has had particularly stark consequences for families of color struggling to access basic needs like diapers that cannot be bought using other targeted social assistance programs.

A social safety net that provides less support to poor families of color is one way racism shapes inequitable diaper access and affordability for Black mothers like Aisha. Another is how long-standing racist housing practices and policies like redlining have consolidated community and public resources in neighborhoods according to race. Due to residential segregation and the tendency for public services and commercial shops to be in predominantly white neighborhoods, families of color are less likely to live in or near areas with ready access to diaper services and big-box discount stores where they can purchase diapers in bulk at reduced prices. When their diaper supplies run low, parents of limited means are more likely to buy smaller packages of diapers for higher surge prices. Poor predominantly Black urban neighborhoods have the fewest supermarkets that sell discounted household goods like diapers, but more grocery and convenience stores that sell diapers at higher per-unit rates.[47] One more reason it's expensive to be poor and Black in the United States: Aisha often paid upwards of fifty cents per diaper, while I rarely spent half as much.

Although several federal bills have proposed providing public diaper assistance and recategorizing diapers as medically necessary, paving the way for tax exemptions and coverage of diapers by public programs, few have passed as of 2025. One promising exception is the federal Diaper Distribution Demonstration and Research Pilot, which began in 2022. Otherwise, during the post–welfare reform period, when many states passed family cap policies intended to limit additional childbearing among welfare recipients, there has been significant policy inertia around supporting this basic need of early childcare.[48] The struggles of caregivers (the vast majority of whom are women) to get enough diapers within a political system that doesn't recognize diapers as one of children's basic needs is perhaps the most perplexing diaper dilemma of all. Diapers certainly aren't the only necessity of early childcare not covered by existing safety net policies. Neither bottles and blankets, nor clothing and shoes are covered. There is no systematic policy that offsets the costs of baby shampoo, Band-Aids, thermometers, and over-the-counter medications. Families are also on their own to get items required by law such as car seats.

Are diapers symbolic of all such items that point to a hole in the safety net around many basic needs of childhood? Or is there something unique about diapers that sets them apart from other essentials families need to properly care for young children in ways our society deems necessary? The answer is both. Diapers are among many things young children need to stay clean, healthy, and safe. Along with diapering, parents are expected to feed, clothe, and shelter their babies, treat them when they are sick, and ensure their safety in and outside the home. Both children and parents suffer when their families don't have what they need to meet these fundamental responsibilities of early childrearing. In this way diapers are especially like clothes. Social norms and child welfare laws dictate that children wear suitable clothing—clean, protective, well-fitted, and seasonally appropriate—while childcare facilities require that parents bring multiple clean outfits for each child. Soiled, wet, tight, baggy, or revealing clothes can cause discomfort, embarrassment, and developmental delays, just as used or uncomfortable diapers can.

Yet diapers are also unique in important ways, leading to distinct concerns and differential costs linked to diaper insecurity. Early childcare items fall into two categories: durable and nondurable goods. Durable goods, such as cribs and car seats, are designed to last for several or more years and be used repeatedly over a long time. Nondurable goods like soap and food are consumed quickly, used once, and need to be replaced frequently. Diapers are a quintessential nondurable good. Babies go through multiple diapers daily starting at birth, upwards of twelve each day, requiring parents to stock up and replenish their diaper supplies early and often. Diapers are among the most expensive nondurable infant goods and a persistent rather than intermittent need. A bottle of baby shampoo that can last many months costs a few dollars, a bulk box of adhesive bandages for the occasional cut or scrape about the same. Most infant fevers, colds, and rashes go away quickly, making over-the-counter medications and creams, despite being expensive, only sporadic needs. But families must often pay fifty dollars or more on diapers at least every few weeks.

Clothes and food, especially infant formula, are nondurable necessities of early childhood most like diapers. Yet diapers still differ from both in ways that can make diapers harder to get for cash-strapped families. There are public programs that offset the cost of food, including WIC, which helps meet the nutritional needs of two in five infants in the United States.[49] Like diapers, clothes require constant changing but not as frequently, and there are many strategies families use to reduce children's clothing costs. Reusing clothes on multiple children, borrowing from others, hand-me-down networks, yard sales, thrifting, seasonal sales, buy-nothing groups, and children's charity closets are all common methods for accessing cheap or free kids' clothes. It also helps that infants get bigger fast, quickly moving from one size to the next and generating an abundance of barely used clothes. These strategies don't work as well for getting diapers, even cloth diapers. Due to hygiene concerns, charity and consignment shops typically won't accept or sell previously worn cloth diapers, which are categorized as used underwear even if clean. Except when donated to specific organizations like cloth diaper banks, many second-hand cloth diapers are sold by weight for converting into industrial rags.

Diapers are also unique as a basic need due to taken-for-granted presumptions that they are cheap, widely available, and have easy alternatives—namely cloth diapers. Yet they are increasingly expensive, hard to get if you lack funds, and don't have many socially acceptable, truly effective substitutes. For these reasons diapers and difficulties getting enough of them shape daily rhythms of family life during early child-care in ways that other basic needs often don't. That a young child needs to wear diapers around the clock only adds to the constant stress and strains of diaper insecurity, and running out can be a full-family crisis. We must mend the diaper-shaped hole in the US social safety net, which has been inadequately responsive to the needs of the country's youngest, poorest, and most marginalized residents. Fortunately there is a special group of people committed to leading those efforts.

THE NEW CBO ON THE BLOCK: THE EMERGENCE OF THE DIAPER BANK

To cope with growing diaper insecurity, families turn to a relatively new type of community benefit organization (CBO): the diaper bank. Diaper banks work like food banks by collecting monetary and in-kind donations for distribution to partner organizations and families in need. Since the first US diaper bank opened in 1994, hundreds of diaper banks have emerged across the country and thousands more organizations directly distribute diapers to families along with other services. Many diaper banks use a community partner model whereby they distribute diapers to agencies that address other family issues, including homelessness, food insecurity, refugee resettlement, and domestic violence.[50] It is no coincidence that the proliferation of diapers banks across the country coincided with welfare reform and the decades after, when the number of children living in deep poverty doubled.[51]

Diaper banks typically provide a supplemental supply of diapers to make up the difference between what families experiencing diaper insecurity can afford and how many diapers their children need. Known as the "diaper gap," most diaper-insecure families are short about ten to twelve diapers per week, and therefore need at least fifty diapers per child per month.[52] However, some distribute far fewer diapers, like the charity from which Aisha received only a couple days' worth of diapers. Others provide entire boxes of diapers intended to meet a child's full need. The nation's largest diaper banks operate out of massive warehouses, have multiple full-time paid staff, and distribute millions of disposable diapers each year. The smallest consist of lone unpaid volunteers who strive to serve at least a handful of families, sometimes by distributing a few hundred diapers each month from their homes or car trunks.

People who found and run diaper banks—self-referred "diaper bankers"—cite various personal and social reasons that inspired them to start diaper banking. Primarily women who are mothers and grandmothers, some experienced diaper need themselves with their own children and want to prevent other families' diaper despair. Faith motivates others to support their spiritual communities by offering diapers as a necessary item, almost like a tithe. Many are involved in philanthropic causes and clubs that specifically target health and economic needs of families, women, and children. Despite a wide variety of political affiliations and inclinations, almost all have come to see diaper banking as a tangible and necessary way of addressing an all-too-common problem of poverty in a system ill designed to meet basic needs of society's youngest and most vulnerable members. From their perspectives, handing out diapers can be a way to pay good fortune forward, serve a higher power, fortify the financial position of needy families through philanthropy, and resist inequality and oppression as a political act.

The growing network of diaper banks across the United States can therefore be understood as a social movement consisting of organized collective efforts intended to alter a fundamental aspect of society.[53] In 2016 the nation's more than three hundred diaper banks distributed fifty-two million diapers to more than 277,000 children, meeting 4 percent of the estimated need.[54] The number of diapers distributed annually has continued to increase, especially during the COVID-19 pandemic, when diaper banks reported two- to six-fold increases in diaper requests.[55] Diaper banks have become a significant part of the growing community-based safety net comprised of private and nonprofit organizations that help families meet basic needs unmet by government policies and programs. And many do more than distribute diapers. Diaper bankers are leading efforts to raise awareness of causes and consequences of diaper need and advocating for policies that can address it and similar inequities.

Founded in 2011, the National Diaper Bank Network (NDBN) represents an alliance of hundreds of member diaper banks and is the largest national organization advocating on behalf of policy solutions for diaper need. Funded as part of the philanthropic arm of Kimberly-Clark, maker of Huggies diapers, the NDBN allows community organizations to purchase truckloads of Huggies diapers for mere pennies each. The NDBN hosts an annual conference, organizes lobby days for diaper-related proclamations and policy proposals, and sponsors research on diaper need. As their advocacy work has unfolded, it has focused on diapers as only one issue of unmet basic needs among families. Claiming that a diaper is more than a diaper, the National Diaper Bank Network has been instrumental in shaping public conversations around diaper despair as a window onto the workings of American inequality and the need for public basic needs assistance.

In addition to federal diaper bills, lawmakers in most states have considered at least one diaper policy proposal as of 2025, many involving funding for direct diaper assistance or diaper voucher programs and/or reducing or rescinding sales taxes on diapers.[56] Few of these bills have made it past initial committee deliberations. As diaper bills encountered policy inertia, diaper bankers ramped up diaper distribution efforts to serve the growing number of families facing diaper despair. All states and almost all major US cities and metropolitan areas now have diaper banks, with more emerging each year as leaders of community organizations, hospitals, and maternal and child health programs work to address diaper need.

More people are getting involved in the diaper distribution movement's efforts to draw public attention to diapers' role in the well-being of children, families, and society. They see diaper banking as having a twofold goal—one part exceedingly practical, the other ambitiously political. They seek to get desperately needed diapers into the hands of parents and on babies' bottoms as well as to change the social, economic, and policy structure of diapering. Most of these advocates will tell you that this must start with politically defining diapers as *necessary*, paving the way for tax exemptions, coverage by existing public programs, and earmarking money for diaper support. The average state diaper tax of fifty dollars per year amounts to weeks' worth of diapers families could get if diapers were tax-exempt, just like food and medicine we've deemed essential for health and well-being.

Officially recognizing diapers as necessary would also validate Aisha's struggle and help resolve diaper dilemmas faced by millions of parents across the United States like her who sacrifice their own needs to diaper their babies. Diapers aren't a discretionary item that parents buy simply because they're convenient. They are necessary for health, dignity, and full social inclusion. They are essential for employment and caregiving among parents who must provide them. They are a moral imperative for a society designed around the assumption that all young children wear diapers. That our policies deny these demands harms parents, children, and us all. This book shows why and what we can do to fix it.

UNDERSTANDING AND RESOLVING DIAPER DILEMMAS THROUGH INTERSECTIONAL JUSTICE

A diaper is indeed more than a diaper. Diapering is an inherently sociological phenomenon with significant physical, emotional, relational, and moral significance for children, parenting, and the social organization of carework. Yet diapers have no place in our national social safety net, and the social and political repercussions of diapering shaped by intersecting gender, race, and class inequalities have until now been overlooked, leaving a significant gap in sociological understandings of how poverty affects marginalized families with young children. Diapers are a powerful case of how basic needs are foundational for families' complex needs of affection, social acceptance, education, living wage work, democratic participation, and human dignity. Diapers are part of reproductive justice, involving not only the right to a safe abortion but also access to a healthy pregnancy, delivery, and caregiving relationship. Applying an intersectional reproductive justice lens to the case of diaper insecurity reinforces the importance of sufficient and equitable access to caregiving resources, which is a form of reproductive freedom that has historically depended on wealth and white privilege in the United States.[57]

Access to sufficient diapers is also an important social determinant of health or nonmedical factors, such as the social conditions in which people live, that influence health outcomes. Many social determinants of infant and child health are framed as the result of personal decision-making by individual parents who presumably have the agency and resources to make the right choices about infant feeding, diapering, and sleeping. As gender scholar Laura Harrison explained about the promotion of infant sleep safety guidelines, the neoliberal health-as-individual responsibility paradigm permeates our public understandings, rhetoric, social policies, and laws related to early childhood health outcomes.[58] Despite extensive research finding that class, race, and access to housing, healthcare, high-quality childcare, food, and other resources best predict infant health, parents are ultimately held responsible for babies' well-being. Yet parents who are unable to meet white middle-class norms of parenting, especially mothers of color living in poverty, are surveilled and criminalized based on presumptions that they fail to care for their children. This is why Aisha feared that Shannon could be taken from her if a social worker or judge decided that Shannon was not wearing a proper diaper. Diapering is an intersectional reproductive justice issue that demands we create equitable conditions for childrearing, rather than police poor parents like Aisha for making impossible decisions rooted in deprivation and despair.

As a highly visible and expensive single-use item needed to contain the excreta of young children, diapers are emblematic of the recurring, and presumably wasteful, costs of childbearing among those often deemed undeserving of parenthood. That diapers are not systematically subsidized—or even officially recognized—by existing safety net policies reflects assumptions that families can simply choose alternative diapering methods, such as cloth, that are purportedly cheaper. Yet these assumptions belie the conditions of racialized and feminized poverty that intersect to limit diapering options, especially among low-income mothers of color like Aisha, and subject them to heightened scrutiny and surveillance of their diapering habits and parenting practices. A disposable diaper is not absolutely necessary for infant survival. But we live in a society where it's socially unacceptable for an infant to urinate or defecate anywhere other than a toilet or diaper, where most parents of young children must work outside the home (sometimes as a condition of receiving public aid), and where parents can be declared unfit if children are deemed inappropriately clothed or unclean. A diaper is thus more than a diaper, not because diapers are necessary in absolute terms but because they are essential for living up to socially constructed norms of proper caregiving, hygienic childrearing, and good parenting.

Framed by an intersectional justice perspective, this book draws on three primary sources of empirical data, which I describe in greater detail in appendix A. First, to understand diaper despair, I interviewed seventy mothers who experienced diaper insecurity. Most were women of color, and almost all were living in poverty according to government definitions based on family size and annual household income. Despite significant targeted efforts to recruit fathers, I was able to interview only three men, reflecting the highly gendered nature of managing diaper need and leading me to focus analysis on women's experiences. I spoke with mothers about their family's financial situations, their diapering habits, and how diaper need affected them and their children. Second, to get an inside view of the diaper bank movement, I interviewed forty-five diaper bankers and diaper advocates from across twenty-five states. Most were founders and/or directors of their respective diaper banks, which ranged in size from small diaper pantries that distributed hundreds of diapers monthly to large banks that distributed millions of diapers annually. My interviews with diaper bankers focused on their views of diaper need, experiences working with parents and partner organizations, and participation in political activities related to diapers. Most diaper bankers were white middle-class women who were directly involved in local, state, or national diaper advocacy.

Third, from 2017 through 2024, I closely tracked diaper legislation and political activity at the federal and state levels and have become personally active in diaper banking and diaper advocacy. As part of this research, in 2019, I founded Diapers for Degrees, a diaper pantry for student parents and caregivers at my university. This firsthand experience has deeply acquainted me with the politics of diapering, both formal bills and official policies, as well as the ideologies and power struggles that shape the political context of diaper need and public efforts to address it. As a self-identified diaper banker and supporter of public diaper assistance as an issue of morality, equity, and social inclusion, I make no claims to neutrality. What I can claim is unique ethnographic insight based on hundreds of hours spent in diaper banks, speaking with parents and diaper bankers, and writing and speaking about diaper need to supportive and critical audiences. Using this insight, I hope to convey a deep historical and sociological understanding of how we got into these diaper dilemmas and how, with the right political will, we can find our way out of them.

OUTLINE OF THE BOOK

To that end, the following chapters are organized in two parts: problems and potential solutions. Chapters 2 through 5 focus on the problem and consequences of diaper insecurity. Keeping in mind the end goal of diaper justice—inclusive and equitable access to diapers and opportunities they enable—we must first understand the historical underpinnings of diaper injustice. Chapter 2 traces the social history of diapering to reveal how diapering practices and ideologies are historically and culturally situated and reflect changing hygiene norms, technological advancement, and gendered dynamics of parenting labor. Scanning time and space to show how disposable diapers became a costly necessity for families, it reveals how lacking something as seemingly mundane as a diaper becomes a personal and public health crisis.

Chapter 3 provides insight into how diaper insecurity affects mothers and how they manage the problem of diaper need through *diaper work*—the physical, emotional, and cognitive labor of calculating, saving, and sacrificing to do daily diaper math as well as cope with the stress and stigma associated with diaper despair. Using the case of diaper work, I show how marginalized mothers strategically perform what I call *inventive mothering*—that is, childrearing practices that creatively compensate for deprivation and protect children from poverty's harms and indignities. Inventive mothering illuminates diaper work as a previously unacknowledged form of childcare labor created by poverty, one that reveals the complexity, agency, and inventiveness of marginalized mothers' strategies, logics, and moral meanings as they raise their children amid intersecting inequalities of class, race, and gender.

The environmental impacts of diapers and cloth diapering are the focus of chapter 4. A practice many consider to be a cheaper alternative to disposables and a feasible solution to families' diaper need, cloth diapering is often more expensive, especially for low-income mothers of color who face the constraints of poverty, low-wage work, and gendered and racist stigma. This chapter explores whether and when cloth is a "greener" alternative to disposables, struggles to create truly environmentally friendly and affordable single-use diapers, and the limits of cloth diapering as an answer to the problems of diaper insecurity and despair.

Chapter 5 underscores how individualistic ideologies of parenting, growing family inequality, and limited public support for childrearing in the United States intersected to shape political conditions ripe for diaper despair. It explores why existing public programs like WIC were never

designed to cover hygiene items like diapers and why work-focused welfare reform increased diaper need and led to policy inertia around early
diaper policy proposals. Drawing on interviews with mothers who found
that neither work nor welfare could fill their diaper gaps, this chapter
details how there came to be a gaping hole around diapers in the US social
safety net.

The final two chapters turn to how we can resolve these diaper dilemmas. Chapter 6 takes us inside diaper banks. Based on interviews with
diaper bankers and mothers and participant observation of diaper bank
activities, I trace the history of the diaper bank movement and the landscape of diaper-focused charities and community-based organizations in
the United States. Some diaper bankers view diaper need as a short-term
emergency, while others see it as a reflection of deeply entrenched inequalities. This divergence leads to distinct goals within the diaper bank
movement, whereby some diaper bankers understand the value of their
work as distributing diapers so that parents can go to school, work, and
become economically "self-sufficient," while others view diaper banks as
centers of community improvement needed to address root causes of diaper insecurity. With lessons for sociological understandings of direct aid
for poor families, this chapter analyzes community diaper distribution as
a political and material response to inequities as well mothers' varied
experiences seeking diaper assistance.

The concluding chapter 7 proposes a plan for how to systematically
mend the diaper-shaped hole in the safety net. It does so by drawing on
mothers' lived experiences of diapering their children, doing diaper work,
and seeking diaper support described in prior chapters. Taking a cue from
mothers who explained which diaper programs and policies would be
most useful to them, this final chapter explores possible solutions to diaper need, recent progress regarding antipoverty policies for children and
public diaper provision, as well as continuing challenges.

Appendix A provides contextual information and demographic details
about the parents and diaper bankers I studied along with methodological
information about the study and data analysis strategies. Beyond comparing experiences and outcomes of social groups, the goal of intersectional
research is to uncover oppressive conditions to identify, validate, and create opportunities for social justice; to that end, study findings must be

linked to structural and political solutions that ameliorate oppression of the study group.[59] Respecting these tenets of intersectionality—guiding principles that call upon us to not only study but work to fix social problems that harm and stigmatize marginalized individuals—I describe in appendix B how interested readers can engage in activities that address diaper need in their own communities. I provide succinct talking points that readers can use to raise awareness of diaper need and refute common myths about families that experience it. From donating diapers and organizing diaper drives, to writing government representatives and creating diaper pantries, readers will find ideas for how to get started should the book inspire their own advocacy.

.   .   .   .   .

Each subsequent chapter addresses issues central to Aisha's story with which we began. How did disposable diapers become a necessity of early childhood for infants like Shannon? What is it like to experience diaper insecurity and despair, and how do mothers like Aisha cope by doing daily diaper work to protect their children from deprivation and discrimination rooted in inequities like diaper need? What keeps mothers like Aisha from using cloth diapers to solve diaper insecurity? Why do existing safety net policies not cover diapers, and what hope is there that more policies soon will? Why have diaper banks and pantries popped up across the United States in recent years, and how can they best serve families? How are diaper need and despair symptoms of larger problems with possible solutions pointing to how we can do better by families with young children? Practically, what can we do to accomplish that?

The answers to these questions teach us a lot about how our society tends to ignore the very basic human needs of the most marginalized families. By shedding light on these all too common, yet often invisible diaper dilemmas, those answers teach us how we can create better social, economic, and political conditions of childrearing in which we all have a stake.

2. From Leaves to Luvs

THE EVOLUTION OF DIAPERING

Marion Donovan was tired of changing wet crib sheets while her baby cried. Like the millions of other US mothers with infants in the 1940s, Donovan basically had two diapering options: use only cloth or paper diapers that leaked or put tight rubber pants on top that prevented leakage but often caused skin rashes. Donovan's light bulb moment came while standing in her bathroom staring at her shower curtain. She pulled the curtain down and cut it into pieces. Using her attic sewing machine, she fashioned those pieces into the first waterproof breathable diaper cover, one ingeniously fastened with snaps instead of traditional safety pins. The "Boater" was born. A precursor to the modern disposable diaper, the Boater was a diaper cover made from parachute nylon fabric that kept liquid in while letting air out and included a panel insert for absorbent cloth, or occasionally disposable paper, that parents used for diapers at the time. Recorded in 1951 as US patent #2,556,800, Donovan's Boater "diaper wrap" was so named because Donovan thought that when unfolded it resembled a boat and helped "babies stay afloat." She also hoped it would help laboring mothers stay afloat by reducing their laundry load.

Speaking to Barbara Walters on a 1975 television show featuring inventors of famous everyday products, Donovan described her futile initial efforts to sell the Boater to owners of major US paper companies, who were all men. They laughed, boasting that there was no market for a niche diaper product among American housewives. Donovan recounted, "I went to all the big names that you could think of, and they said, 'No, we don't need it. No woman has asked us for that. We don't need it at all. They're very happy. They buy all of our baby pants.'"[1] After many men told her that she had invented a product mothers neither needed nor wanted, Donovan partnered with a lingerie manufacturer and produced it herself. First sold at the high-end Saks Fifth Avenue department store in 1949, the Boater was such a hit with upper-class mothers that just two years later, Donovan sold her company and patents for $1 million, worth $13 million in 2025. Now seven decades later, the global diaper market Donovan's invention helped launch is worth an estimated $76 billion.[2]

Donovan's innovation solved one of the biggest diaper dilemmas of that era. Mid-twentieth-century cloth diapers functioned more like a wick that pulled liquid away from skin than a sponge that merely absorbed it, making leaks through the outer layer of the diaper inevitable. Adding rubber baby pants as a top layer created an airtight seal to stop leaks but caused irritating and painful chafing, sores, and rashes. The quandary was how to hold the wet in but not keep the air out. Promising to solve this dilemma and using a blue sailboat as the company insignia, early advertisements for the Boater claimed that it was "brilliantly fashioned to give comfort to baby—bind-proof, leak-proof, it has plenty of freedom for action. Fold disposable or regular diapers into its waterproofed nylon pocket and snap on. Takes a few minutes to launder."[3] Donovan's 1998 *New York Times* obituary described her as "a onetime Connecticut housewife who had to change one damp diaper too many . . . and . . . helped spearhead an industrial and domestic revolution."[4] This was no exaggeration. Donovan's invention liberated mothers from the time-consuming, tedious task of washing and drying baby clothes, crib sheets, blankets, and other linens soiled by drippy and smelly uncovered diapers. Because breathable Boater-covered diapers could be worn longer, even overnight, babies used fewer cloth diapers that mothers had to scrape, soak, scrub, wring, hang, fold, and put away.

With its humble beginnings as a shower curtain in the hands of an enterprising and exhausted mother, the modern disposable diaper is a stunning feat of technology. Within its many layers is a story of technological progress that revolutionized caring for young children. To fully grasp this, one must understand what a diaper is, and more fundamentally, what a diaper does. A modern disposable diaper may seem like simple, cotton-soft, paper underwear wrapped around something resembling toilet paper. But it's really a sophisticated multilayer garment specially designed to hold one hundred times its weight in liquid while maintaining both a dry inner liner touching the baby's skin and a dry outer cover that encounters everything else. Within these layers unfolds another story—one of urbanization, capitalism, and changing norms of cleanliness, parenting, and childhood rife with class, race, and gender inequalities. This chapter tells that story, starting with a multigenerational account of my own family's diaper choices. Babies' bodily processes have remained constant. Yet our understanding of what babies need and social contexts in which parents strive to meet their needs have changed radically, with serious implications for the nearly half of parents with infants in the United States who struggle to afford diapers.

PARENTING WITH "PAPER DIAPERS" THROUGH THREE GENERATIONS

The same year that Marion Donovan sold her diaper company in 1951, my maternal grandmother, Patsy, gave birth to the first of her four children. As a seventeen-year-old working-class mother in rural Texas, she experienced life and parenting far removed from the upper-class New England mothers buying Boaters at Saks Fifth Avenue. Although disposable diapers, or what my grandmother called "paper diapers," were available in department stores like Sears and Montgomery Ward, no one she knew used them. "I loved my kids too much to put them in paper diapers," she told me. "Using cloth diapers showed a lot of love because I had to wash them." As was common for mothers in the 1950s, Pasty didn't work outside the home during the six years her four children were in diapers. She slept next to their bassinet and changed diapers in the middle of the night when wetness woke them. When they were outdoors, she put plastic pants over cloth to prevent leaks. During the rare occasion a neighbor or her mother babysat the kids, they too used cloth diapers or rags.

Patsy scooped the contents of soiled diapers into the toilet and soaked them in a bucket of soapy water each evening. Handwashing and line-drying the dozen diapers each child used daily made laundry an everyday chore. My grandfather suggested she use paper diapers when the babies had loose stools, but my grandmother wouldn't consider it. She had no memory of my grandfather changing a single diaper. Two of her children were fully potty trained by their first birthdays, and all four were out of diapers by fifteen months. Of potty training, Patsy simply said, "cloth made them feel the wet, so as soon as they could walk, they loved to go to the bathroom and sit on their little toilet." Even when her children were all in or nearing their seventies, my grandmother could still remember how to fold an eighteen-inch-square cotton muslin cloth into a diaper, something she did more than twenty thousand times over those six years.

By the time I was born three decades later in 1981, parents could buy several major brands of disposable diapers in most stores, which had entire aisles dedicated to baby items. Like many of her generation, my mother, Bridget, used a combination of cloth and what she also called "paper diapers." She remembered that cloth diapers were cheaper and meant "you weren't always throwing something away." She can still fold a cloth diaper from muscle memory and secure it with safety pins. The pastel yellow teddy bear–shaped diaper pins she used to fasten my diapers are among keepsakes from my infancy she has tucked away in a memory box. She vividly remembers running those pins through her long red hair to make them slicker so they wouldn't get stuck when pushed through the diaper cloth. My mother bought two dozen cloth diapers at Sears before I was born and used them for eighteen months, noting how "then kids didn't stay in diapers like they do now." When I was a newborn, like her mother Pasty before her, Bridget used only cloth diapers and handwashed and line-dried each day after soaking in a bleach water bucket kept in the bathroom.

A crucial difference marked my grandmother's and mother's experiences, one that fundamentally shaped their distinct diapering choices and those of most parents since: my mother returned to work six weeks after I was born. Until I could walk, she relied on a friend, a neighbor, my aunt, and my grandmother for full-time childcare. Although my aunt and grandmother diapered me in cloth, just as they did with their own children, my mother said of nonfamilial care, "I didn't want them to mess with the cloth diapers. It was just easier." Once she started using disposables for outings and when I was in others' care, she came to appreciate fewer nighttime changes and spending less time on weekends washing cloth diapers. Moreover, my diaper rashes weren't as bad when I wore disposables. By the time I was six months old, only half of my diapers were cloth. Every other mother she knew used a combination of cloth and disposables, Bridget explained, because it minimized both laundry and diaper expenses.

Had my mother not already transitioned to using mostly disposables as I was nearing my first birthday, another change in my care arrangement would have necessitated the switch. The daycare center I attended required disposables. My mother has little recollection of potty training and credits my daycare providers with teaching me to use the toilet by eighteen months. I never wore a diaper overnight past my second birthday. Save for the dozen or so diapers my father changed during the rare times he "babysat" me, women—my mother, my grandmothers, my aunts, the neighbor, and the daycare workers—changed, washed, and disposed of all the diapers I used.

Three decades later, as I was preparing for the arrival of my daughter Bridget in 2015, few of my family and friends used cloth diapers. I could have read the many books and blogs on cloth diapering to learn. But using disposables seemed more like a foregone conclusion than a choice after considering diaper options, which had proliferated since my grandmother and mother diapered their infants. In the common parlance of describing different diapering methods, "diapers" now means disposables, and "cloth" requires qualification. I knew that cloth diapers had become more sophisticated than cotton squares secured with safety pins of the kind my mother resourcefully rubbed through her hair. I also worried about the excessive garbage disposables created. Yet, as with my mother, my return to paid work happened mere weeks after my daughter's birth. I didn't want to burden her caregivers (her grandparents at first and then daycare workers) with handling soiled cloth. Admittedly, given the challenges of transitioning to new parenthood—my daughter had early health problems, struggled with breastfeeding, and rarely slept through the night until she was two years old—I couldn't imagine adding that extra work to everything else.

Besides, having seen thousands of diaper advertisements by the time I became a mother, I'd been primed as a disposable diaper consumer. By 2015 two corporate titans of disposables, Procter & Gamble (maker of Pampers) and Kimberly-Clark (maker of Huggies) had created and cornered a large and ever-growing US national and global diaper market. I received Pampers and Huggies samples via mail almost immediately after my first prenatal doctor's visit, and the hospital where my daughter was born put on her first Pampers when she was an hour old. As intended by diaper marketing campaigns, I never bought another diaper brand or type for two years until I purchased her first disposable training pants. Fortunately I had more diaper-changing support than my grandmother and mother. My daughter's father changed just as many diapers as I did (honestly, probably more), and changing tables had by then become common, if not universal, in women's and men's public bathrooms. By the time I became a parent, diapering was less strictly something only mothers and other women did, and public diaper-changing stations suggested some social recognition of, if not social support for, children's diapering needs.

The economics and culture of diapering evolved significantly from the time my mother wore cotton muslin squares to when I purchased disposable diapers by the hundreds for my daughter sixty years later. Factors specific to my family influenced their diapering habits, including my grandmother's and mother's rural working-class background, which meant they certainly had more options than many but fewer than some, and their experiences aren't generalizable to all mothers. Nevertheless, my family's own intergenerational trajectory tracks larger trends in diapering and toilet-training practices of American parents during the past half century. In the early 1950s fewer than 1 percent of infants in the United States wore disposable diapers. By the early 1980s about half of infants wore disposables most or all the time, and many families used a combination of cloth and disposables. Now, nearly 95 percent of US infants and toddlers wear disposables for most or all their diapering needs.[5] Pivotal social and economic shifts undergirded these changes. Parents of my grandmother's generation were most likely to use disposables if they were employed, affluent mothers who shopped at expensive department stores like Saks Fifth Avenue that sold Donovan's Boaters. Today those most likely to use cloth diapers are affluent families who own their homes, have in-home washers and dryers, can afford expensive start-up costs, and include stay-at-home, married mothers.[6]

The past half century also saw the average age of potty training in the United States rise by about a year per generation. My mother and her siblings were trained around their first birthday, me by my second, and my daughter closer to her third. Some people, like my grandmother, are quick to blame elongated diapering on the rising popularity of modern disposables, which keep babies' skin drier longer in ways that would have astounded Marion Donovan and her contemporaries. Yet the real reasons require a historical and global perspective to grasp fully the social, economic, and cultural factors that converged to make disposable diapers, which my grandmother considered a superfluous luxury, a necessity for today's families with young children.

THE HISTORY OF MAKING BABIES' ENDS NEAT

Diapering rituals for protection, modesty, and containing excreta have varied considerably across time and space in response to changing cultural norms, economic conditions, material availability, and even weather. In colder climates, the earliest objects used for what we now call diapers included American Indian milkweed leaf wraps and Inuit moss or grass packed under animal skins.[7] In warmer climates, where children often went naked, caregivers learned to sense when infants were about to urinate or defecate and placed them over a container or ground space for excrement. For centuries in rural northern China, where water was scarce and caregivers worked in agricultural fields for most of the day, parents placed infants in bags of fine sand to absorb urine and feces.[8] Swaddling infants between their legs using strips of fabric to contain waste was depicted in many fifteenth-century European paintings and architecture. Among the most notable are the ten bambini mounted on the arches of the Ospedale degli Innocenti, Italian for "Hospital of the Innocents," a historical building in Florence, Italy, that housed one of the world's oldest organizations for the care of abandoned infants.[9] An infant wearing nothing but swaddling cloth on their lower torso still serves as the insignia of many child-focused organizations, including the American Academy of Pediatrics.

The etymological roots of *diaper* had more to do with fabric than any intended use. *Diaper* derives from the Greek *diaspros* (*dia* "across" and *aspros* "white") and the Old French verb *diapre*, meaning "to pattern cloth with small, repeated designs." The Middle English word *diaper* also originally referred to a fabric pattern of rhombic shapes that created a series of diagonal lines and by the late sixteenth century came to mean the white linen or cotton fabric bearing the pattern. Not until the mid-nineteenth century did garments intended for swaddling infants' bottoms sewn from this patterned linen come to be known as *diapers*, a usage that persisted in the United States following British colonization of North America. In the United Kingdom *nappy* (a diminutive of *napkin*) became the most popular word for infant undergarments intended to contain waste. The English version of *diaper* as a verb meaning "to put on a diaper" was not used until the mid-twentieth century, when my grandmother wrapped her infants in plain white muslin cotton cloth.

As with much of American history, diapering as we now understand and practice it has roots in settler colonialism. Early American diapers were as much about piety and morality—and more specifically European notions of civility—as they were about containing children's excreta. The rising popularity of diapers reflected common colonial views that linen-clad bodies were more modest and healthier than uncovered bodies that were frequently bathed. Pilgrims and Puritans wrapped children in tight bands of linen to create a diaper clout that caught urine and feces, holding waste exceptionally close to the body for long periods of time. Conversely, many American Indians constructed infant garments with openings between the legs that let evacuations easily flow away from the body while allowing access to fresh air.[10] The Indigenous practice of keeping babies unswaddled for unfettered defecation and urination offended the religious sensibility of white Europeans, who equated a fully linen-clad, if rarely washed, body with cleanliness and propriety.

During the seventeenth century, when both soap and cloth were scarce, diapers were rarely washed. "Dry" cleaning that involved rubbing skin against clothes was preferred over removing dirt via immersion in water. Medical theories of the time posited that outer skin protected the inner body from disease, defilement, and putrefaction, and that certain fabrics, notably linen made from flax or hemp, absorbed bodily toxins released through urine, feces, sweat, and menstrual blood. Though diapers were seen as especially contaminated, they were rarely washed and merely hung to dry in front of fires before reattaching them on infants using string, buttons, and needles.[11] In the eighteenth century, as bathing and laundering became more common, especially among upper-class households, linen undergarments lightened from their natural beige or gray color through bleaching became associated with fashionable respectability, high social status, and racial notions of whiteness. Extremely labor intensive—and therefore expensive—to produce and clean, white linen became a precious commodity, one that demanded extensive laundering labor of women who had to haul water and wood, build fires, make soap, soak garments in lye, stir hot kettles, wring and hang wet garments, and iron and mend damaged cloth. A white, clean, crisp linen garment, including a neat diaper, came to represent affluence and access to laundress services, as most colonial households couldn't afford to redirect a significant share of women's labor from the homestead production of food to laundry.

Common beliefs during the preindustrial era, such as ideas that cotton flannel—which eventually replaced flax linen as the primary material used to make diapers—didn't require washing and that urine salt from wet diapers strengthened a young child much like salt in brine toughens a herring, supported minimal diaper-cleaning practices through the eighteenth and nineteenth centuries.[12] Drying diapers were a common fixture on hearths in households with infants, and their stench a taken-for-granted smell of family life well into the twentieth century.[13] Unfathomable by modern standards, one was unlikely to notice the particular pungent smell of rarely washed diapers. Vats of cleaning lye made from concentrated urine, rural farmyards and city streets littered with livestock excrement, sweat-stiffened adults' work clothes, and chamber pots made ammonia and skatole (the organic compound primarily responsible for fecal odor) common olfactory characteristics across households of all classes. Other inequities were stark, such as access to chamber pots for containing urine and feces and emptying diapers. The expression "without a pot to piss in" harkens back to this time when abject poverty or enslavement meant that one couldn't afford a chamber pot, the contents of which even the wealthiest families threw out the most convenient door or window.[14]

The late eighteenth century brought new cleanliness norms, notably a growing sensitivity to smells emanating from rarely washed chamber pots, undergarments, and diapers. Failure to appear appropriately clean, as evidenced by soiled garments, could seriously compromise an individual's and family's social status and community standing. Mothers faced growing class-based and racialized imperatives to embody refinement, cleanliness, and health through meticulous and labor-intensive care of their and their children's bodies. These expectations were especially strong for garments that came into direct contact with urine, feces, and menstrual blood, the substances thought to be most toxic and polluting. Cloth and women's labor were instrumental for meeting these heightened cleanliness standards, resulting in more and more frequent laundry. A grueling household task done several times a year or at most monthly during the seventeenth and eighteenth centuries, laundry became a weekly chore by the 1800s.

Monday was the universal day for washing household linens, a term that came to mean any fabric that regularly touched the body. A Monday wash day ensured that housewives had sufficient time for drying (Tuesday), sewing (Wednesday), ironing (Thursday), and storing (Friday) before religious observance on Sundays, after which the cycle started again. A family's social reputation and class- and race-based authority hinged in part on how well mothers maintained clean children, especially the symbolic whiteness reflected in the literal whiteness of children's skin, teeth, and freshly laundered linens, including diapers. Cleanliness evidenced by white linens, access to which was deeply rooted in class privilege and white supremacy, became a way for white upper-class families to differentiate themselves from Indigenous peoples, later immigrants, and enslaved individuals—those most often responsible for the arduous labor required to produce and clean white diaper linens.[15] As "clean" was increasingly associated with "classy," family laundry turned into an especially tedious task and, according to historian Suellen Hoy, Monday became "the blackest day in women's domestic calendar."[16]

Bodies and linens also became the focus of moral reforms and public health campaigns intended to rid the social body of dirt and disease. Despite how pungent urine and fecal odors were a taken-for-granted sensory quality of social life prior to the twentieth century, it was still widely believed that "miasma" or noxious smells in bad air were sources of life-threatening illnesses. Due to its pivotal role in one of the most influential cholera outbreaks in human history, a diaper ultimately put this miasmic contagion theory of disease to rest. In late summer of 1854 a scourge of sickness struck the Soho neighborhood in London, leaving surrounding areas surprisingly untouched. On an early Monday morning, five-month-old Frances Lewis began vomiting and emitting green, watery, acrid stools. As her mother, Sarah Lewis, waited on the doctor's house call, she soaked the infant's soiled cloth diapers in a bucket of lukewarm water, some of which Sarah dumped into the cellar cesspool in front of the cramped single-family house they shared with twenty people. Intended to be a trap but functioning as a dam that interfered with normal water flow to the sewer, the cesspool was lined with decaying bricks placed just thirty-two inches from the Broad Street well used by thousands as their primary source of drinking water. Hundreds of neighbors contracted cholera by that Thursday. By Saturday, dozens, including baby Frances Lewis, were dead.[17]

Low population density had mostly kept bacterial diseases like cholera, which cannot be transmitted through air or most bodily fluids, in check. But as urban areas became increasingly populated and commercially connected, cities became epidemic breeding grounds. At Broad Street, just as Dr. John Snow created a map of the neighborhood's cholera cases, local minister Henry Whitehead recalled Frances Lewis, how her illness predated the outbreak by a day, and that her address at 40 Broad Street was one of the closest residences to the well. Identifying Frances as the index case and the diaper bucket's contents as the transmission source supported Snow's theory that the deadly outbreak, which ultimately killed 616 people, came from germs in fecal-contaminated water.[18] Owing its discovery to a dirty diaper, the germ theory of disease revolutionized public health and sanitation as social issues and laid the ideological foundation for public garbage removal, sewer, and clean water infrastructure. Subsequently, cholera was eradicated in most large cities by the 1930s.

Growing acceptance of germ theory in the context of increasing urbanization also transformed diapering and toileting.[19] The earliest toilets were rudimentary ground ditches intended to separate and conceal human excrement that could mark individuals and communities as unclean and profane. For most of human history toileting was a decidedly social event in collective spaces with adjacent communal latrines where people sat near others during simultaneous defecation.[20] Well into the nineteenth century, most Americans still lived in low-population rural areas that relied on individual outhouse toilets. As cities grew during the first half of the 1800s, so too did public water systems and focus on hygienic habits as ways to minimize disease transmission. The availability of potable water differentiated city from country life, and the upper classes from everyone else. Before the advent of widely available indoor plumbing, water for cooking, cleaning, and bathing had to be laboriously carried from one spot to another, and only the wealthiest families could afford water lines connected directly to their houses.

The impetus to find increasingly discrete and sanitary methods for disposing of human waste led to the invention of the flush toilet in the last quarter of the nineteenth century. For the next fifty years, private in-house toilets requiring sophisticated plumbing remained a luxury of the wealthy, while the poor continued to suffer effects of living in close quarters with their own and neighbors' excrement. With the advent of indoor plumbing, one could plausibly pretend that bodies didn't excrete, and private defecation, like clean linens and bleached diapers, signaled wealth and whiteness. Interior water closets, as they were then called, allowed the affluent privacy while ridding the body of urine and feces, which could immediately be flushed away out of sight and forgotten. During this time, peeing in public was a privilege for which one paid. Through the mid-twentieth century in the United States and England, use of public bathroom facilities intended for affluent, able-bodied, adult white men came with a hefty cost (though urinals were often free). Installed in 1910 in Terre Haute, Indiana, the first US pay toilet cost a nickel per use, or roughly $1.65 in 2025. The poor and women could rarely afford to use public bathrooms even when they could access them, and changing tables and family bathrooms were unthinkable, largely due to assumptions that women and children had little reason to be in public.[21] Public bathrooms were among the social spaces most stringently segregated and policed in the Jim Crow South, where racialized social control denied Black people access to equitable toileting based on racist ideas that marked anyone not white as unclean and contaminated.

These race, class, and gender inequities of toileting had enormous consequences for diapering. With the ascendancy of upper-class ideas and hygiene habits, the connection among privilege, privacy, and prestige around toileting became stronger, while speaking of bodily functions that produced excrement and the items that contained it became taboo. With ever-increasing population density, containing excreta became a moral imperative and civic responsibility, though the labor associated with doing so, much like the excrement itself, was thought best left hidden and unspoken. According to historian Kathleen Brown, toileting and diapering, by this time considered entirely private, were profoundly shaped by social processes and standards for health and decency and reflected deep cultural convictions about the meanings of civilized sociality. Diapering especially became part of what Brown called *body work*, the cleaning, healing, and caring labors necessary for managing the inevitable corporeal by-products of physical bodies believed to be sources of dangerous, defiling pollution.

Gendered labor has always been integral to creating and maintaining the "civilized" body, one subject to public scrutiny and expectations for keeping all evidence of grotesque corporeality and its polluting by-products—gas, urine, feces, vomit, blood, mucous, and genital secretions—contained and concealed so as not to violate social norms of propriety. A clean, refined body came to be seen as a matter of moral choice, social superiority, and individual responsibility that revealed a person's inner virtue, and in the case of infant diapers, a parent's worth and ability.[22] Behind every refined body was the labor of women—wives, mothers, enslaved people, and domestic servants—who became what historian Suellen Hoy termed "agents of cleanliness."[23] It was in this social context that disposable diapers as a commonly used baby care item were born.

THE BIRTH OF DISPOSABLE DIAPERS, PRICELESS CHILDREN, AND INTENSIVE MOTHERING

Cloth diapers were first mass produced in the United States in 1887, just as rising standards of cleanliness cemented expectations that all household linens should be laundered regularly.[24] Doctors started to advocate for washing, boiling, and sun-drying diapers between each use, tasks made especially difficult for the three in four Americans who still lived in homes without running water at the turn of the twentieth century.[25] As indoor plumbing became universal, first for urban areas in the 1930s and a decade later for most rural areas, the ever-increasing burdens of cleanliness fell to women presumed to be naturally best-suited to ensuring orderly, healthy, and clean homes and children.[26] Affluent women who could afford to outsource laundry labor usually did, mostly to low-paid women of color domestic workers. Commercial laundries were popular until in-home electric washer and dryers became common among middle-class families starting in the 1930s, after which few relinquished the autonomy and privacy sacrificed by washing clothes in public laundry facilities.

The 1930s also saw the emergence of laundry services specifically for cloth diapers. One such business, Dy-Dee Wash Diaper Service in Wisconsin, opened in 1937 and advertised to young mothers as specializing "entirely in a laundry for babies." After a bout of unemployment during the Great Depression, owner Karl T. Hellerman moved to Milwaukee, where his brother Paul worked at Eureka Laundry and came across a story in the trade publication *Starch Room Laundry Journal* about parents of the famous Dionne quintuplets using a professional laundry service. Hellerman reasoned that mothers with smaller broods would also appreciate a paid service that reduced arduous labor associated with hand-powered wringer washers and line-drying methods commonly used to clean cloth diapers at that time. In the six months it took Hellerman to get the local service up and running in Milwaukee, they shipped garbage containers of dirty diapers by railways to Chicago, where diapers were cleaned and sanitized. Karl's wife, Lorraine Hellerman, who like many women of the time lost her job upon marriage, became central to the business. While serving as president of the National Institute of Diaper Services in the 1950s, she invented the cotton prefolded diaper my grandmother and mother later used.[27]

During World War II, mothers of young children were employed in record numbers, increasing the demand for diaper services like Dy-Dee Wash that delivered clean cotton cloth diapers directly to homes. Many diaper services continued regular operation through the war, even when cotton rationing compelled parents to use sugar and flour sacks to make diapers. Parents could also stretch cloth diapers by using the gauze or paper pad liners many companies sold in the 1930s and 1940s. The post-war baby boom was good for business, as Dy-Dee Wash laundered upwards of fifty thousand cloth diapers daily at its peak in the 1960s. Yet business declined steadily as more women started to work outside the home for pay, more children went to daycare, and the disposable diaper market took off. When the Hellerman family sold Dy-Dee Wash in 1990, it was washing about 160,000 cloth diapers a week, less than half of normal business two decades prior. The operation closed a few years later after new owners took over and acquiesced to a rapidly declining market for cloth diaper services. By 1997, 75 percent of reusable diaper services in the United States had gone out of business.[28]

The early success of companies like Dy-Dee Wash was due to the fact that in the late 1950s disposable diapers accounted for less than 1 percent of the billions of diaper changes in the United States each year and even fewer internationally. This wasn't because disposable diapers didn't yet exist. In 1948, Johnson & Johnson produced and marketed the first fully disposable diaper made of multi-ply cellulose with padding that resembled a paper towel encased by plastic film. Sold under the brand-name Chux, its no-frills moniker was perhaps too on the nose for consumers unaccustomed to wrapping their infants in something one step removed from garbage. Like my grandmother, American mothers were initially averse to putting their babies in "paper diapers." This aversion to disposables was unusual given the growing preference for throwaway over durable goods in the service of cleanliness and hygiene. Other disposable paper products—including paper shirt collars, toilet paper, and paper cups and towels—were commonplace by the turn of the twentieth century, especially in public spaces. Prior to this, before wood pulp and other nonrag papers were widely developed, disposable products were prohibitively expensive.[29] As paper prices dropped, more people could afford the privilege of disposability. Advertising for single-use paper products promised American housewives and consumers a lifestyle of laundry-free luxury and leisure once available only to wealthy white women with servants.

But as Johnson & Johnson's Chux proved, creating a market for disposable infant diapers presented a unique set of challenges that neither cheaper paper products nor promises of leisure could solve. Diaper disposability didn't really take off until the mid-1960s when, shortly after Marion Donovan's diaper inventions were deemed unnecessary and impractical, a man named Victor Mills—chemical engineer, inventor of Jif peanut butter, and innovator of Pringles stackable potato chips—developed the world's first commercially successful disposable diaper. Assigned to the diaper task force at Procter & Gamble in 1961, Mills was a new grandfather inspired to combine (or as many believe, appropriate) two of Donovan's innovations: the waterproof plastic outer layer of the Boater with an absorbent inner layer made of paper. The result—Pampers—hit the market in 1966 and has been the best-selling diaper brand worldwide ever since.

A watershed year for diapering, 1966 was also when Carlyle Harmon of Johnson & Johnson and Billy Gene Harper of Dow Chemical filed nearly identical patents for superabsorbent polymers, a technology that fundamentally changed the personal hygiene product market. Superabsorbent polymers are tiny plastic flakes with a chemical structure that can absorb up to three hundred times their weight in liquid "insults," the diaper industry term for infant urine. Although urine salt reduced the absorption rate by three-quarters, the invention revolutionized diapering in two ways. One superabsorbent diaper could hold a baby's entire overnight output of urine, and polymers converted fluid to solid gel that stayed intact within the diaper layers without leakage. Before this, manufacturers added more permeable paper—"fluff" in diaper industryspeak—to increase disposable diapers' absorbency. But more fluff meant larger diapers that sagged when wet and took up more space in boxes, shipping trucks, warehouses, and supermarkets shelves, which allotted limited space to each product category. Superabsorbent diapers were half the size with twice the capacity of bulkier paper fluff-filled diapers. Despite how superabsorbent diapers weren't toilet-flushable and could severely clog sewer systems, sales of diapers and related products with polymers, including those for adult incontinence, grew nearly 50 percent annually throughout the 1970s and 1980s. Lighter, thinner, more absorbent diapers enhanced their market appeal to storeowners who could stock more units per box on limited shelf space and to parents who had to lug fewer diaper boxes home, where they now enjoyed less laundry and more uninterrupted sleep.[30]

These technological advances coincided with significant cultural shifts to rapidly increase disposable diapers' appeal. First, a growing consumer culture of disposability spurred by innovations like superabsorbent polymers shaped preferences for and meanings attached to different diaper types. According to historian Susan Strasser, products intended for single use were opposed to "traditional reuse and recycling [connected to] poverty and backwardness."[31] Influenced by growing tastes for novelty and beliefs that unused things represented progress and modernity, Americans' relationships to waste and trash transformed during the first half of the twentieth century. Aspirations for leisure, luxury, and cleanliness—long associated with upper-class, white respectability and social distinctions based on economics and race—replaced commitments to the durable, washable, and reusable. Having a pristine white diaper for every change and not needing to wash dirty diapers were privileges only few could initially afford. Consequently, a single-use disposable diaper became a status symbol of wealth and social esteem, specifically not being poor. It signaled that you had enough money to simply throw away every dirty diaper.

Second, changing ideologies of childhood and good parenting, especially proper motherhood, played a crucial role in the growth of diaper disposability. As sociologist Viviana Zelizer described, a child's birth in the eighteenth century meant the arrival of a future family laborer and greater security for parents later in life—that is, if the child was fortunate enough to escape high infant mortality rates and live to adulthood.[32] A new perspective of childhood emerged during the late nineteenth and early twentieth centuries that transformed views of children from unsentimental but economically useful nonadults to emotionally priceless, exalted young treasures with unique value, desires, and needs. As children's sentimental worth increased, concerns over their well-being, happiness, and comfort became private and public health priorities. Sacred children couldn't wear diapers that were rarely changed or barely washed.

Third, this reimagining of childhood led to increasing commercialization of children's lives and products and even higher expectations of parenthood, tasking mothers with protecting vulnerable children from contamination and illness. With the ascent of what historian Rima Apple called *scientific motherhood* starting in the mid-nineteenth century, medical childrearing advice replaced intuition and traditional knowledge passed down through generations.[33] This redefined what it meant to be a good mother who, instead of trusting maternal instinct and know-how learned from her mother and grandmothers, thought of maternal love as a skill developed through training based on medical expertise and adherence to professional advice. As the "good mother" turned to modern science to inform her childrearing choices, practices like infant feeding, bathing, and diapering became subject to medical study and treatment.[34] Scientific motherhood found its footing in advice from popular early twentieth-century childrearing experts and texts, which discouraged play with infants under six months of age and recommended strict eating, sleeping, and toileting schedules. As raising sacred children turned into a scientific enterprise, *childcare* became a distinct and definable task separate from other housework. Specifically, diapering and toilet training were understood not as household duties leading to laundry labor for mothers but as childrearing priorities requiring expert-informed strategies and consumer choices to ensure healthy child development.[35]

Venerating children, and by extension childcare, turned childrearing into a moral undertaking through what sociologist Sharon Hays termed *intensive mothering*.[36] Incorporating norms of scientific motherhood about heeding the directives of childrearing professionals, intensive mothering as a gendered model of parenting demands that mothers prioritize children's needs through practices that are child-centered, self-sacrificing, labor-intensive, expert-informed, and emotionally engaged. Diaper companies immediately capitalized on ideas of scientific and intensive motherhood, which gained cultural currency throughout the mid-twentieth century and laid the ideological foundation for conceptualizing childcare, including diapering, not as work but as an expression of expert-guided motherly love. Mounting commercial innovations and profit motives intersected with growing moral and medicalized understandings of mothering to create a huge disposable diaper market within the span of a mere decade.

SELLING A MOTHER'S LOVE, NOT LESS LAUNDRY:
ADVERTISING DISPOSABLES DURING A GENDERED
WORK AND FAMILY REVOLUTION

To find evidence of disposable diaper companies' primary marketing strategy, just take a quick trip down any store's diaper aisle. With images of happy babies, many held by adoring mothers, dominant brands like

Huggies Little Snugglers, Pampers Swaddlers, and Luvs that allow one to "Parent Like a Pro" adorn store shelves. Early brand-name contenders for Procter & Gamble's disposable line—Dri-Wees, Larks, Solos, Tads, and Winks—didn't evoke ideas of parental devotion and expertise.[37] Pampers were so named based on focus groups with mother-consumers who felt the name Pampers best conveyed maternal love and tenderness. Shortly after Procter & Gamble launched Pampers, Kimberly-Clark entered the disposable diaper market in 1968 with Kimbies, the first disposable line to replace pins with a tape closure system. Kimbies' sales dropped after Procter & Gamble introduced Luvs with side tape closures in 1976, prompting Kimberly-Clark to create Kleenex Huggies, the first diaper with elastic leg cuffs promising a more comfortable fit and fewer leaks. These brand names were only the beginning of disposable diaper advertising's focus on providing optimal care and comfort for babies over parents' convenience.

This focus might seem inopportune and ironic given how rising expectations of cleanliness meant that by the 1930s mothers with cloth-diapered babies spent many laborious hours each week scraping, washing, hanging, drying, ironing, and folding an endless supply of cloth diapers expected to be clean, white, and soft. Already one of the most daunting aspects of early twentieth-century housework, laundry that included cloth diapers was particularly dirty, smelly, and unceasing. Yet the power of this strategically savvy brand message centering mother's love rather than less laundry becomes clearer when understood in connection with larger social and economic changes in mothers' employment, caregiving arrangements, and growing expectations of intensive mothering. The earliest Pampers ads emphasized that with no need to wash, they made the dirty work of diapering "disappear." Rather than couched in benefits of less labor and mess for mothers, ads extolled the virtues of disposables for freeing up maternal time and energy for taking even better care of babies. The best part of Pampers, one early television ad proclaimed, was that "every day they give you so much more time to play with your baby and be with your family," while emphasizing mothers' selfless devotion to keeping babies happy and dry.[38] Another 1960s Pampers ad showed one mother saying to another, "I heard cloth diapers are better, if you don't mind the trouble." To which the other mother responded, "Frankly, I'd do almost anything to keep my baby comfortable. And I'd wash a million cloth diapers myself if they kept his skin as dry as Pampers."[39]

Contrasting Pampers with "diapers," which at the time meant cloth, became a very commercially successful depiction of disposables that took a sharp turn from original advertising strategies. Initial disposable diaper test marketing revealed that parents envisioned using them only for travel, babysitting, and special occasions. But diaper companies stood to lose significant profit if parents used disposables only part time. An ad executive hired by Proctor & Gamble in the 1960s recalled that "we were inclined to build our campaign around the product's convenience advantages. . . . We concluded that there was a more promising potential in positioning Pampers as a superior diapering system. We believed the marketing objective should be to replace cloth diaper usage on a full-time basis with no specific attempt to encourage part-time or convenience usage."[40] Yet how to advertise disposables as superior, especially without showing actual urine or feces, presented challenges. Based on more market research with mothers, Procter & Gamble decided to highlight cloth diapers' discomfort for babies and acumen among mothers who knew better than to keep their beloved children in inferior cloth.

Pampers boxes in the 1960s declared right on the packaging "Instead of a Diaper . . . Pampers." One television ad included a baby's voiceover as their mother gently placed them on her shoulder: "My mommy loves me. She cuddles me, and boy am I lucky, she never makes me wear diapers. I wear Pampers instead. Pampers—Procter & Gamble's discovery that makes diapers seem old-fashioned."[41] Another ad showed an image of two bare-butt babies sitting atop open diapers—one on leaky cloth, the other on Pampers with a dry top sheet. The tag line, "Pampers, for drier, happier babies," remains a popular ad slogan to this day. These ads ignored how cloth diapering involved smelly, unpleasant labor involving consistent intimate contact with another person's excrement. As historian Jessamyn Neuhaus found, advertisers have long depicted diapering in relation to a highly idealized image of women as devoted mothers and guardians of family health and well-being, rather than household laborers whose carework is actual *work*.[42]

Notably, the few early diaper ads focused on convenience targeted fathers who "babysat" their children during mothers' rare trips outside the home.[43] A 1967 Pampers print ad read: "The nicest change—they're flushable. Won't Dad love that? (And won't *you!*). No more rinsing soiled diapers. No more soaking and washing and fetching and folding. No more diaper pail." An early-1970s commercial similarly portrayed several fathers standing outside a hospital nursery window. One turned to a new dad handing him a Pampers, "Here, start 'em off right, . . . It's not a diaper! It's a Pampers. Better for babies. Besides, it'll save the little woman from washing diapers." Although ads portrayed fathers occasionally changing diapers while the "little woman" was out, they never equated using disposables with fatherly love or optimal paternal care. Diapering and buying the best diapers for babies were clearly sold as mothers' domain.

Disposables were also marketed as a tool to help mothers stay relaxed and playful. A 1967 magazine headline read: "The first six months with a new baby: Pleasure or Panic? If you're like most mothers, you'll soon discover that anxiety is contagious. That the best thing you can do for both of you is relax and enjoy yourself. . . . It's easier today to keep baby comfortable and yourself relaxed—even when it's time for a change. . . . Pampers make it a playful time." Pampers ultimately promised a cleaner, healthier, and happier baby, one who slept through the night, contracted fewer germs, developed fewer diaper rashes, and had calmer, more present mothers. Another late-1960s Pampers advertisement featured a mother's voiceover asking, "Is there anything more satisfying than to pick up your crying baby and turn his tears into smiles? But how nerve-racking when he cries and nothing you do seems to help. . . . Sometimes, though, the reason is obvious: chafing and rash in the diaper area. That's when you ask yourself, 'Do I change him fast enough? Am I doing everything I can to help prevent this?'"[44] Ads portrayed Pampers as the answer to these vexing questions and antidote to maternal guilt and anxiety. In doing so, they vilified cloth diapers as messy, irritating vectors for filth, diaper rash, and maternal distress.

Implicit in early diaper ads was that white, upper- and middle-class, stay-at-home mothers were the target consumers for disposables. Early Pampers commercials emphasized "only a nickel a piece" as an ostensibly low price point, but this would buy fewer than two diapers for a dollar in 2025 currency. One of the first Pampers television commercials showed a white mother's pristinely manicured and bejeweled hands effortlessly dunking a soiled top sheet in a toilet prior to flushing. Later commercials stressed the freedom and flexibility Pampers allowed as white, middle-class families moved into new suburban homes, took older siblings to little league games, leisured in parks, and played poker and bridge.

In the 1970s disposables advertising started to appeal to medical authority and expertise by portraying Pampers as going beyond being an expression of mother's love to becoming an extension of it in ways that adhered to scientific motherhood.[45] Ads emphasizing hospital-endorsed diapers were especially compelling for immediate postpartum mothers separated from newborns who spent their first days in hospital nurseries. One magazine ad showed a young, white, married mother with her arms wrapped tenderly around her newborn with copy that read:

> A newborn spends so little time in his mother's arms. And so much time in diapers. So 1,694 hospitals use Pampers. . . . he can't be in your arms all the time you want because so much of the time he's in the hospital's hands. So the hospital does lots of little things to make him feel loved, wanted, and comfortable too. One thing is Pampers. . . . Many hospitals think Pampers are the best all-around way to diaper babies. After you use them, you'll think they're a little bit of love you can wrap your baby in—when he's not in your arms.

Trusted by parents and hospitals alike, the ad claimed, disposables allowed mothers to love their babies even when they couldn't physically be with them. This was a particularly compelling brand message for mothers striving to live up to norms of scientific and intensive motherhood. Major diaper companies have since expanded their reach to expectant and new mothers through sponsorships of childbirth classes and prenatal health-care campaigns and samples distributed via hospital labor and delivery wards.

The primary reason mothers during the 1970s and 1980s were separated from their infants was their jobs. Yet rarely did disposable diaper ads of that era acknowledge mothers' employment. One for Pampers showed a new mother returning to her office's secretarial pool. An expectant mother coworker asked her, "Don't you miss your old typewriter?" Another coworker responded, "She's too busy washing diapers!" The new mother exclaimed, "Diapers?! No, Stacy wears Pampers!" Although few diaper ads of the time portrayed employed mothers, one in three married mothers were in the labor force in the mid-1970s when this commercial aired. Only a decade later, half of married mothers with children younger than one year were employed, with employment rates for Black mothers and nonmarried mothers even higher.[46] Like my own mother, who returned to paid work when I was six weeks old, employed mothers increasingly relied on disposable diapers preferred by caregivers and required by daycare centers.

Given steeply rising rates of mothers in the paid workforce, it may seem odd that disposable diapers were never marketed as a convenience commodity that enabled mothers' employment and reduced their housework. However, this strategy makes sense when understood within the context of gendered ideologies of good motherhood that coincided with the influx of mothers of young children into the labor market. Intensive mothering expectations tasked mothers with putting their children's needs and well-being ahead of their own convenience, which left them feeling time-pressured, inadequate, and guilty, especially when they combined paid work with childcare.[47] Intensive mothering expectations intersected with what law professor Joan Williams called the "ideal worker norm," part of the gender system of domesticity that assumes model employees (men) have limited (if any) carework responsibilities.[48] As women were increasingly expected to be ideal workers in addition to intensive mothers, they had to manage a precarious and exhausting balancing act between the first shift of paid work with what sociologist Arlie Russell Hochschild called the "second shift" of childcare and housework.[49] Disposables reduced mothers' second shift in ways deliberately marketed as child-centered, expert-informed, and emotionally engaged. Put another way, they were a "little bit of love" in which employed mothers could wrap their young children when working at their first-shift jobs.

It's no coincidence then that the disposable diaper market grew exponentially as the share of stay-at-home mothers in the United States declined rapidly.[50] Affluent and middle-class women earned more college degrees, leading to more and better employment opportunities. Many women from lower-income families, especially women of color, had long been in the paid labor force for reasons of economic necessity. The 1970s saw unprecedented growth in economic inequality, with rising inflation and higher costs of living made worse by declining unionization rates and lower inflation-adjusted wages for Americans on lower rungs of the socio-economic ladder.[51]

There was a better payoff for affluent women's employment, while poor and working-class women's wages became necessary to offset declines in noncollege-educated men's incomes and racialized wage gaps for men of color. These trends collided to make dual-earner families and employed single mothers the norm rather than the exception by the early 1980s. As was the tendency for earlier generations, it wasn't only mothers of school-age children who went to work. The employment rate of mothers with children ages zero to three had doubled since disposable diapers hit stores shelves in the mid-1960s.[52] This meant many fewer stay-at-home mothers with children of diapering age who could feasibly use cloth diapers most or all the time. A tool in the small arsenal of employed intensive mothers' resources, disposables that didn't require constant washing became more important as childcare demands grew. Despite worries that mothers' employment would interfere with childcare, women's time spent with their children actually doubled from about fifty-four minutes per day in the 1960s to 104 daily minutes by the 2010s.[53] Ironically, my cloth-diapering, nonemployed grandmother likely spent *less* time directly engaged with her children than my mother did with me, even though my mother was employed full time throughout my childhood.

Disposables only got better as employed mothers faced gradually tighter time binds trying to balance their first and second shifts. In the 1980s, major diaper companies introduced two core features of the modern disposable diaper: hourglass-shaped diapers tailored to babies' bodies and elasticized bands that created leak seals around babies' legs.[54] Many diaper ads of the era showed mothers and fathers espousing the benefits of Pampers to others, including their own parents who were presumably too old-fashioned to appreciate the wonders of disposables. Indeed, stay-at-home mothers like my grandmother who used cloth diapers became outdated. But it wasn't because cloth seemed passé and less sophisticated than disposables with new-age polymers, side-adhesive closures, hour-glass shapes, and elasticized leg cuffs. It was because disposable diapers of the time held more, leaked less, and became readily available just as mothers were becoming desperate for any way to manage the dual demands of work and care that produced deep-seated feelings of maternal exhaustion, guilt, and inadequacy.

Diaper companies have capitalized on these feelings among a growing sphere of mothers ever since. Crafting a brand message of universal motherly love, 1970s Pampers ads portrayed Black and Latina mothers praising Pampers as the diaper of choice among hospitals, childcare experts, and experienced mothers.[55] Several 1970s Pampers commercials featured African American actresses, including Phylicia Rashad, who would later find fame as the beloved fictional mother Clair Huxtable on *The Cosby Show*. Part of a larger ad campaign intended to address consumer concerns about Pampers' cost, in one television spot, Rashad played "Mrs. Taylor," the "budget director" of the Taylor family who wanted the best for her baby daughter, Judy, and claimed that "for the same money, you just can't buy a dryer diaper than Pampers."[56] Another commercial featuring Rashad showed her applauding a mother-to-be played by African American actress Debbie Allen for choosing Pampers because of the stay-dry lining, concluding with the tagline, "You're going to be just terrific! . . . [male voiceover] Doesn't your baby deserve Pampers' dryness?"[57] Most of these commercials portrayed Black mothers talking with other Black moms, but some showed mixed-race groups of parents discussing the benefits of disposables, including one 1970s commercial depicting a baby care class for new fathers in which both Black and white men discussed with enthusiastic awe the improved Pampers stay-dry lining.

There were also many Spanish-language Pampers ads during the 1960s and 1970s that featured nods to Latin culture, including a christening celebration, *abuelos* and *abuelas* (grandparents), a fiesta band, and foods like paella. In an effort to appeal to the widest array of consumers, Procter & Gamble targeted many groups, hoping their brand message would translate across racial and ethnic boundaries and easily incorporate racially diverse images that powerfully linked Pampers with maternal know-how and love rather than mothers' convenience.[58] Cognizant that much of the potential market for disposable diapers was composed of Black and Latine families, Procter & Gamble strategically focused disposable diaper advertising on the shifting demographic composition of the United States, where in the 1960s and 1970s the white population was in numeric decline. This was prescient given increases in the US Black and especially Latine populations that tend to have higher birth rates than whites in the United States where now every one in two babies born is a child of color.[59]

Although diaper ads have continued to portray racially and ethnically diverse mothers, they have never focused on class differences and only recently started to feature diversity that increasingly characterizes American families. Just like earlier diaper advertisements in the 1960s, today's ads exclusively feature two-parent nuclear families, usually hetero-sexually married parents, as evidenced by mothers and fathers wearing highly visible wedding rings. Yet over the past sixty years, it has become less likely that children will be born to and grow up with two married par-ents. In 1960, 87 percent of children were living with first-married fami-lies, which fell to 61 percent by 1980 and 46 percent by 2014; two in five babies in the United States are now born to parents who are not mar-ried.[60] A 2017 commercial for Luvs was the first and still one of the only diaper ads to feature two parents of the same gender, both white men married to one another. Although single mother–headed families have been on the steepest rise since disposable diapers hit the market, diaper ads have very rarely featured women in their varied roles as employees, students, caretakers, and household laborers. Given these growing and often competing demands on mothers' time, maternal convenience as a selling point for disposables would have made sense. But it would also have been at odds with intensive mothering expectations that "good" mothers prioritize their baby's health and comfort above all else even, and perhaps especially, when they had to leave their children in someone else's care to go to work.

Parental convenience as a marketing strategy for disposables was only ever emphasized for fathers, who diaper advertising has historically por-trayed as secondary parents and playmates at best, and worse as incompe-tent, less committed caregivers.[61] A 1970s Pampers television commercial showed a father changing his infant daughter's diaper while watching a football game as his friend Buddy said, "That's the spirit, George. Don't let wet diapers interfere with watching football." Intensely focused on the tel-evision, George waved to a box of Pampers and replied, "I never do. Because these are Pampers." "So?" Buddy retorted, as George picked up the baby, gently patted her bottom, and concluded, "Keeps them drier in the end zone."[62] A similar ad of the same period depicted dads playing poker while "babysitting" their infants, the message being that disposables kept babies drier longer, allowing fathers to focus on fun activities they prioritized over childcare. The bottom line: For mothers, disposables were about love. For fathers, they were about leisure.

Fast-forward almost half a century to 2012, when Huggies maker Kimberly-Clark produced a series of diaper commercials that made headlines for invoking a different but no less problematic message about fatherhood.[63] Huggies promised to put their product through the "toughest test imaginable" by leaving fathers alone with their infants for five days. In one television spot upbeat music played while mothers handed over babies to their dads. Fathers struggled to entertain, feed, and keep their infants clean, and changing diapers caused looks of befuddlement, intimidation, and disgust. Much like earlier Pampers ads, the Huggies spot framed fathers as babysitting their own children, positioning women as primary parents who are rarely given a day off. The ad also poked fun at fathers as clueless, comical, bumbling oafs when it comes to the most basic care needs of their children. The Huggies ad met swift backlash from fathers who wanted their contributions to family labor recognized and taken seriously. Selling diapers as so good that they even pass the "dad test" seriously missed that mark.

Criticism of the Huggies dad test ad pointed to how the rising popularity of disposables unfolded during a time of significant changes in the gendered division of parenting labor, as fathers increasingly do more childcare, including diapering. But as reflected in diaper advertising, gendered stereotypes and stark gender inequities in parenting persist. The typical US father in 1965 spent twelve minutes a day on childcare, barely enough to do a single diaper change. Today's fathers report on average just under an hour, or about half of what mothers do.[64] Fathers' time with children is still more likely to be characterized as ancillary to mothers' and as play rather than work. Reflecting this characterization of dad as playmate, a 2018 television spot for Pampers Pure opened with singer John Legend changing his daughter's diaper, smiling, and singing a song as other dads wrangled toddlers and changed diapers. The lyrics rhymed children's "stinky booty" with dad's "diaper duty" as fathers tickled and swayed their children's legs to the upbeat, silly tune. The commercial ended with a message from Pampers, thanking fathers for "making every moment special." Although the ad portrayed fathers as competent coparents who share diaper duty, dads' diapering was still portrayed as mostly fun and something men do only when mothers aren't around.

Contrast this style of playful paternal diapering with the message of another 2018 Procter & Gamble Pampers Swaddlers ad. Marketed as the softest Pampers diapers available, the television spot showed a doctor placing a tiny, crying newborn on her astonished mother's bare chest immediately after delivery as she embraced the baby. A loving, feminine voiceover proclaimed, "From the first loving touch, everything that touches your baby should be this comforting." Pampers is "the #1 choice of hospitals," "two times softer," and "wraps your baby in our most premium protection." Rather than fun with dads, this diaper ad sold the idea that, just like mothers, disposable diapers love, hold, and protect babies. A similar 2015 Kimberly-Clark Huggies ad campaign emphasized the "Power of Hugs" and appealed to scientific authority and maternal intuition by claiming that "over 600 medical studies on the effects of human touch prove what moms have always known: Hugs are important. . . . After your first hug, let the second thing that touches your baby's skin feel just as good."

More than half a century after Procter & Gamble launched Pampers, a man was first featured on a diaper box in 2019 for the Kimberly-Clark Huggies Special Delivery line. Despite recognition that diapering is something dads do too, diaper companies continue to highlight the connection between healthier, happier, and smarter babies and loving, attentive moms who nurture them by choosing and using disposables. This remarkably successful gendered message is among many reasons that disposables quickly overtook cloth as the dominant diaper type across the United States and throughout the world.

THE GLOBAL REACH OF THE "DIAPER WARS"

A diaper innovation tug-of-war between Procter & Gamble and Kimberly-Clark sparked what industry insiders dubbed the "diaper wars," generating continual improvements in disposable diaper technologies between the two major disposable diaper manufacturers that dominated both national and international markets. By the mid-1970s, Procter & Gamble's Pampers had captured a 75 percent share of the US disposable diaper market and expanded to seventy-five countries.[65] Capitalizing on this vast success, in 1976, a decade after a profitable initial launch of the Pampers line, Procter

& Gamble introduced Luvs, the first "premium" hourglass-shaped diaper with elastic leg cuffs, which sold for about 30 percent more than regular Pampers. After Kimberly-Clark's Huggies surged to 30 percent market share in the early 1980s, Procter & Gamble introduced Ultra Pampers with new proprietary absorbent gel and leak-proof waist shields. Capital and marketing investments totaling nearly $750 million paid off when many consumers switched back to Pampers, but not enough to hand a definitive win in the "diaper wars" to Procter & Gamble.

Due to Procter & Gamble's efforts to differentiate their two main diaper lines, Luvs, the brand once considered top-of-the-line luxury among disposables, became a simpler, more basic diaper in the mid-1990s. Now known as the "economical" mainstream diaper line, Luvs price about a dime less per diaper than Pampers or Huggies, which sell for about twenty-six to thirty-three cents per size 3 diaper and cost half of what they did in the mid-1960s after adjusting for inflation. As they became more functional and affordable, disposables also became cuter and more fashionable. In 1984, Cabbage Patch Kids cartoons appeared on the first designer diaper, sparking a trend of popular character-imprinted disposables. The following decades saw even more diaper innovations, driven mostly by Procter & Gamble's and Kimberly-Clark's efforts to one up each other in a fiercely competitive US diaper market where the infant population was growing at about only 1 percent annually.[66]

When it came to how to care for babies' bottoms and effects it would have on their parents' bottom lines, perhaps even more important than industry diaper wars was the larger battle between cloth and disposables. By the turn of the twenty-first century, disposables had clearly overtaken cloth as the diaper type of choice among most American families. Instead of encouraging parents to choose single-use diapers over reusable cloth, advertising emphasized new disposable diaper technologies, which ranged from umbilical cord cutouts and sex-specific diapers with extra padding where "boy and girls need it most," to stretch waistbands and Velcro fasteners on thinner, more absorbent diapers with a clothlike feel. The earlier focus on babies' butts shifted to an emphasis on babies' brains, when ads in the 1990s and 2000s portrayed disposables as central to healthy childhood development by enabling more comfortable play and mobility and longer sleep for cognitive growth. Yet the related message that calmer, slumbering infants allow stressed-out, sleep-deprived mothers to rest has never been a focal point of diaper advertising. The dominant US brand message of optimal maternal care over convenience persisted through all these technological and cosmetic innovations, as diaper companies found more ways to sell the promise of better mothering through disposables.

Efforts to break into, or rather deliberately create, other national disposable diaper markets have been fraught with challenges. In China, disposable diaper companies had to convince parents not only that their diapers were best but that parents even needed disposables at all. Historically many Chinese children were potty trained starting at six months and wore split-crotch *kai dang ku* pants, a practice enabled by communal childrearing and constant availability of mothers, aunts, grandmothers, and other caregivers always on hand to help children squat and clean up.[67] Not until the highly successful 2007 "Golden Sleep" campaign was Procter & Gamble able to tap into the large Chinese diaper market. Touting corporate-sponsored research that babies who wore disposables instead of cloth fell asleep 30 percent faster and slept an extra half hour every night, Procter & Gamble linked extra sleep to better cognitive development. This proved to be a powerful marketing strategy for Chinese parents looking for opportunities to boost children's academic achievement.[68] By 2010, Pampers dominated the diaper market in China, where just a decade earlier disposables barely existed.

Pampers is now the top-selling diaper brand in India where, as in China, if infants wear disposables, it tends to be only one per day. Pampers strategically placed kiosks that sell one- and two-diaper packs all over India and Southwest Asia.[69] Procter & Gamble also initiated healthcare outreach, baby care programs (including door-to-door diaper samples), and Pampers-UNICEF vaccination campaigns throughout India and Africa to promote the Pampers brand. Pampers manufacturing plants are in twenty-five countries, with Pampers sold in more than one hundred, and Procter & Gamble has become well known for effectively tweaking its brand messages for different national markets shaped by distinct parenting norms. Market research has found that convenience as a selling point for disposables doesn't resonate for Indian mothers who tend to believe that only "lazy" moms use disposable overnight diapers. As Pampers brand manager Vidya Ramachandran said in a video for Pampers employees, "We really had to change that mindset and educate [mothers] that using a diaper is not about convenience for you—it's about your baby's development."[70] Selling disposable diapers as best for babies over less work for mothers transcends national contexts and cultural differences.

Advertising for disposables remains a key lens through which to understand changing norms of diapering as influenced by larger social, economic, and demographic trends in family life. The year 2021 marked the first time that a diaper ad made an appearance during that most coveted commercial spot, the Super Bowl.[71] Featuring infants born around the globe on that very day, Huggies assured parents that their diapers would help babies eat, sleep, and move with ease and acclimate to a world increasingly connected through globalization. Highly visible advertising, especially to a huge mixed-gender audience, reflected concerns over US parents having fewer babies that require diapers and efforts to make greater inroads into other national diaper markets. Since 2008, US birth rates have been declining, on average, about half a percent each year; 2020 saw a particularly steep 4 percent decline in birth rates, an anomalously large bump in a longer-term trend.[72] Despite concerns that falling birth rates due to the COVID-19 pandemic would cut into diaper company profits, sales for both Huggies and Pampers were up about 5 percent during early 2021 by the time the "Welcome to the World, Baby" Super Bowl commercial aired. This was due in part to an ever-growing cross-national preference for disposables over cloth diapers that major diaper companies deliberately cultivated.

Disposable diaper technologies continue to proliferate as parents face a vast array of brands, materials, types, and features. Parents can now buy swimming diapers, diapers specially made for children of color with "melanated skin," and even smartphone-enabled diapers that use embedded moisture sensors and special textiles to signal wetness and weight to cell phones and computers. Although Kimberly-Clark and Procter & Gamble still dominate national and international markets, the Honest Company, Costco's Kirkland, Walmart's Parents' Choice, Cuties, Hello Bello, Baby Cozy, Mama Bear, and many other smaller diaper companies occupy a significant market share. Yet not all disposable diaper inventions have taken off. In 1987, actress Jaime Lee Curtis patented the "Dipe and Wipe," a disposable diaper with an outer moisture-proof pocket for holding wet cleaning wipes. Curtis was issued another diaper patent in 2017 for a similar plastic pocket feature that could be unfolded and wrapped around soiled diapers prior to disposal.[73] As an environmental activist, Curtis opted not to capitalize on the patents until they can be mass-produced using biodegradable materials. As discussed in chapter 4 about environmental concerns over diapering, many parents increasingly look to "greener" diaper options, including those made of reusable organic cotton and bamboo. As more parents seek to reduce their environmental impact and diaper costs, cloth diapering has experienced a resurgence in recent decades, with a small but significant portion of parents in the United States eschewing disposables.

DITCHING THE DIAPERS: POTTY TRAINING AND THE DEMANDS OF CAPITALISM

The same changing ideologies of childhood and socioeconomic conditions of childrearing that revolutionized diapering also fundamentally reshaped how parents think about when their children should be out of diapers. Like diapering, toilet training, considered an important aspect of early childhood development and major milestone for both parents and children, is a psychological, physiological, and sociocultural process.[74] Later toilet training became more practical during the mid-twentieth century, when disposables were invented and many families acquired access to electric in-home washers and dryers that made laundering cloth diapers less intensive.

Starting in the 1960s, leading childcare experts like Dr. Benjamin Spock and Dr. T. Berry Brazelton recommended that mothers take a flexible approach to toilet training or else risk psychologically harming children.[75] Perhaps influenced by commercial interests, these experts noted that children would start using the toilet when they were ready. Procter & Gamble featured Dr. Brazelton in a 1998 commercial introducing a size 6 diaper for children thirty-five pounds and over with Brazelton, chair of the Pampers Parenting Institute, advising, "Don't rush your toddler into toilet training or let anyone else tell you it's time. It's got to be his choice." The American Academy of Pediatrics concurred. Yet other nationally recognized experts of the time advocated that children should be out of diapers sooner, even as early as their first birthday. The "toilet-training wars" have been raging ever since, with the age at which children become diaper-free rising steadily each generation. In the 1950s almost all—92 percent—of children age eighteen months and older were toilet trained.[76] Now most children in the United States are closer to their second birthdays before they even start potty training, though many show readiness signs, such as expressing discomfort when their diaper is wet or dirty, starting at eighteen months.[77] The rising age of potty training has been attributed to the popularity of disposables, a preference for short-term convenience over longer-term benefits, and the luxury of no longer having to wash cloth diapers by hand.

Yet various social and economic factors influence when and how children learn to use the toilet. Parents in the United States report an average of 20.6 months as the age toilet training should be initiated, with white parents and higher-income parents reporting older ages than Black and lower-income parents.[78] In addition to the widespread use of disposables, the growing emphasis on child-oriented parenting approaches and higher employment rates for mothers have likely contributed to the rising age of being diaper-free in the United States. As mothers' education and family income increase, so too does the age by which her children are toilet trained.[79] Moreover, many children in the United States learn to use the toilet according to norms and practices dictated by childcare facilities on which working parents must rely.[80] Diaper companies have responded, and likely contributed, to the rising age of toilet training by expanding product categories for larger diapers, as with size 6 Pampers advertised by Dr. Brazelton in the "child readiness" campaign. Size 7 diapers for children weighing forty-one pounds or more are now readily available, as are training pants intended for children up to fifty pounds, the average weight for seven-year-old children in the United States.[81] There is also growing recognition of reasons that some children need to stay in diapers or training pants longer or indefinitely, including developmental delays, neurodivergence, and physical challenges or disabilities that make urinary and bowel control difficult or impossible.[82]

Families in other parts of the world toilet train their children at much younger ages, and often forgo diapers entirely due to limited infrastructure, economic conditions, and climate. More than two billion people in the world still lack access to basic plumbing, and most of them necessarily practice open defecation.[83] In places where parents don't have easy access to diapers and resources needed to clean them, most children are potty trained by one year. Potty training at older ages is also associated with how far families live from the equator, suggesting that warmer climates encourage children to go diaper-free much younger than their colder climate counterparts.[84] Moreover, age and method of toilet training depend heavily on cultural norms and social support. In Nigeria, the majority of parents start toilet training their infants before the child's first birthday by removing children's diapers and asking them to urinate at specific times each day.[85] Similarly, many Iranian families start taking one-year-old infants to the toilet at regular intervals and encouraging them to urinate or defecate.[86] Yet in Norway, where the average age of toilet training is much older, parents tend to believe that children should initiate the process by showing signs of readiness, a belief supported by widely available and subsidized cloth and disposable "nappies," public changing tables, and large public and private networks of infant caretaking.[87]

A particularly noteworthy case of how socioeconomic conditions influence toileting is in Côte d'Ivoire on the coast of western Africa, where many Beng women are farmers, no daycare system exists, fathers rarely participate in infant care, and mothers start infant bowel training a few days after birth when they must return to long days in the fields. When newborns' dried umbilical cords fall off, mothers administer bulb syringe enema laxatives each morning and evening, usually during bath time.[88] Once children can walk, they are toilet trained, which typically means learning to defecate in forests and urinate in village outskirts. Using enemas on newborns may seem extreme among those in social contexts where extended diaper-wearing is common. However, like throughout much of the Global South, in Beng villages disposables are unavailable or prohibitively expensive among subsistence-farming families. While their mothers work in the fields, young infants spend their days strapped to mothers or caregivers, who understandably do not want feces running down their backs. With no tradition or technology for diapers, toilet training from birth helps ensure that mothers can provide adequate food for their families. According to anthropologist Alma Gottlieb, this method is completely rational within the sociocultural and economic context of Beng society.[89]

Lest we condemn infant enemas, Beng parents would likely find the common American technique of tightly adhering absorbent plastic and cloth to children's bottoms and leaving them to sit in urine and feces, sometimes for hours, to be just as odd. Both practices are deeply influenced by diaper availability and affordability rooted in larger structures of gendered labor and childrearing values and norms. In both contexts the demands of work, especially women's labor, dictate diapering and toilet-training methods and timelines.[90] In the United States, where most families of young children depend on extrafamilial care, parents' diapering choices are greatly influenced by daycare center requirements that children wear disposables or be toilet trained by a certain age. Mothers who have access to extended leave from paid work or don't work outside the home have more discretion and time to use cloth diapers and potty train according to timelines they deem best. As with many aspects of childrearing, diapering and when parents can ditch the diapers via toilet training come down to money, time, and what seems normal—all factors shaped by local context and differential access to resources and choices.

Nowhere is this more evident than with another diaper-free practice: elimination communication. Also known as "assisted toilet training" and "natural infant hygiene," elimination communication is customary in most parts of the world, including Africa, Asia, and South America.[91] Often starting with the newborn stage, parents learn to recognize infants' involuntary muscle contractions in the bowels, also known as peristaltic movements, and other signs that they are about to pee or poop. When they sense these signs, a caregiver will hold the infant over a container and gradually habituate the child to excrete in a toilet on cue. In Kenya, for instance, Digo mothers place children on their laps, make a hissing sound, and reward infants when they pee; using this method, most Digo babies learn how to urinate in position and on command by five months of age.[92] Many Vietnamese mothers use a similar sound-association method, whereby they pay attention to newborn kicks and cries linked to peeing or pooping and put their children over a toilet and whistle as they go. Using this strategy, mothers plan for their infants to use the toilet around nine months of age by whistling to cue the babies' bladder and bowel movements.[93]

In the United States elimination communication—or what some call "diaper-free parenting"—has a small but devoted group of advocates who promote it as more natural, comfortable for babies, environmentally friendly, and good for parent-child bonding.[94] Where diapers are not readily available and sanitation infrastructure is sparse, diaperless babies are a necessity for parents, caregivers, and employers.[95] However, in a society like the United States where infants are rarely toilet trained before two years of age, many babies must be placed in daycare, and most mothers lack an extended network of family and friends to watch an infant around the clock, elimination communication becomes an extreme form of intensive mothering dependent on time and energy resources many American mothers lack. Disposables for the first several years of a child's life have thus become the preferred diaper type and method in many parts of the world. Suffice it to say, Marion Donovan's detractors didn't understand the varied physical, cultural, social, and economic diaper dilemmas parents would eventually face.

·   ·   ·   ·   ·

U.S. News and World Reports hailed innovators Marion Donovan and Victor Mills, often credited as the mother and father of disposable diapers, no less "pioneers of women's liberation than Betty Friedan and Gloria Steinem."[96] This raises the question: from *what* exactly did disposable diapers liberate women? Much has changed since Donovan invented the Boater and my grandmother diapered her children in muslin cotton fabric and potty trained them all by fifteen months. Mothers of subsequent generations were much more likely to be employed when their children were very young. By the early 1980s my mother's return to work when I was a newborn was a necessity for our family, just as it was for millions of working-class mothers in the United States like her who absorbed the shocks of rapidly growing class divides with few public provisions to support their childrearing efforts. In other ways, however, little has changed as the US social safety net frayed and supportive family policies stagnated during this revolution toward working families. Three-quarters of a century after the disposable diaper was born, the evolution of diapering has been nothing short of astounding. We've gone from square paper diapers secured with sharp pins and covered in uncomfortable, leaky plastic, to diapers expertly tailored to babies' shape that feel comfortably dry for hours without leaking and can communicate with computers. Yet the United States still lacks fair-wage laws, universal paid family leave, guaranteed flexible work schedule mandates, permanent child allowances, and adequate basic needs and cash assistance.

Gender ideologies of parenting have also been stubbornly slow to change. Employed moms like mine who returned to work due to financial necessity when their children were very young were vilified as lesser mothers lacking full commitment to their children. What was really lacking were social, economic, and political supports for working families. Within this context disposables didn't just mean less laundry for moms. They became one of the few stopgap measures mid- and late-twentieth-century working mothers had at their disposal to manage the precarious balancing act between their first and second shifts. This is hardly women's liberation. Some question if disposables are a better product that filled an unmet consumer need, or if diaper companies deliberately created that sense of need. In any case, driven by profit motive in an untapped growing consumer market, disposable diapering evolved in response to changing demands of work, care, and cleanliness. This met a need for working families, especially employed mothers who no longer had to wash cloth diapers, but it created new problems and needs in its wake. As our global society transitioned from rural and agricultural to more urban and industrialized—bringing with it vast changes in sanitation infrastructure, hygiene and disposability norms, the social organization of gendered labor, and ideologies of proper parenting—disposable diapers became a taken-for-granted requirement of late capitalism.

American families, and increasingly those in other countries, now work and parent in social contexts that presume access to disposables. Long gone are the days when my grandmother's muslin squares would suffice as acceptable diapers. Any form of diapering and even alternatives, such as elimination communication and early potty training, depend on intersecting forms of privilege that many families don't possess. Diapers' history foretells a great deal about the disastrous contemporary consequences of not having them, which is where our diaper story unfolds next.

3. Love and Labor of Diaper Need

INVENTIVE MOTHERS DOING DIAPER WORK

Food, toilet paper, and tampons. These were just a few things Patricia went without each month to save money for diapers. Aluminum cans, food stamps, and her blood plasma. These were things Patricia sold for diaper money. Keeping a careful diaper log, closely tracking her toddler's liquid intake, and letting her daughter go without diapers on warmer days while at home. These were tactics Patricia used to stretch her limited diapers. Each of these strategies involved innovative diaper math, the sacrificing, scheduling, selling, and stretching parents do to meet children's diaper needs.

Patricia, a thirty-two-year-old Black mother of three, including eighteen-month-old daughter Sofia, had a quickly dwindling diaper supply when I interviewed her, and there was still over a week to go until the second of the month when her next cash aid check would arrive. That check could cover a 120-count box of size 5 diapers at the closest supermarket for thirty dollars, almost all of what would be left of Patricia's welfare money after she paid her portion of rent, bought food that WIC and food stamps wouldn't cover, and put gas in the car. Most months Patricia had to scrape together change to buy single one-dollar diapers at the corner store. Recalling an old adage her own mother used—"not a lot of money left at the end of the month"—she told me, "When it comes to diapers, there's usually a lot of month left at the end of the money."

"Diapers are the thing we buy first because it's the thing we can least do without," Patricia said about why she always bought mid-priced diapers right after cashing her check. She'd tried the cheapest brands, but Sofia always got rashes, and they held less and leaked more than pricier diapers. When Sofia didn't have a bowel movement, a diaper that held more liquid and kept her drier could be worn longer, marking a critical difference between a 120-count box that lasted three weeks versus one that might be stretched to the second of the next month. As a last resort, Patricia used pillowcases, T-shirts, and paper towels secured with duct tape and hair ties to create makeshift diapers. Patricia worried most when Sofia had diarrhea. In addition to a sick baby, she explained, "that means more diapers." Patricia was starting to potty train Sofia, who was about a year younger than most toddlers in the United States who initiate toilet training. "I'm potty training early so we can cancel the diaper cost, but she's not really ready," Patricia admitted.

Sharing why she sacrificed so much to provide Sofia's diapers, Patricia said, "Diapers are a need because that's a bodily function they have. They're not a luxury. Every child needs diapers, from the poorest of the poor to the richest of the rich. Even the richest babies poop, and even the poorest babies need and deserve a clean butt." Patricia used the word *need* four times in explaining why diapers are important, describing them as a necessity of early childhood that transcends class lines—"from the poorest of the poor to the richest of the rich"—and one for which Patricia was readily willing to go without her own needs to secure enough. What struck me most was the specificity with which she answered when I asked, "How many diapers do you have now?" Patricia replied straightway, "I have seven in the house, two in my purse, and one hidden for an emergency. Based on how often [Sofia] goes to the bathroom, I know those diapers will last me about thirty-six hours before I run out and have to get more."

Patricia's answer was telling, but not just because of the few diapers she had. It was that she knew to the hour how long her limited diaper supply would last. I could only imagine the energy, effort, and forethought needed to know that ten diapers would last exactly a day and half. But when you don't know where your baby's next diaper is coming from, Patricia reasoned, you do what you must. Not keeping a constantly running mental diaper tally is a privilege. If you had asked me when my daughter was in diapers how many I had at any moment, I would have estimated a couple boxes in the closet, a pack on each changing table, several in the car, and a handful in each diaper bag. Until I met Patricia and mothers like her struggling to get enough diapers, I took these guesses for granted. As Patricia poignantly explained to me, diapers are a need not a luxury. Yet the ability to buy ahead, stock up, and not give much thought to running out is.

The previous chapter explained how the disposables Patricia struggled to afford and stretch each month became a basic need of early childhood. Heightened hygiene expectations combined with modern norms of intensive mothering and sacred childhood make a clean diaper seem like something, to paraphrase Patricia, all babies need and deserve. Patricia mentioned potty training "early" even though Sofia wasn't "ready" yet, reflecting a historically and culturally specific understanding of when children should be out of diapers and anxieties over how long families must buy them to adhere to norms of appropriate toilet training. Like Patricia, mothers born after the mid-1960s have been raised on incessant disposable diaper advertising on television, in magazines, via direct-mail promotions, and even in hospitals and pediatricians' offices. Ads convinced generations of women that buying and using name-brand disposables is about being a "good" mother who loves her children enough to keep them clean, comfortable, and healthy, enabling optimal childcare, sleep, and development. Just as decades of deliberate diaper advertising intended, Patricia never spoke of disposables as more convenient for her but rather as best for Sofia.

Providing children's basic needs often requires poor mothers like Patricia to do more labor than affluent mothers. Although all parents must contain and dispose of children's waste, managing limited diapers is a complex physical, cognitive, emotional, and social process for financially strapped parents. I call this multifaceted labor *diaper work*, an overlooked class-based component of early childcare involving more than purchasing or procuring diapers and disposing of or cleaning used diapers. For mothers I interviewed, this work entails a specific form of care labor necessary to oversee limited diapers supplies, invent and use diaper-stretching strategies, and manage the physical, economic, and cognitive toll of material shortages and stigma. Diaper work illuminates the parental stress and strain of unmet childcare needs and the lengths to which mothers will go to protect their children from deprivation, discomfort, and discrimination. Diaper work also shows how dominant ideologies of parenting don't always acknowledge forms of childcare labor created specifically by conditions of gendered and racialized poverty and stingy social safety nets that don't account fully for families' basic needs. That Patricia knew she had exactly ten diapers reveals a lot about diaper need specifically. More generally, it is a window onto how inequalities shape modern mothering.

Mothers across social classes assume they should put their children's needs first and, when necessary, sacrifice their own needs and wants to provide for their children's. Sociologist Sharon Hays called this ideology "intensive mothering" when it compels women to devote tremendous time, energy, and money to raising their children.[1] Beyond this, diaper work reveals the agency and inventiveness of low-income mothers' parenting strategies, logics, and moral meanings as they raise their children in the context of poverty, racism, welfare state curtailment, and limited public support for basic needs. Diaper work demands a particular approach to parenting that I call *inventive mothering*, which, in addition to being child-centered, time-consuming, and self-sacrificing, is innovatively resourceful, harm-reducing, and stigma-deflecting. In this chapter I draw on mothers' diaper work stories to highlight the complexity and rigor of coping with diaper need as part of inventive mothering.

Mothers' efforts to manage diaper need as a specific type of scarcity provide insight into larger issues that characterize parenting in poverty in the United States. The first is how diapers, which may seem like any other optional household product, become essential and come to have profound material as well as symbolic value. The second is how physically and mentally taxing it can be to manage deprivation of basic needs day in and day out, especially when poverty itself creates additional costs for cash-strapped families. Finally, doing diaper work is associated with racialized stress, stigma, surveillance, and social exclusion that all shape parenting experiences of mothers of color in particularly harmful ways. By showing how each of these issues influences mothers' inventive efforts to raise their children at the intersection of class, gender, and race inequalities, this chapter explores how and why Patricia knew precisely that she had ten diapers on hand—and the significant social, psychological, and economic costs that come with doing this kind of diaper math.

"CHOOSING THE DIAPERS IS CHOOSING MY KID": WHAT DIAPERS MEAN TO MOTHERS

As undergarments intended to contain and conceal urine and fecal waste, diapers may seem to be simple objects that do little more than keep babies from being dirty. Yet, according to anthropologist Mary Douglas, "dirty" doesn't have absolute meaning but rather reveals cultural conventions of hygiene intended to ward off disease and social disorder.[2] Cleanliness norms—or what Douglas calls "pollution beliefs"—are both instrumental and symbolic in how they create unified social experiences and demarcate claims to social status based on being "clean." One near-universal pollution belief is that sacred beings are most in need and deserving of protection from defilement and dirt. Sociologist Sharon Hays subsequently theorized how American norms of intensive mothering task women with protecting young children in this way, or risk being judged a maternal failure.[3] That is, a baby in a "dirty" diaper not only violates sacred norms of childhood; it denies their mother social status as an attentive and intensive parent.

Sufficient clean diapers are therefore both instrumental for protecting children from disease and discomfort and symbolic of mothers' maternal work on behalf of their children as precious and adored. For both reasons diapers become central to mothers' parental presentations of self. As sociologist Jessica Collett discovered when observing and interviewing parents about their children's clothes, mothers differentiate between "old" and "new" dirt on children when judging their and others' maternal fitness. Normal "new" dirt accumulates on children's bodies and clothing within a few hours as they do typical kid activities like play and eat. Regular cleaning and bathing of children are part of being well cared for by dutiful, devoted mothers who love them. Yet a child in "old" dirt with smelly, soiled clothing and grime on their face accumulated over a matter of days or weeks wears the mark of neglect—and thus being the child of a lesser mother.[4] Diapers fall into a unique liminal space in this "new" versus "old" dirt typology. They are intended to cover a young child's most delicate, intimate body parts and be a barrier between their tender skin and polluted bodily substances. According to dominant cleanliness norms, soiled diapers should be changed right away and often. Mothers come to fear being judged as bad, neglectful parents when children smell of urine or feces or are seen wearing a "dirty" diaper that is swollen, sagging, or leaking.

Although their children's soiled diapers were almost always "newly" dirty, mothers told me they constantly feared the stigma of "old" dirt when it came to diapers, which had even greater significance than clothes for mothers' presentations of self as "good" parents. Soiled children's clothing bearing food and milk debris, mud, and other evidence of children's normal daily activities was never seen to be as unclean as diapers marked with urine and feces, both of which mothers described as the smelliest and foulest kind of "dirt" children's bodies could accumulate. Maria, a thirty-year-old Latina mother of four, noted, "I don't have a lot of money for diapers. . . . But I can't leave them on too long either. I can't have my baby smelling like pee. I don't want *that smell*. It's a strong smell, and I just can't have other people smell that on him." For many mothers the thought of their children's skin having contact with urine or feces for any period of time was unsettling, not only because of the health risks and physical revulsion associated with excrement but also because of the social revulsion associated with dirt and odors linked to being lower class.

Trina, twenty-nine, white, and a mother of two, explained, "I'll go without food, but I'm weird about my kid sitting in a diaper that has any pee in it, even a drop." Trina knew she could stretch her diaper supply if she let her daughter urinate several times between changes. Yet a clean diaper wasn't just about vigilant hygiene for her. It represented a baby who was comfortable and respectable, despite other scarcities the family, and especially Trina herself, faced. Similarly, Kelly, a thirty-two-year-old white mother of three, said, "I'll cut other things in the budget to buy diapers because I don't think a baby should be in a dirty diaper. It's not healthy, and it smells and looks bad. What will people think if they see your kid in a dirty diaper? No one wants their baby to smell like pee or poop, especially to other people." Mothers rationalized not buying clothes, toys, or fancy baby care items or even food and hygiene items for themselves, but they couldn't let their children be dirty—neither in the physical sense of being touched by or smelling of excrement nor symbolically being marked by polluting social stigma.

In prioritizing their children's hygiene and working to deflect classist and racist stigma associated with being physically or socially contaminated, mothers were in a bind between wanting to change their children's diapers frequently and constantly stressing about running out of diapers. Many mothers described the hypervisibility and odor of diapers, specifically how the stench of stale urine is redolent of deprivation, a top note of the smell of poverty that marks someone as unclean and "trashy." Distinguishing between the lived experiences of food insecurity and diaper scarcity, several mothers noted that although a hungry baby and a baby in a dirty diaper are both tragic, only the latter is immediately obvious. You can't always sense when a child is hungry, and a dehydrated or malnourished child can take days or weeks to show signs of need and neglect. But you can immediately see, feel, and smell when they wear a soiled diaper. Consequently, more than half of the mothers I interviewed told me that diapers were the household expense they worried about most, even more than food or housing. Mothers prioritized diapers among their children's most basic needs, as evidenced by their descriptions of diapers as central to mothering and by how diapers were often the first item they bought after receiving aid or income. Sonia, a thirty-three-year-old Latina mother of two, described diapers as "part of babies' developmental and physical needs, which means it's really scary for a mom not to have diapers. You have to have them to be able to function properly with your child as a mother."

Natasha, a thirty-five-year-old Black mother of four, explained why diapers trumped other childcare and household necessities when money was tight. "You can cut back on his baby formula as they get a bit older, but Pampers don't go away. . . . Then you find yourself in that situation where you only have ten dollars left and you gotta get Pampers or food." Mothers often chose diapers, as most (79 percent) told me they regularly went without other necessities, including food, to afford diapers. Tellingly, Natasha and other mothers used "Pampers" as a proprietary eponym, when a brand-name becomes a common generic referent for all products in that category.[5] Disposables have become such a ubiquitous and taken-for-granted aspect of modern childcare and "good" parenting that mothers put "Pampers" on par with food in their accounting of household expenses.

Mothers also worried about diapers more than food because, in their view, there were fewer coping strategies available when diapers ran low or out. They reported fewer food shortages due to receiving WIC and SNAP and access to food banks. Food assistance programs didn't cover all their families' nutritional needs, and many mothers reported spending money out-of-pocket on food, especially infant formula. But public assistance and compensatory tactics for managing diaper need were limited compared to strategies mothers had devised for dealing with food insecurity. Mothers justified going without food themselves or eating mostly low-cost foods like tortillas and dry cereal as tactics they could anticipate and manage. Yet they struggled to do the same with diapers when rationing was less predictable and meant depriving their young children of something needed to stay clean and dignified. As Melissa, thirty-two, Asian, and a mother of three, shared: "As long as you portion sizes and know how much your children eat, you know how much food you're buying. But diapers, it's uncontrollable because you don't know how many times they're going to pee or poop a day. If they're sick and have diarrhea, they're going to go through way more. I don't worry as much about food because I can manage it with food stamps. I worry more about diapers because there's no support, and they go like no tomorrow." Melissa got fresh produce through her job as a fieldworker and knew family members and friends with fruit trees and gardens that produced excess food. But she had fewer sources of in-kind diaper support and felt guilty asking for diapers or diaper money from friends and family experiencing similar financial constraints.

Cora, a thirty-five-year-old Black mother of five, worried "about diapers more than food because we can portion our food. We get some food stamps, always have at least a can of something. You can't really portion your diapers in the same way and say, 'Okay, I'm going to use only three diapers today.' What if your kid goes poop four times?" Like Cora, many mothers received food stamps and housing assistance, but very few received diaper assistance due to limited public provisions for diapers. This made it difficult to cover costly diaper expenses with dwindling cash aid and low wages earned from work. With two kids in diapers, Cora faced especially dire diaper need:

> [My husband] gets side jobs to pay for the diapers, but if we start running out, I will only change the diaper when the baby poops or fills it all the way up totally with pee. . . . I know I shouldn't leave it on too long. That might make me seem like a bad parent, but it's hard to change a diaper all the time because if you run out then that makes you a bad parent too. People assume that you're spending money on stuff you shouldn't have. I worry about being out in public and people making comments or judging me for what my kid's diaper looks like. People look at you funny when the diaper looks a little bit big because he just went to the bathroom, and it's already sagging, like, "Why aren't you changing the kid's diaper?" They don't know. They have no idea.

Cora's dilemma was common. She felt like a bad mother for delaying diaper changes, but without stretching them she risked running out and being judged a bad mother for lacking diapers. It was a damned if you do, damned if you don't diaper-changing situation.

Although mothers like Melissa and Cora told me they worried more about diapers because they could get food in other ways, many also shared stories of going hungry or limiting their own food intake to save diaper money, suggesting that they couldn't always utilize other food access strategies or aid. This aligns with other research finding that caregivers who struggle with diaper need report higher levels of food insecurity and skip meals and buy less food and lower-cost foods as common ways of coping with diaper need.[6] Mothers admitted to relying on these tactics to save diaper money, while emphasizing that their diaper work related to food involved minimizing only their own eating and food costs, never their children's. According to mothers, the only exceptions were when they avoided feeding children foods that tended to cause diarrhea and giving them "extra" liquid to drink, especially around nap or bedtime.

Nora, a twenty-three-year-old Latina mother of two, said, "At night, I'll just give my son a bottle, and then I won't give him anything else extra to drink so his diaper will go all night without being changed." Briana, a twenty-year-old Latina mother of one, was also attentive to how her daughter's drinking and eating habits affected diaper use: "I have to wait to change her diaper until it's really full. I feed her a lot, but I try to reduce after she's eaten, and I try not to give her foods that upset her stomach and might cause her to poop more." Mothers reasoned that reducing the number of diapers used was ancillary to ensuring that their children had comfortable digestion and sufficient good sleep, an important consideration given that diaper need is associated with disrupted and shorter sleep for infants and toddlers.[7]

Mothers also admitted to not changing their babies immediately after urination, but only after they'd figured out exactly how much each diaper could absorb without irritating infants' skin. Yazmin, a twenty-eight-year-old Latina mother of three, said, "As long as I know she's not going to get a rash, I'll hold off for about an hour or so to change her. If I bathe her, and she hasn't used the diaper, I reuse the same one she had before the bath, so I don't waste a diaper." Mothers like Yazmin invested significant cognitive labor into learning which diaper brands and sizes could hold the most without causing their children discomfort or pain. The primary criterion shaping mothers' diaper brand preferences was the likelihood of skin irritation, with price a secondary consideration. Although they could barely afford to buy any diapers at all, mothers frequently bought the most expensive ones because they held more while keeping their children drier, rash-free, and more comfortable. Mothers often covered the extra costs by buying cheaper versions of their own needs or going without. Natalie, a twenty-nine-year-old multiracial mother of three, simply said, "I will always choose my kid over other expenses. Choosing the diaper is choosing my kid."

Mothers understood these diaper work tactics as necessary steps for shielding their children from material deprivation. Yazmin confided, "I don't want them to be traumatized by certain events. If you really knew my backstory, I still try to keep my kids away from it. That's why the diapers, the kids, their comfort, come first." Yazmin's conflation of "diapers" and "kids" pointed to the practical and symbolic significance of mothers' diaper work as about living up to a child-centered, self-sacrificial ideology of parenting in the context of poverty. Yet unlike intensive mothering focused on children's enrichment, the mothers I studied spoke of inventive mothering as necessarily prioritizing their children's humanity and security, often at the cost of meeting their own basic needs.[8] In articulating their perspectives on childrearing inequalities, mothers described diapers as more than mere pieces of plastic and cotton. Ramona, a twenty-one-year-old Latina mother of one, lamented not being able to buy pricier diapers. "I see other parents, they have their life together, and my daughter's the same age as their kid, but she's not wearing the [expensive diaper brand]. She's wearing these four-dollar diapers that I can barely afford. It's right in my face with diapers that their kids' future will probably be better than mine, especially if I don't get it together fast." Ramona "splurged" on name-brand Huggies or Pampers when she had money to give her daughter a chance to experience a small part of middle-class childhood by wearing softer, more absorbent diapers with imprinted popular mainstream cartoon characters.

Diapers thus became symbolically important for mothers' inventive efforts to provide equal opportunities for early childhood experiences of comfort, consumption, and status. This was a primary reason mothers avoided cloth diapers. Beyond expensive start-up costs and money and labor associated with laundering, mothers were reluctant to use a type of diaper they feared others would associate with filth, poverty, and maternal unfitness. When describing cloth diapering, mothers didn't envision colorful, reusable diaper covers with smooth snaps and washable inserts, the kind commonly used by affluent mothers. They imagined prickly diaper pins used to secure cheap pieces of stained fabric that leaked urine and feces and held lingering foul smells that couldn't be washed out. Hence part of diaper work was a hyperfocus on keeping children in dry, powder-scented, disposable diapers that could be readily changed and immediately discarded. This meant that some mothers experiencing diaper need changed their children more often than affluent mothers with greater access to diapers.

Mothers ensured that their children had disposables as both a material need and status symbol that was less a marker of middle-class affluence and more about deflecting classist and racist criticisms of their children as unhygienic and not well cared for. While they were not in a financial position to give their children everything that more privileged parents could provide, mothers reasoned that they could at least offer clean, comfortable diapers as part of a secure and dignified early childhood experience. Understood in this way, diaper work became a powerful strategy for marginalized mothers to exercise agency and stake a positive maternal identity, two things often denied to them. Evidence of this was in how mothers emphasized their creative approaches to diaper work especially when recalling stigma they faced as parents who fell outside the normative bounds of "proper" motherhood defined by age, marital status, class, education, and race.

Alexis, a twenty-three-year-old Asian American mother of four, explained, "As a teen mom, people would look down on me all the time, while I'm over here paying myself through school with a minimum-wage job fending for myself and my kids. Moms, we figure it out with the diapers. We just mold into these people that make it work." Diaper work was a practical but also profoundly moral way mothers deflected criticisms about their employment, receipt of government benefits, and childbearing choices. As Alexis noted, mothers without privilege must be innovative and adaptable in ways that more affluent parents don't have to be, by "mold[ing] into these people" who make parenting in poverty work. They do so by working low-wage jobs, scrupulously managing limited resources, and devising creative and laborious strategies to meet children's needs in the face of extreme financial stress. Ultimately, diapers' significance goes beyond that of garments for containing children's excrement, especially when parents struggle to get enough. Diapers are a unit of time when parenting in poverty, each one representing a ticking clock of despair and deprivation measured in how long a parent has until their last diaper becomes too full to use. Diapers are a crucial currency of caring for young children, with significant negative repercussions when in short supply. As a basic need of early childcare that poor and low-income mothers painstakingly manage through extensive diaper work, diapers are part of living up to tenets of sacred childhood and intensive mothering.

Even agreeing to talk with me was part of mothers' efforts to add more time to their diaper clocks and increase their diaper currency. The mothers I spoke with each received twenty-five dollars in cash to recognize the value of their time and to offset any costs associated with the interviews, regardless of how many questions they answered. Mothers' stress levels, tight budgets, and constant concerns over diaper calculations were evident when they shared without my asking how they would use the money. They told me that although they would have done the interviews anyway, getting twenty-five dollars allowed them to buy diapers immediately when they were already at or nearing the point of using their very last diaper. Sharing their stories was part of their diaper work, which entailed creative and varied—as well as time-consuming and emotionally intensive—strategies for getting diapers or diaper money.

Another common use of the twenty-five dollars in cash was covering other expenses incurred from buying diapers with money initially budgeted for rent, bills, gas, or food. Mothers planned to pay overdue phone or electricity bills, buy groceries and toilet paper, and settle debts to family and friends who had fronted them diapers or diaper money. Conveying how much each minute matters and every cent counts when it comes to managing diaper insecurity and other forms of material deprivation, mothers expressly thanked me for paying the incentive in cash rather than check or gift card. Cash doesn't come with fees that would have reduced the value of the incentive by several dollars, a seemingly small amount of money to some, but substantial for those who could stretch a few dollars to cover more days' worth of diapers. These calculations were just a small part of the daily diaper math mothers did to diaper their children.

"ALWAYS THINKING ABOUT DIAPERS": DAILY DILEMMAS OF DIAPER MATH

As disposable diapers became a marker of mothers' love and care, diaper need became a strong predictor of maternal stress, anxiety, and depression.[9] Quantitative research on diaper need has found that lacking diapers is a form of material deprivation specifically associated with worse maternal mental health outcomes.[10] Public health expert Megan Smith and her colleagues suggested several possible explanations for this. Diaper need may be associated with other factors, such as low income and social isolation, that are known to negatively affect psychological well-being; diaper need and maternal mental health problems may share common causes, such as children's health issues and economic challenges; or diaper need alone may negatively impact mothers' well-being.[11] My interviews with mothers suggested that all three mechanisms are likely to blame. Diaper work takes a significant mental, emotional, and physical toll on mothers, contributing to maternal anxiety, depression, and sense of parental failure. The shame and stigma of lacking diapers as a mother primarily tasked with caring for young children hinders parental pride, dignity, self-efficacy, and sense of self-control. Interviews also revealed that common ways of managing diaper need—missing work, school, and medical appointments, going without other basic needs, and skipping shopping and socializing—can mean less income, less access to healthcare, and fewer social interactions for parents and children. Ultimately, daily diaper work strategies mothers described to me required not just money but other limited resources. Diapers are certainly expensive. But not having them can cost even more in mothers' time, energy, and mental space.

Scarcity is likely to blame. As described by economist Sendhil Mullainathan and psychologist Eldar Shafir, living in poverty and managing material deprivation depletes individuals' psychological resources and emotional energy. Scarcity of any kind—too little money, time, or human connection—taxes mental capacity, or what Mullainathan and Shafir call "bandwidth."[12] Like a physical muscle, pressures on and overuse of bandwidth strain cognitive abilities. Poverty especially reduces bandwidth. People constantly worried about money have less time and mental energy to focus on other aspects of their lives. More specifically, time and energy spent budgeting down to the last penny and coping with the emotional toll of deprivation detract from other things, like being an attentive and engaged parent. This is likely part of the reason why many mothers shared that diaper insecurity led to feelings of guilt and anxiety about their parenting abilities. Several mothers confided how every diaper change that depleted their diaper supplies could trigger anxiety attacks or depressive episodes.

Melissa, a thirty-three-year-old Hmong mother of three, recalled an anxiety attack brought on by shopping for $100 worth of diapers. She stocked up and bought cheaper diapers in bulk when she had money, but even this was stressful because she worried her daughter would outgrow that size before using them all. Most days Melissa could make the diaper math work in her favor but not always:

> You think you're okay when you're lifting your baby, and you look at her. You're like, "I'm okay, sometimes I think you need more than I can give, but you don't." But then you're holding the baby and all of a sudden, you're not

enough. There were moments when I didn't want to hold my baby because of my depression. In those moments diapers always come into mind, like, "Oh, did I get your diapers? Do I have enough? Did I use too many? Oh my gosh, I don't actually have enough. Or I have too much of the old size, but I don't have any bigger ones. I have to finish the smaller ones before I can afford new ones." It's all so triggering. The diaper stuff is always on my mind.

Days when the diaper math didn't work out led to severe anxiety attacks and feelings that Melissa wasn't worthy of motherhood. She was among many mothers who intentionally left a diaper or two in inconspicuous places—cars, family members' houses, tucked away in hidden zipper pockets in purses and diaper bags—so that when they ran out, they could use them as backups.

Stashing diapers was a strategy mothers used to maintain a sense of agency over a situation that otherwise felt out of their control. "This is silly," Natalie explained, "but I'll even stash diapers. When I have extra money, I'll buy two or three packs and stash a pack. If I'm running low, I'll find that pack. When I don't have money in the future, I'll say, 'That's right, I stashed that pack of diapers.' I find myself doing that a lot recently with my son, running on constant mom brain." Hiding diapers helped Natalie manage the cognitive burden of "mom brain" in overload when money and diapers ran low. Jessica, a thirty-seven-year-old white mother of five, could only afford to buy small diaper packs every three or four days. She too hid a diaper in her purse, allowing just enough time to get to the corner store and buy another small pack. She confided:

> It's that feeling when you're down to your last two diapers, you're waiting for your check to come tomorrow, and your baby is a little bit wet, but you don't want to change them right now because you might run out of that last diaper. That, and we don't have gas in the car until tomorrow, and I can't go to the store to use the little gas I have to buy diapers. I'm always thinking about diapers, making sure the babies have diapers, or if they only have one diaper left, when I can get to the store. It's always kicking in the back on my brain. Worrying about it becomes second nature.

Without pause, Jessica explained all this in one long breath, conveying a frazzled feeling of constantly gnawing concern about diapers "always kicking in the back" of one's consciousness, so much so that diaper despair becomes "second nature."

Many other mothers described the utter relief of discovering forgotten diapers when they thought they had run out, including Toni, twenty-nine, Latina, and a mother of four:

> One day, we were down to two diapers. I didn't get paid until the next day, so I was doing everything to make those two diapers last until I could get paid, get to the store, get her diapers, and change her then and there. But then I found one diaper just laying around. You know you just put them in your purse, you have them everywhere. I just opened my son's drawer, and I found one. I was like "Thank you, Lord! Thank you, Jesus!" She had on that last diaper, and I was like, "Please, please don't poop, we can make it, you know?" The diaper thing, it's killing me.

Deliberately hiding diapers or discovering one final diaper in emergencies became psychological cushions that helped mothers manage the emotional fallout of diaper need. In these urgent moments of diaper math, mothers reasoned that one diaper wouldn't last long but at least allowed additional time to get more. That a single diaper could provoke such gratitude reveals how dire mothers' lived experiences of diaper despair could be.

Using their last diaper was its own source of distress that triggered mothers' feelings of despondency. Joanna, eighteen, Afro-Latina, and a mother of one, explained:

> I psych myself out when he's on the last diaper. I'm already a mess emotionally. I just had a baby. I felt like I was going crazy in the head, my emotions were everywhere. Diapers and the money situation are a big trigger for me. I can change him only when he really needs to be changed, not when he's barely wet, just to save on diapers. I think, "It's okay, he can go like thirty more minutes." If I'm down to my last ten or fifteen diapers, I won't go out. If I stay home, I can make those diapers last longer. I'm embarrassed because that's my baby. . . . It takes a big toll on my overall mental health. . . . When I'm in the zone with him, and he's just the light of my life, then I do of course get that peak of happiness, but that's not very often. But if I'm having a bad day, the diapers are running really low, it's harder to interact with him, to get my mind off things.

Joanna poignantly captured the psychological toll of limited and dwindling diaper supplies that many mothers described. The postpartum period coincides with when infants tend to require the most diaper changes—around ten to fifteen per day—and skin is particularly delicate and prone to rashes. Joanna's experience also pointed to how insufficient diapers contribute to social isolation when mothers' diaper work involves avoiding public spaces that could offer support and alleviate their mental health struggles.

Mothers also worried about not using diapers "all the way," which meant ensuring they held the maximum amount of urine before changing. This involved figuring out exactly how much a diaper could hold before it leaked, started to smell, or caused discomfort or rashes for the child, and whether the cost of diaper barrier cream was worth what it bought in additional diaper wear time. Jill, a thirty-six-year-old multiracial mother of four, shared, "I know it sounds horrific, but for pee only, I wait for a while. I just put some of that rash stuff on them, so they never get a rash." Some mothers also admitted to taking a diaper off, wringing it out, and putting it back on as a last-ditch effort to stretch a diaper to its maximum capacity.

Aurelia, twenty-five, Latina, and a mother of three, had resorted to diaper-wringing by the time we talked. The six diapers she had on hand when I interviewed her had to last until her boyfriend's payday, which was still two days away. "I'm trying to reuse the diapers and limit his drink because if he drinks a lot, he'll use all six of those diapers in a day, and I just don't have that many." Yet this was not Aurelia's most stressful diaper math problem. The month prior, her son had an intestinal health condition that caused loose stools and bowel incontinence when not treated with medication. Their healthcare coverage would only pay for so much medicine every thirty days, and they were running low. Aurelia used the money she'd saved for diapers to buy the medicine, but by that point her son had skipped some doses, causing moderate diarrhea. Struggling to stretch the few diapers they had left set off a cascade of problems. Without enough diapers Aurelia couldn't take her son to daycare or leave the house, causing her to miss work and lose several days' pay. She also needed someone to pick up her older children from daycare, but they couldn't risk losing the money if her boyfriend, the children's father, left work. Aurelia's uncle finally picked up the kids, and she concluded: "It's just safer if he's without a diaper at home. I just clean it up. I can't clean it up at school when you have people around you watching. They all have kids and most understand, but you still have parents that give you this look. . . . It has really affected my physical and mental health. You just stress over it because you're going back and forth in your mind thinking, 'How am I gonna do it? How am I gonna do it?' It wears you out." The exasperation in Aurelia's voice was palpable, underscoring the stress of constantly balancing diapers with other basic needs like medicine and why staying home, even if it meant less income, seemed like the only viable option given her family's constraints.

Molly, thirty-one, Black, and a mother of two, similarly described the mental toll of daily diaper math and the effort, energy, and embarrassment associated with diaper work:

> Couponing and going to different stores to get diapers involves a lot of math, gas, and time. And it's embarrassing to ask for diapers. I haven't run out yet because I try to stay ahead of the game. When we're at home, I let them go without diapers, and one time, I even stretched my daughter's medicine for diapers. I'm currently down to my last pack of diapers now, and I'm thinking I have a shelf I may be able to sell. . . . I'm stressed out a lot. It definitely takes a toll on [my husband and kids]. I try not to let them see it, but sometimes it's unavoidable. Last month, I went through a bad depression for a week. It was nonstop crying because all I was thinking about was money. "How am I gonna buy diapers this month? How I'm gonna buy the food *and* diapers this month?" There's no outlet for moms.

Molly's diaper work involved a complex process of simultaneously looking for sales and saleable items she owned, stretching her children's diapers and other needs, and managing not only diapers but also maternal stress and strain on family relationships created by constant worry over the household budget. Overseeing diapers was a rigged game that was easy to lose, cost a lot to win, and offered few opportunities to release pressure that ensued. Ultimately, for many mothers, depression and anxiety were the endgame.

Some mothers even coached children to signal when diapers became irritating. Keira, a twenty-three-year-old multiracial mother of one, described "training the baby to indicate when the full diaper is uncomfortable. I admit I buy the more absorbent diapers so they will last longer." Disposable diaper technologies described in chapter 2 (superabsorbent polymers, wicking stay-dry top sheets, and elasticized leg cuffs that prevent leakage) enable these modern diaper work strategies. They also contribute to class-based understandings of what it means to *use* a diaper and to change a *full* diaper, as poor and low-income mothers necessarily relied on these technologies to stretch diapers that can be worn longer with lower risks of rashes and stigma associated with being visibly soiled. But this meant that mothers had to do another kind of difficult diaper math. They carefully weighed buying the cheaper, less absorbent diapers that leaked more against buying the more expensive ones that could be kept on longer.

Yet, mothers noted, this only worked with urine, not with feces that were unevenly absorbed by the diapers and partially adhered to children's skin. Moreover, loose stools exacerbated mothers' diaper stress when worries over sick babies coincided with diaper despair. Nora shared that she agonized "a lot more about the diapers when the kids get sick because I think, 'This is like the fifth diaper he just went through. I'm down to eight diapers.' I never thought I'd have to worry about counting every last diaper all the time, about my kids not having enough. It weighs on you and brings you down." Diana, twenty-nine, white, and a mother of five, described similar unrelenting concerns. "I just pray and hope the kids don't get sick, that by the time I get paid, I can get the diapers right away. . . . We have to wait for the diaper to get very, very full as it's nearing the point of leaking, and then change them right away. It wears you out having to worry about every last diaper."

Like Nora and Diana, who used the language of diaper despair "weighing on you" and "wearing you out," many mothers described the incessant anxiety about running out of diapers as a particularly stressful form of deprivation that constantly occupied their thoughts and led to feelings of depression "bringing you down." Down to her last diaper for her two young daughters during the hour of our interview, it was hard for Jill to focus on anything but how "we're literally about to run out in less than an hour, and I'm stressing hard about it. I can feel it in my body, the thoughts are always there." Part of these persistent thoughts was mothers' tracking, often to the hour, when their last diaper would be too full or dirty to use. Like Patricia, whom we met at the beginning of this chapter, many mothers noted how many diapers they had and exactly how long those diapers would last. This high degree of specificity was especially telling about the unique labor of diaper work. Not just having fewer diapers, diaper math was about how much effort and energy mothers put toward calculating, saving, and stretching limited diaper supplies as far as possible.

Maria, thirty, Latina, and a mother of four, logged each diaper change on a chart, tracked her son's food and liquid intake and urine output by the ounce, and set a daily diaper quota with different limits for when her son had diarrhea and when he didn't. Based on this data, she kept a strict diaper budget to predict the date and hour when she would need to open a new box and how long that box had to last. Maria's careful diaper math and budgeting inventively increased her diaper supply:

> Diapers are lasting longer because I know when my son pees, how many times, how much he pees each time, and how many times fill up a diaper. . . . I count every diaper, write it down, track every little thing, so I know how much money and how long each box will last. Diapers is the number one concern for me right now, so I have to think about this stuff in this way. I can't go over my daily limit. If you don't have the money to stock up, you have to live month to month. It's hard living paycheck to paycheck, living diaper to diaper. But I budget, compare, stretch things, figure out prices, the best deal for the most diapers. I'm a pro at this now with my fourth child. But I still get stressed out if we run out of diapers. I don't want my baby smelling like piss all day.

In Maria's experience "living diaper to diaper" demanded creative and exhausting diaper work strategies and logics—having to "think about this stuff in this way"—involving significant physical, emotional, and cognitive labor. Maria and others were proud of their innovation and ingenuity around managing diaper need. More than a survival strategy, they viewed diaper work as a productive practice rooted in hard-earned knowledge and as a form of childcare expertise developed through resourcefulness. Maria took pride in becoming a diaper work "pro" who could get the "best deal for the most diapers" using creative diaper math to make diapers and diaper money last longer.

Mothers' extensive management of limited diaper supplies profoundly shaped the daily rhythms of family life in other ways, including interactions with children and how mothers planned their work and social schedules. A third of mothers I spoke with had reduced their work hours or time children spent in childcare facilities due to lacking diapers. More than half of them had foregone running errands, attending social events, or leaving their homes because of diaper need. These tactics were often necessary when mothers had no diapers at all. Christine, a fifty-two-year-old Black custodial grandmother of three, devised the cleverly dubbed "potty game" for when she ran out of diapers for her three grandchildren, ages one, two, and three and all in diapers. The children played diaperless on the linoleum kitchen floor as Christine nervously waited the few hours it usually took for her sister to arrive with an emergency pack. At half-hour intervals each child received a piece of candy for sitting on the toilet and an additional piece if they peed or pooped. Watching if any of the children were about to urinate or defecate before their turn required Christine's constant, careful attention, but it hid the gravity of the situation from the kids who never knew they ran out of diapers.

What troubled Christine most was that her sister could afford only a single diaper pack, forcing Christine to choose the one size that could best accommodate her barely walking one-year-old granddaughter and her three-year-old grandson, who weighed twice as much. A common problem for families with multiple children in diapers, Jill also had to split single-size diaper packs for her eighteen-month-old who wore size 4 and her two-year-old in size 6, despite size 5 not fitting either child well. As Christine did, two in three mothers I interviewed had borrowed diapers or money explicitly intended to buy diapers from others in their social networks, including family, friends, coworkers, and neighbors. Asking family or friends for diapers or diaper money was also the most reported diaper need coping strategy in other research on diaper insecurity.[13] This borrowing strategy aligns with research finding that those facing economic hardship are most likely to turn to network resources when they lack staple necessities for children, like food or diapers, with immediate impacts on well-being.[14]

Yet mothers confided to me that they were reluctant to ask for diaper help and usually only did so as a last resort in the direst situations. Aversion to asking for help was rooted in mothers' identities as self-reliant parents committed to sacrificing and stretching for their children. Shaped by cultural narratives of self-sufficiency and parental responsibility, requests for diaper assistance came at a psychological cost to mothers' pride, sense of independence, and parental self-efficacy. Audra, a thirty-two-year-old white mother of five, said, "It's sad to need diapers. You don't want to feel like you're failing as a parent." The embarrassment associated with asking for diaper help, even (and sometimes especially) from others they knew well, prevented many mothers from asking at all. "I will never ask my mom for diaper money again because she doesn't get it," Toni shared. "Neither does my sister. They look down on me about it. It gets thrown in my face. I can't live down that I asked them for diapers." Although their social networks typically had more resources, employed mothers, mothers with more education, and white mothers reported facing greater social censure when asking for diapers or diaper money and fearing that others attributed their diaper need to bad budgeting.

Hence mothers didn't ask just anyone in their social networks and kept close tabs on not only who could afford to help but also who would be willing to help with no judgment, especially fellow parents who had similarly struggled and empathized with the practical and emotional pressures of diaper scarcity. Natasha, a thirty-five-year-old Black mother of four, explained how her neighbors helped struggling moms with diapers by buying in bulk when they found sales. While most of the neighbors didn't currently need diapers themselves, they had experienced diaper insecurity when their children were younger and knew the value of being able to reach out to those living nearby when diaper supplies ran low. "My neighbors help with diapers because they know I'm trustworthy," Natasha noted. "If you don't have a job, you won't be able to get Pampers, and you need someone to love you, help you get them." By "trustworthy," Natasha meant her neighbors knew she was working hard for her kids and spending her limited funds responsibly only for crucial items. That she still needed diaper help despite this was not a failing, she reasoned, but rather about prioritizing raising her children over taking any low-paid job. Natasha valued this understanding as much as the diapers, a form of support so significant that she described it as "love."

Children's fathers were a particularly important source of diaper support, especially when they didn't live with children. Research on child support paid by nonresidential fathers has focused on cash payments, either formal support through courts or informal support given directly to mothers.[15] As a noncash good, diapers are a common and crucial third type called in-kind support. Low-income fathers are especially likely to provide more support through in-kind goods intended specifically for their children rather than formal child support they struggle to afford that could be garnished by the state. Cash-strapped dads with very young children often take responsibility for providing highly visible, costly, and necessary items, most commonly diapers and formula. Ensuring that their children have these two baby basics serves symbolic and relational purposes in addition to providing necessities. It can be a way of informally claiming paternity, "stepping up" for one's child and proving paternal responsibility to mothers and extended family, and making a down payment that promises more support when economic situations improve. Ultimately diapers dads provide can be a relational tool to create, sustain, or mend bonds with their children.[16]

Providing in-kind support through diapers served these purposes for many of the mothers I interviewed. When dads brought diapers, mothers were more inclined to let them see or spend time with their children because the diapers signaled a commitment to their kids and providing something of great need and value to mothers. Marissa, a forty-one-year-old Latina mother of seven, explained how she and her youngest child's father agreed, "I get the milk, the formula, and he gets the diapers and the wipes. We both budget. Money for this stuff gets put aside first, and it means a lot that he always takes care of this one thing." Although they had broken up shortly after their daughter's birth, Marissa worked hard to maintain an amicable coparenting relationship with her baby's father, whom she believed proved his paternal commitment by providing diapers.

On the flip side, fathers' refusal or inability to bring diapers signaled lacking or waning responsibility for their shared children and failure to acknowledge mothers' stresses and sacrifices in taking on the primary share of both financial providing and caregiving for kids. At the very least, mothers reasoned, dads could find a way to pay for and bring diapers if they were doing everything else. Trinity, a forty-two-year-old Black mother of three, shared that "her father helps, but not really. He's not really around. I've been with him on and off for a long time. By the time we had the baby, I assumed from our conversations, and we had two miscarriages, that he wanted the baby. But once she came, he was just out, no diapers, no nothing." In these cases diaper transactions were a barometer of the quality of coparenting relationships, and diapers a currency used to prove fathers' commitments and negotiate their involvement. Being partnered seemed to mitigate mothers' diaper despair, but only to a point. Half of the married and cohabiting mothers I interviewed had an employed partner who contributed income to the household, which accords with research finding that many families experiencing diaper need include at least one working adult.[17] An additional residential parent allowed partnered mothers to more easily buy diapers, access diaper giveaways, and be full-time caregivers at home, where children could go diaperless.

But two-parent families were not immune from diaper stresses. Some mothers shared that husbands' and boyfriends' questioning about money spent on diapers exacerbated their diaper stress. Partnered mothers tended to purchase and change more diapers than fathers, some of whom, according to mothers, were unaware of diaper expenses, how many diapers children used, and the labor of managing limited diapers supplies. Diapers sometimes played a role in parents' conflicts, adding to mothers' diaper work and despair. Sonia, a thirty-three-year-old Latina mother of two, said, "I had never been without income. Her father and I separating dampened our situation. When he was around, he was helpful with her and diapers, but when we didn't have [diapers] that added to our fighting. As we were breaking up, I was worrying about diapers."

Regardless of relationship status, mothers constantly worried about diapers and decided which of their own needs they could sacrifice as part of their diaper math calculations. A quarter of respondents reported going without food or eating cheaper foods as part of their diaper work, while more than half talked about not buying their own period products, toilet paper, medicine, underwear, clothing, or shoes. "When I get paid," Toni explained, "I pay my bills, then go to Walmart and get whatever my kids need, like diapers. If there's any money left over, then I can think about if I need shoes, socks, or underwear, like, 'Crap, my underwear is all holey, or my bra broke.'" Similarly, Audra, a thirty-three-year-old white mother of five, shared, "I can't think of the last time I bought something for myself. Well, I bought tampons yesterday, but I got the cheap brand so the kids can have their good diapers. You work around your stuff, not theirs." Mothers saw their own needs as discretionary when it meant affording diapers for their children.

Even more than what they sacrificed, mothers emphasized their resourcefulness in managing diaper insecurity. Tracy, a twenty-five-year-old multiracial mother of three, described her skill at reconfiguring her household budget around her son's diapering needs. "I always figure things out," she said. "With my bills and diapers, it's a picking and choosing game. You have to reserve the rent space, so that's a priority. Your child needs food, so you use food stamps when you can, instead of paying cash. You think, 'How much do I have for this box of diapers for this day? I don't have to pay taxes when I use my food stamps. How much of that can I put on the diapers? What will that leave for tomorrow? Is there something I need that I can put back to buy the diapers?'" Feeling confident in her ability to play this game, Tracy usually chose to pick something she could do without when her son needed diapers. Through their innovative efforts to prioritize diapers in their accounting of household and personal expenses, mothers' diaper work reflected all the tenets of intensive mothering by being laborious, self-sacrificial, and child-centered. Beyond this, diaper work required ingenuity in the face of poverty, especially when being poor increased diaper costs.

THE DIAPER POVERTY PENALTY: WHEN BEING POOR COSTS MORE

Another difficult aspect of mothers' diaper math was higher diaper costs when budgets were tight. Mothers described diapers as especially expensive for their families for three primary reasons. First, buying diapers used a greater proportion of their overall income and aid. Second, mothers often had to pay more per diaper due to financial, geographic, and racialized aspects of poverty. Third, running out of diapers and last-minute efforts to get more added opportunity costs that worsened families' economic situations. In a vicious cycle of diaper despair, poverty can make diapers more expensive for families, which contributes to diaper need, thereby exacerbating family poverty.

High diapers costs disproportionately hurt poor families. The poorest 20 percent of families in the United States spend 14 percent of their income on diapers, while the richest 20 percent spend only 1 percent of

Richest quintile ▱▱▱ 1.0%

4th quintile ▱▱▱▱ 2.1%

3rd quintile ▱▱▱▱▱ 2.8%

2nd quintile ▱▱▱▱▱▱▱▱▱ 5.0%

Poorest quintile ▱▱▱▱▱▱▱▱▱▱▱▱▱▱▱▱▱▱▱▱▱▱▱▱▱ 13.9%

|0% | 2% | 4% | 6% | 8% | 10% | 12% | 14%|

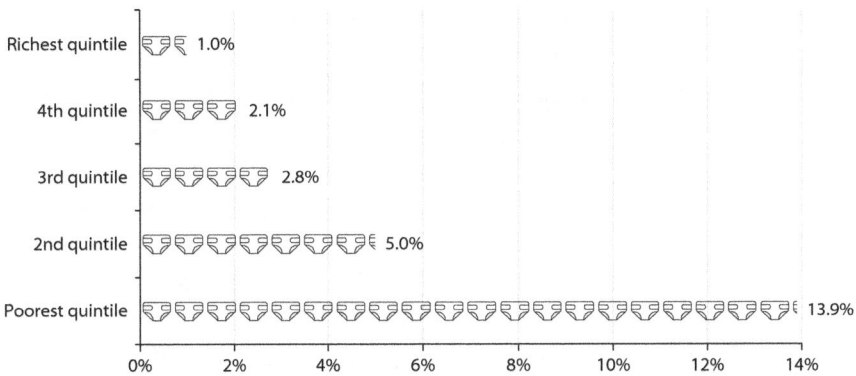

Figure 1. Share of after-tax household income spent on diapers in the United States, by earnings quintile. *Source*: Cashman (2015).

their after-tax income purchasing diapers.[18] Referred to as the "poverty penalty," diapers circulate in a consumer market where the poor shoulder relatively higher costs, compelling them to buy lower-quality products, pay more for similar-quality goods, forego purchasing certain products, and engage in catastrophic spending.[19] Mothers' diaper work involved all these consequences. "Even if you buy cheap diapers because you can't afford the pricey ones," Trina explained, "you're gonna be using just as much or more as if you buy the better ones. When you buy cheap ones, you're constantly changing them because the cheap diapers just won't hold." Mothers' average monthly diaper cost was $66, or 8.3 percent of monthly income and aid, which averaged $797. However, as mothers shared, they necessarily reduced diaper costs by stretching diapers, reusing soiled diapers, or going without diapers. These strategies all come with their own physical, economic, and psychological costs. One study found that parents who cannot provide diapers for daycare missed, on average, four days of work or school per month, risking lost wages, lost jobs, and lost opportunities for upward mobility.[20] Many mothers who spoke to me struggled with accessing childcare due to diaper need. Alicia, a twenty-two-year-old Latina mother of two, shared, "There has been times I couldn't go to work. I didn't have gas because I needed to buy my son diapers instead of going to work. I used a sick day for that, almost lost my job over it."

Given that mothers are especially likely to bear burdens when budgets can stretch to cover only food *or* diapers, maternal hunger and food insecurity were also common penalties of diaper poverty, pointing to why diaper need and use of food assistance programs go hand-in-hand.[21] Ashley, a seventeen-year-old Latina mother of one, matter-of-factly said, "Lots of the time I don't eat a whole day, or sometimes I'll just eat one part of the day because I'm trying to save money for diapers and I'm so stressed." Melissa, who told me she worried more about diapers because she got food stamps, shared details about what this really involved. "I just worry about the girls having enough food because I can go on a diet and deal. But because I was breastfeeding and didn't eat, I would get really bad headaches. Then the baby would be fussy. All that milk I'd be pumping, it's all my energy." Similarly, Kiera, a twenty-three-year-old multiracial mother of one, explained, "By the end of the month we literally have nothing, no food, no money, low diapers. They'll be three or four days where I'll go without eating, just drink water. It makes me angry and sad, and not eating adds to the stress."

Ashley, Melissa, and Kiera paid for diapers using currency of their own hunger, stress, and discomfort. Diapers were also costly in this way for Lila, a twenty-four-year-old multiracial mother of three, who sold her blood plasma twice weekly to afford diapers for two of her children:

> I was going two times a week so I could get the twenty-five dollars and then the forty dollars. I did it for three, almost four months, donated blood. My boyfriend made me stop because he was worried it wasn't good for me. It was hard because my hemoglobin always seemed to be so low. I was trying to eat kale, boiled eggs, oatmeal, orange juice trying to make sure I was high [in hemoglobin] before I went. I was turned down once because I was two points too low. It was so stressful, like, "How am I going to get these diapers if I can't get the money for the blood?" I was breaking down crying because I didn't know what I was going to do.

After her boyfriend convinced Lila to stop "donating" blood when he noticed problems with her energy, sleep, and mood, she turned to other means for making diaper money. Lila participated in diaper market research and wrote to diaper companies, lowering her voice when she confided that "this part sounds horrible, but another way I've gotten diapers is by emailing the companies. I emailed Huggies, Pampers, Seventh Generation. I did Cuties and Luvs. They'll usually send you coupons for half the amount of diapers if you complain and tell them your kids got a rash. Sometimes they'll send you free diapers. There have been times when I've used my mom's or sister's addresses, but I've only done that when I'm really struggling and desperate."

To Lila, earning diaper money by selling her blood—though neither she nor the plasma donation center she visited more than twenty times used remunerative language of *buying* and *selling*—didn't evoke the same sense of theft or duplicity as did making false claims to diaper companies with billions in annual profits. Between buying food to increase her hemoglobin levels, hours spent in waiting rooms, and lost energy, these "donations" were incredibly costly to Lila. Still, several mothers shared that they bought diapers with blood money earned via plasma "donation" for pay, a legal practice in the United States but banned in other countries. Plasma "donation" centers are more common in areas like where Lila's family lived—that is, poor neighborhoods with larger proportions of Black and Latine residents.[22] Diaper availability and pricing also track with the geography of racialized poverty. Reflecting the legacy of racist redlining, neighborhoods with fewer retailers that sell diapers are more likely to have Black residents, renters, and dwellings not up to housing codes.[23] Much like many low-income families live in "food deserts" where access to healthy and affordable food is limited, they also live in what could be described as "diaper deserts" where few stores sell diapers and those that do charge higher per unit surge pricing.[24]

As of 2025, a box of size 5 diapers can be bought from a discount retailer for nineteen cents per unit on average.[25] But several privileges are embedded in this "bargain." To save this much on diapers, families either must live within walking distance of discount stores or have transportation. They also need twenty to thirty dollars it typically costs to buy a large-quantity box of diapers. To purchase diapers at bulk shopping membership-based clubs, such as Costco or Sam's, they must pay upfront fees, which typically range from $60 to $120 a year. To buy diapers through online discount retailers like Amazon, shoppers need a valid credit card, internet access, and an address for secure deliveries. Families with more resources can comparison shop and benefit from multiple product discounts, such as buy-two-get-one-free deals and sales on diapers that can be stored for later use. However, low-income families face liquidity constraints, or limited access to on-hand, immediately usable cash.[26] Consequently, they are less able to take advantage of intertemporal savings strategies, which include buying in bulk, stocking up during sales, and spending more money at a single point to take advantage of "free" products.[27] Ultimately, "saving" money on diapers can be prohibitively expensive for poor families.

What then must poor parents do to get diapers? First, they either pay for transportation or buy diapers closer to where they live. The lowest-income Americans spend nearly $300 a month to own and drive a car.[28] The average adult fare for a one-way bus trip is $1.71.[29] Residents in low-income neighborhoods would, on average, need to take two buses and walk eleven minutes to travel one way to the nearest big-box store that sells diapers in bulk at lower per-unit prices.[30] For either car expenses or bus money, it costs about seven dollars just to get to and from the store where parents can buy cheaper diapers. Many resort to buying single diapers or smaller diaper packages near their residences, usually at convenience and corner stores with high-markup pricing; this costs parents, on average, $0.50 per size 5 diaper, and up to $1.49 for unpackaged single diapers.[31] All told, diapers cost up to six times more when you're poor.

Most mothers described paying more per diaper either because they couldn't afford to get to cheaper stores or because they didn't have enough money to buy larger packages. Brenda, a twenty-five-year-old Asian American mother of three, stayed up late many nights searching for diaper sales and coupons. When she couldn't find a good deal or she ran out of money, she asked her grandmother, who also lived on a limited income. Brenda explained, "I would sit there and cry, and my grandma would say, 'I can do twenty dollars right now. Can you make that work?' I can but instead of buying a box—boxes are twenty-five, thirty dollars, even more, and she couldn't spare enough for a box—I would go around the corner to Walgreen's and buy two small packs of twenty for eighteen dollars. With tax, I could get about forty diapers and try to make that last until I get paid again." The diaper poverty penalty was costly for Brenda. If she'd had ten dollars more to spend on diapers, she would have gone to Target, where the same diapers were cheaper, and bought a 120-count box of diapers for thirty dollars, or about a quarter each. Yet because she had just twenty dollars, she could only afford the two twenty-pack deal at Walgreens, which cost twice as much at fifty cents per diaper.

Mothers recounted stories of scrounging up change for single diapers. Lisa, a thirty-year-old Latina mother of four, collected recyclables from neighborhood trash cans, and in dire situations she borrowed money for diapers from her children. She shared:

> When I'm down to my last fifteen [diapers], I'm starting to see if I have money, what's my next step, how am I going to go about this? When fifteen hits, I'm on it, collecting cans, figuring out something. Sometimes I can borrow from my neighbor, but I have to give clean diapers right back. There were times I went three hours without diapers. I was doing my best to get them, but Grandma was out of town, so I had to get all the change out of the piggy bank, literally break my kids' piggy bank. I can buy two diapers for one dollar at the store a six- or seven-minute walk from here to give me more time to figure things out. It's frustrating, but so far frustration ain't bought me any diapers. You gotta do what you gotta do.

Some mothers noted travel times to corner stores that sold minipacks, while others bought single "loosie" diapers for one dollar each from street sellers who pocketed high-markup profits from diaper-desperate families. Ultimately, mothers I interviewed often spent more on diapers than higher-income families for several distinct but interrelated reasons. Even if everyone paid the same amount, diapers cost poor and low-income families a greater share of the little money they do have, leaving less to spend on other needs. Yet because lower-income families can't use many of the savings strategies better-off families do, such as buying in bulk and shopping for better deals, they rarely end up paying the same price for diapers. They pay more, both relatively and in absolute dollars.

Moreover, not having enough diapers also costs poor mothers. The diaper poverty penalty included lost income when mothers couldn't work due to lacking diapers and interest when diapers were necessarily bought on credit, not to mention the stress, strain, and struggle of diaper work. Although harder to quantify, these opportunity and indirect costs associated with diaper insecurity were no less real to mothers who incurred them, making what they truly paid for diapers disproportionately and exceedingly expensive. Mothers' diaper work thus involved tracking who in their social networks could offer diaper assistance on short notice and knowing where diapers could be purchased in a pinch. In the absence of a public safety net for diapers, mothers necessarily relied on these inventive strategies and their private safety nets, which had particularly negative consequences for mothers of color.

"EXCUSE TO TAKE HER": RACIALIZED STRESS, SURVEILLANCE, AND SOCIAL EXCLUSION OF DIAPER NEED

Mothers of color described racialized experiences of diaper insecurity, including racist stigma that contributed to diaper-related stress, surveillance, and social exclusion. Compared to white mothers, mothers of color were more likely to report that diaper need took a significant negative toll on their mental health and maternal self-efficacy. They were also more likely to have had complicated pregnancies, traumatic and/or preterm births, and postpartum depression and anxiety, with many mothers of color attributing the latter in part to worries about diapers as an adverse postpartum experience. As Toni explained, "I feel like I'm a bad parent when diapers run low because it's like I'm not a good provider. I'm so anal about them going out in public looking like a hot mess, like people might say, 'Ugh, they're ghetto welfare babies.' I've had anxiety attacks worrying about whether people think I'm a bad mom if the baby has a saggy diaper. That's why I can't buy the cheap ones. Two pees and they drop." Toni's reference to a saggy diaper being indicative of "ghetto welfare babies" pointed to racist ideologies contributing to negative psychological impacts of diaper need. She was among several mothers of color who shared that they purchased more expensive diapers and changed diapers more frequently, thereby exacerbating their diaper insecurity, because they feared that a child in a soiled diaper marked a mother as "unfit."

Carrie, a thirty-three-year-old Latina mother of four, also described the racialized judgment she received mostly from white individuals whom she feared think, "'Why do you have kids if you can't provide for them?' You see all these things on social media, shaming mothers for asking for things they need for their baby, but at least I'm doing what I got to do to get the diapers." Cognizant that others might assume they had more children to get welfare or that their children were unintended results of promiscuity, mothers of color were quick to counter that their children were planned and that they worked hard, spent money responsibly, and sacrificed their own needs to afford diapers. Similarly, Jocelyn, a thirty-one-year-old Black mother of two, told me, "I don't get my hair or nails done, none of that. I just stay in the house and spend money on the kids. I even went out and stole diapers, risked my freedom for my kids. I don't have to do that all the time, but if I have to, I will. I never take the whole pack, just get the couple she really needs until I know we can get more money for diapers. I know to never leave diapers on too long, to prevent rashes, and who might see." Jocelyn knew that diaper theft risked her incarceration, especially as a poor Black woman. She was also acutely aware that a baby with rashes presumably caused by a mother who didn't adequately change her risked equally catastrophic claims of child maltreatment and maternal neglect.

Mothers of color were particularly attuned to public perceptions of their children's diapers and fears of involvement with the child welfare system due to inappropriate or insufficient diapers. They were less likely to leave their homes where they could use common diaper-stretching strategies, including letting children go without diapers, creating make-shift diapers using other household materials, and using the same diaper for longer. Mothers saved their limited disposables, the type they believed would be recognized as "normal" and proper diapers, for times their infants spent in public or childcare. Like Jocelyn, many mothers of color described rarely leaving their homes, missing work and medical appointments, and not going grocery shopping or to social events because of a lack of diapers. Avoiding public places required fewer diapers, allowed children to stay close to personal restrooms for toilet training, and subjected mothers to less surveillance and scrutiny of their diapering habits.

Diaper work required mothers to consider intersecting gender, class, and race stereotypes of parental fitness as mothers weighed risks of diaper need against potential consequences of their efforts to manage it. Latina and especially Black mothers described facing more stress and stigma, and possibly lost custody, if their children wore soggy or smelly diapers. Heightened surveillance of poor families of color by law enforcement and child welfare agencies subjects them to extra layers of scrutiny. According to legal sociologist Dorothy Roberts, the child welfare system is designed to detect and punish poor parents when they cannot provide for children's basic needs but largely ignores the failings of middle-class and affluent parents whose shortcomings are not defined as "neglect" or "child mal-treatment" in the same way.[32] Being deemed "unfit" can have disastrous consequences for poor mothers of color, whose children are more likely to enter the foster system and receive inferior services within it.[33]

Several mothers I interviewed knew this all too well. Numerous moth-ers, all of them Black, had grown up in foster care and/or lost custody of children to the child welfare system. They emphasized the importance of having babies in clean diapers and not asking for more government aid that might raise suspicion of their parenting capabilities. The ever-present threat of family separation compelled their inventive mothering strategies for managing the outward appearance of diaper need. Several Black moth-ers talked about having ample visible diaper supplies in their homes, where they were more likely to be under surveillance. Lisa, a thirty-two-year-old Black mother of five and pregnant with her sixth child, lost cus-tody of her children due to what a social worker deemed "housing unfit for kids," although Lisa noted the apartment was merely cluttered due to packing for an upcoming move. Claiming that there were already plans to revoke custody of her newborn, Lisa explained, "They're making every excuse to take her. We're trying to get everything, really the diapers and wipes, to make sure they don't. We get food stamps and Housing Authority is paying the full rent. We're keeping our head afloat, but we need lots of diapers so they don't take her away." Lisa counted on food and housing aid to convince social workers of her ability to provide these basic needs for the baby. But with no public support for diapers, Lisa believed that keep-ing custody was contingent on having a "huge stack of diapers" for the social worker's next home visit.

Mothers' diaper work necessarily included these strategies for present-ing a fit mother status in the context of a racially biased child welfare system where poor mothers of color were considerably more likely to expe-rience diaper need as part of racialized poverty. Like Lisa, many mothers of color believed that procuring sufficient diapers was a primary strategy for proving their worth, respectability, and perseverance as good mothers, despite severe hardships they faced. As many mothers described, diaper need can evoke the worst stereotypes of poor mothers of color, notably that they deliberately have too many kids they neglect, they become irresponsibly dependent on public aid, and they engage in reckless behaviors. Respondents' descriptions of their inventive mothering practices, specifically diaper work, intentionally challenged these sexist, classist, and racist assumptions through compelling counternarratives of ingenuity, hard work, and maternal sacrifice.[34]

Mothers' resourceful diaper work was also a bulwark against affronts to their self-esteem and parental self-efficacy. They referenced diaper need management strategies as proof of their deservingness as good mothers when they felt self-doubt or dehumanization by others. Brenda, a twenty-five-year-old Asian American mother of three, shared:

> Sometimes I feel hopeless, like I can't do much at all. But I know I've tried to provide as much as I can for my kids, times when I've gone without or would push a bill out because my son really needed diapers, and I had nobody and nothing else. My [posttraumatic stress disorder] really comes out over the diapers. As much as I need electricity, to keep my kids out of the dark, I need even more to make sure they're comfortable so they won't see my struggle. . . . Diapers are one thing I can do to protect them from all that.

For Brenda and others, diapers represented a secure life unburdened by the trauma of poverty and racism they wanted to give their children. Other mothers of color especially seemed to understand this. Sociologists have long documented the importance of cooperative lifestyles that involve sharing and swapping household items among poor families as adaptive strategies for economic survival.[35] However, expectations of eventual reciprocity for shared goods can put additional strain on poor parents.[36] Yet compared to white mothers, Black and Latina mothers were more likely to describe seeking diaper support as a strategy that solidified social ties, rather than an embarrassing last-resort measure that subjected them to shame or unattainable expectations of reciprocity. Black mothers' more positive experiences receiving diaper support likely reflected a history and valorization of "othermothering," whereby members of the Black community provide communal support for carework.[37] Similarly disadvantaged family members and friends, even those who struggled to afford their own needs, were often the most willing to help with diapers. Black mothers were also more likely to have shared their own limited diaper supplies with others.

As an item necessary for meeting fundamental bodily needs of their youngest children, especially one so closely tied to ideas of cleanliness, comfort, respectability, and racialized parental fitness, diapers had a unique moral import for mothers of color. While mothers sometimes worried that they weren't good role models because they lacked college degrees and high-paying jobs, they felt they compensated by demonstrating innovation, sacrifice, and resilience through diaper work. Winona, a twenty-nine-year-old Black mother of two, said, "I can't be down, knowing I got these kids looking up to me to see how I can handle the diapers. It's challenging, but I'm not letting it break me. Every time I don't go out because I need to save that money for diapers, they see that." Diaper work became a core strategy mothers used to develop a sense of themselves as good parents with agency who had at least some power to resist and counteract the inequalities that shaped their children's life chances.

THE TRUE COSTS OF DIAPER NEED

Diapers are expensive but not having them can cost mothers even more in time, energy, labor, and threats to their social, psychological, and economic well-being. Given a weak social safety net around diapers and how diapers tend to be more expensive for poor families, mothers' diaper math involved a particularly tense set of equations they willingly solved for the sake of their children's health, comfort, cleanliness, and dignity. For mothers diapers played a significant role in presenting young children as provided and cared for. An infant with a clean diaper is a sacred and loved infant; an infant without one is presumably neglected by a bad mother.

It should come as no surprise that mothers viewed diapers in this way. In the previous chapter we saw how diaper companies, healthcare providers, childcare experts, and other authorities have for decades marketed and promoted disposable diapers as a reflection and extension of maternal affection and protection. Recalling the Pampers tagline "a little bit of love you can wrap your baby in," what message does this send to poor mothers who can't afford enough "diapers as tender as a mother's touch"? One result is feelings of parental inadequacy leading to poorer maternal mental health outcomes. The goal of this chapter was to detail these feelings as well as the daily dilemmas and costs of mothers' diaper work, a specific form of childcare labor that parents of privilege never need think about, much less perform. Low-income mothers invest significant labor and love in managing diaper scarcity via diaper work, reflecting their inventive and innovative responses to deprivation and the indignities associated with it.

Diaper work illuminates how intersecting inequities obscure significant aspects of parenting labor, especially their emotional and cognitive dimensions, or what sociologist Allison Daminger calls the mental work of identifying, anticipating, decision-making, and monitoring progress related to family needs.[38] In addition to physical labor of acquiring, changing, and disposing of diapers, diaper work involves cognitive labor of carefully anticipating and tracking children's diapering needs, identifying options for meeting them, making decisions among limited options, and monitoring results. It also involves extensive emotional labor for mothers when options for meeting diapering needs are limited, deciding entails forgoing other basic needs, and monitoring results involves managing gendered and racialized stigma associated with constrained choices.

Intensive mothering ideologies combined with sacred views of childhood task mothers with protecting children from dirt, defilement, and outward signs of defecation.[39] Children's appearances are a core part of mothers' own self-presentations as fit parents, as varying levels of cleanliness among children differentiate "normal" and "neglectful" mothers.[40] Poor mothers therefore devote vigilant attention to their children's hygiene and keeping them publicly clean to ward off critiques of their parenting abilities and not risk losing children to state custody.[41] Parental self-presentations around diapering are especially acute given that diapers cover the most intimate parts of a child's body and contain bodily functions thought to be dirtiest. Intensive mothering ideologies marginalize poor mothers and mothers of color, not just by setting an impossibly high bar for good parenting but by failing to account for how class and race privileges absolve white middle-class mothers from forms of carework demanded by poverty and racism.

Intensive mothering problematically defines "intensity" from the perspective of mothers with a high relative degree of economic security, personal autonomy, and freedom to parent without state interference. Yet just as intensive mothering is concerned with securing children's class position, equally important and rigorous carework strategies and logics focused on accessing crucial needs and protecting children's basic humanity become central to many mothers' experiences of "good" mothering. As sociologist Pei-Chia Lan has shown, parents tend to be adept and adaptable when developing fluid class-specific and context-sensitive childrearing strategies that allow them to cope with uncertainty, changing surroundings, and shifting needs brought on by inequalities.[42] Mothers told me they did everything they could to buffer their children from any ill effects of diaper insecurity, largely by taking its burdens and suffering upon themselves. They skipped eating meals and buying their own hygiene items so that their children didn't go without diapers. They emphasized that any diaper-stretching strategies they used (such as leaving diapers on longer, creating makeshift diapers, and going diaperless) did not harm their children. Almost all mothers explicitly noted their efforts to prevent diaper rash, including buying more expensive diapers and antirash cream and changing diapers more frequently, which increased their families' diaper costs.

Despite mothers' best efforts, they are likely unable to fully protect children from health problems associated with diaper need. Diaper rash is common across all social groups, with up to 70 percent of infants developing diaper rash at least once, accounting for one in four pediatrician visits among children during their first year of life.[43] However, children in families of color and low-income families have higher rates of dermatological and urinary health conditions associated with prolonged diaper wear, including diaper rash, urinary tract infections (UTIs), and yeast infections in the diaper area.[44] Families who report diaper need and seek support from organizations that give out diapers are also more likely to visit pediatricians for infants' diaper rash or UTIs.[45] Like mothers I interviewed, parents have reported in other studies that they cope with diaper need by using diaper-stretching strategies associated with diaper rash. About one in five admitted to leaving diapers on longer, diapering children in paper or cloth that can't wick urine away from babies' skin, and using diapers that are too big or too small.[46]

·   ·   ·   ·   ·

Distrust, stigma, and fear of child welfare system involvement likely lead to underreporting of these common diaper-stretching strategies to researchers and reluctance to seek medical care for diaper-related health problems among economically vulnerable, diaper-insecure families. When parents seek medical care to treat and prevent skin conditions linked to diapers, doctors and health educators recommend more frequent diaper changes, choosing more breathable diapers, and using topical barrier diaper rash creams. These recommendations assume that parents have access to sufficient resources to change diapers more often, choose among different diapering options, and afford additional diaper supplies. Most severely cash-strapped families that struggle with diaper need simply don't have these choices. Without access to these options, mothers do what they can through diaper work involving vigilant attention to babies' bodily rhythms, forging social connections that can help alleviate diaper need, and accounting for every cent of household expenditures. This is a child-centered parenting tactic informed by the classed and racialized logic that a mother's job is to protect children from the injuries and indignities of poverty and racism. Diaper need conjures up ideas of babies left hours or days in the same dirty diaper. What remains invisible are inventive mothers working rigorously and creatively within limited means to provide their children a dignified sense of comfort and security through diapers.

4. Cloth Controversies

A CHEAPER AND GREENER SOLUTION TO DIAPER NEED?

"For more than a decade, the disposable diaper has been a symbol of contemporary child care. Today it is emerging as a symbol of the nation's garbage crisis," wrote Michael Decourcy Hinds in the *New York Times* in 1988.[1] That same year, columnist and humorist Erma Bombeck famously claimed, "As a mother, I'd rather do away with foam cups and have hot coffee poured into my hands and drink fast than do away with disposable diapers." Two decades after Pampers were invented, disposables had become commonplace in American stores, nurseries, and daycare centers, and per Bombeck, indispensable for mothers of young children. Hinds's article drew attention to how disposable diapers had also become common in American trashcans, city waste facilities, and ultimately landfills, where they might never fully disappear.

Although disposable diapers accounted for less than 2 percent of solid waste in the United States in the late 1980s, this period marked a turning point when disposables were roundly condemned as uniquely symbolic of humanity's—and more specifically parents'—reckless disregard for outsized contributions to environmental degradation. By then, the single-use diaper was emblematic of a large and growing garbage problem wrought by increasing disposability, population growth, and a society that buried its trash in the ground without full knowledge of how long it would stay there and what impacts on land, air, and water it had in the meantime. Yet with only about half of infants and toddlers wearing disposables in the 1980s, most parents still had either some experience using cloth diapers or knew others, most likely their mothers, who had exclusively cloth-diapered their children. This first- and secondhand understanding of cloth-diapering amid growing use of disposables contributed to still-common knowledge at the time of how diapering methods differed by cost, cleanliness, comfort, and convenience. Single-use diapers quickly gained the edge for most families, as disposables were credited with allowing daycare centers to function, fathers to become more active parents in the daily (and dirtier) tasks of childrearing, and families with young children to travel more freely away from bathrooms, diaper pails, and washers. By 1988, Judith Nolte, editor of *American Baby* magazine, could confidently conclude, "I can't think of a product that has helped parents more than the disposable diaper."[2]

What some saw as signs of progress for parenting, childcare, and gender equality, others observers understood as glaring evidence of Americans' irresponsible attitude toward trash and impending ecological collapse caused by human-made factors. As soon as single-use diapers captured a significant share of the US diaper market, and consequently a larger proportion of municipal waste, environmentalists critiqued the product as one that had far higher costs than reusable versions, both in terms of more expensive prices for parents and more ecological harms for the environment. Public health advocates were also early critics of single-use diapers, questioning the risks they posed via disposal through sewer and garbage systems. Made of plant-based cellulose fibers, the earliest disposables were largely biodegradable and even flushable. But the features diaper companies designed to make disposables more appealing to parent consumers—latex cores, superabsorbent polymers, plastic fasteners, and oil-infused lotions—significantly reduced their biodegradability. Diaper manufacturers recommended that parents empty feces in toilets prior to trashing diapers so that waste was properly channeled into sewage systems designed for it, but few complied when doing so undermined the convenience factor that made many choose disposables in the first place.

While the 1960s and 1970s were watershed decades for disposable diaper development and innovation, the ensuing decades saw widespread efforts to curb their use and ecological impacts. In the late 1980s and early 1990s, lawmakers in two-dozen states—including California, Florida, and New York—debated laws intended to restrict disposables, while those in Vermont proposed an outright ban. In 1988, Washington state lawmakers considered a bill that would have required disposable diaper packages to carry a health warning that read: "Soiled disposable diapers contain viruses and microbes which may transmit diseases to the general population when disposed of improperly. Fibrous material must not be disposed with garbage or trash." Supporters of the Washington bill claimed that infant waste can contain more than one hundred viruses, including live polio and hepatitis from residual vaccines, posing hazards to sanitation workers, groundwater, and the public through contamination via flies. Diaper companies strongly opposed the bill, noting that soiled disposables hadn't been linked to health or environmental problems when in landfills, where bacteria and viruses didn't survive.

Environmentalists also urged policymakers to create tax breaks for cotton diapers like incentives for recycling that existed at the time. Yet rather than making reusable diapers cheaper, most state policy proposals focused on making disposables pricier. Bills in New Hampshire and Colorado proposed taxing single-use diapers at, respectively, a dime and quarter each (or twenty-eight cents and sixty-nine cents in 2025 currency), which would have doubled or tripled their costs and made them too expensive for most families. Owners of cloth diaper services campaigned for disposable diaper bans and taxes along with environmentalists who targeted throwaway diapers as the ultimate symbol of toxic disposability culture. None of these bills passed. Nor has there been a similar political movement to curtail the use of disposables since. Notably, however, at the height of these efforts in 1990, nearly three in four Americans reported supporting a disposable diaper ban.[3]

In the early 1990s a few bills intended to curtail disposables' use were more successful. New York almost passed a law requiring hospitals to distribute information about cloth-diapering benefits to new parents, and Nebraska passed a law mandating that all diapers sold in the state be biodegradable by 1993. There was a catch. Biodegradable diapers had to be

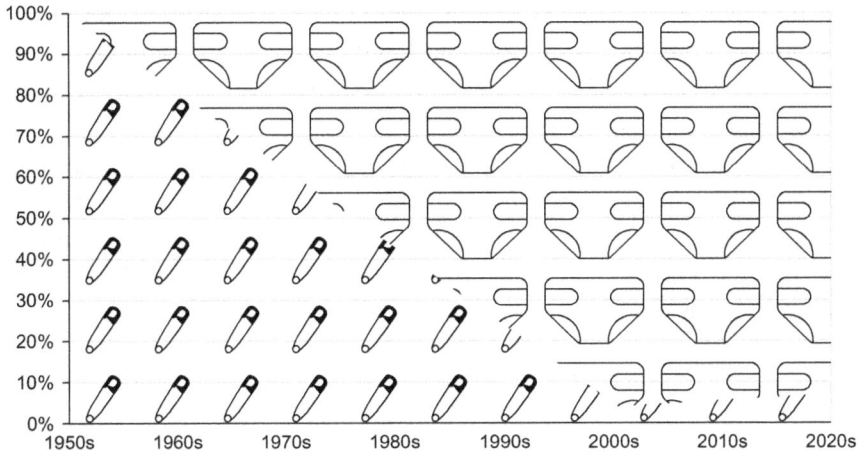

Figure 2. Proportion of primary diaper type worn by US children, 1950s–2020s.
Source: Thaman and Eichenfield (2014).

available through usual retailers at a cost no greater than 5 percent more than the average price for nonbiodegradable diapers of comparable quality. This caveat undercut the Nebraska law for reasons that still prevent most families from using more environmentally friendly diapers: greater cost, less convenience, and a social and economic infrastructure that makes using nondisposable diapers impracticable.

As disposables became a focus of environmentalists' critiques of throwaway society, cloth diapering saw a modest revival in the 1980s and 1990s.[4] Numerous public health campaigns tried to educate parents about the environmental effects of different diaper types and the relative costs of disposables compared with cloth diapers washed at home or by a diaper service. One early 1990s campaign sponsored by the University of Washington School of Nursing estimated that to diaper the average six-month-old baby per week, home-washed cloth diapers would cost $8, diaper services about $9.25, and disposables $12.50 ($20.04, $23.17, and $33.31, respectively, in 2025 dollars).[5] There was a significant uptick in cloth diaper service business in the mid-1990s after the National Association of Diaper Services (NADS) funded a study on environmental impacts of disposables. The Dy-Dee Diaper Service discussed in chapter 2 struggled to keep up with long waiting lists. Yet only a few years later, during the late 1990s, NADS membership had decreased by more than half, and Dy-Dee franchises were shuttered throughout the United States. This prompted a 1997 *New York Times* article to declare: "In the Diaper Wars, Cloth Has Just About Folded."[6]

In a last-ditch effort to save struggling businesses, companies like Diapers Unlimited in Kalamazoo, Michigan, promised free service as part of their "two-and-a-half year potty-training guarantee" urging parents to use "feel the wetness" cloth for faster toilet training. Ultimately, Diapers Unlimited also went out of business, as cloth diapers never regained the foothold they once had before disposables became the diaper type of choice and circumstance for nearly all US families by the turn of the twenty-first century. Still, many have continued to advocate for more sustainable diaper options, starting with questioning what greener diapering would entail.

DRAWBACKS OF DEVELOPING A GREENER DIAPER

Since the 1990s, many life-cycle analysis studies have tried to determine the relative environmental impacts of cloth versus disposable diapers. These studies have considered the full range of resources—energy, raw materials, water—needed to produce, transport, and clean diapers, along with ground, water, and air pollution impacts, threats to public health, and financial costs. In interpreting these studies, many of which were commissioned by diaper manufacturers or the diaper service industry, environmentalists were often pitted against industry experts with economic incentives to downplay disposables' negative impacts. Corporate-sponsored studies concluded that disposables took up less landfill space than assumed and that producing, shipping, and cleaning cloth diapers polluted air and water. Costly public relations campaigns by the two corporate giants of disposable diapers—Procter & Gamble and Kimberly-Clark, manufacturers of Pampers and Huggies, respectively—countered environmentalists' claims that cloth diapers were greener than disposables.

Yet even those with fewer financial stakes in promoting any diaper type argued for closer scrutiny of assumptions that cloth diapers are environmentally benign or unequivocally more sustainable than disposables. They emphasized how trees used for disposables were often planted for that purpose; disposables occupied less landfill space than food waste or used newspapers; and cleaning cloth diapers required a lot of detergent and water, a problem in states like California plagued by frequent droughts. Most modern cloth diapers are prefolded rectangles of cotton fabric inserted into waterproof liners made at least partially of plastic-based materials like polyurethane laminate. Many therefore argue that it remains debatable if environmental impacts of reusable diapers that require a lot of water to produce and clean are significantly less than for disposables, which also primarily consist of petroleum-based plastics and cotton.[7] While early diaper life-cycle analyses offered few definitive answers, one common finding was that designing lighter disposables reduced their impacts. Diaper manufacturers have reduced disposables' size and weight by about 50 percent since they were first invented, if not to assuage environmental concerns, to appeal to consumers wanting lighter diapers that sagged less and could be packaged more tightly.[8] Consumer choices—diapers washed per load, washing water temperature, and using them on multiple children—also shape the environmental credentials of cloth diapering. Ultimately, the environmental impacts of cloth diapers depend largely on use, while those of disposables depend more on design.

What many have proposed as a third option—biodegradable or recyclable single-use diapers—has encountered its own set of challenges. As soon as disposables took over the market, environmentalists called for manufacturers to focus product development on biodegradable diapers made of renewable resources. Biodegradable cornstarch diaper liners were already in development in the early 1980s, but their higher costs, lower absorbency, and questionable decomposability by bacteria in landfills that lacked both oxygen and water prevented them from ever gaining a significant share of the diaper market.

Astutely sensing that urging parents to return to cloth was a futile effort, many municipalities and diaper companies piloted diaper recycling and composting programs in the 1990s, including one in Seattle jointly sponsored by the city's Solid Waste Utility, a local recycling company, and Procter & Gamble. The program used water-filled agitators to separate human waste from paper, absorbent gel, and plastic. Waste and water went into the city's sewer system, while poststerilized gel, paper, and plastic were used in plant nursery soil, recycled cardboard, and park benches and planters, respectively. Although capable of handling seventy-two hundred disposables daily from eight hundred families and thirty-five daycare centers around the city, the program was quickly dubbed a "technological success [and] economic flop," ending after only eight months of operation. A later diaper recycling program in Santa Clarita, California, closed in 2003 for similar reasons: the cost to recycle dirty diapers far exceeded the value of paper pulp and plastic generated. Of 43 tons of used diapers collected by the city, only 3.6 tons, or 8 percent, became useable, saleable materials for which the city could try to recoup the costs of its relatively expensive and laborious diaper-recycling program.

Efforts to design greener diapers have also tried to address diapers' potential health risks via chemicals released through off-gassing. Trapped in diapers during manufacturing, many of these chemicals are volatile organic compounds (VOCs) dispersed in air once diaper packages are opened and exposed to skin when diapers are worn. Many parts of modern disposables and wipes (such as fragrances, inks, absorbents, adhesives, binders, and moisture barriers) contain VOCs. Inhalable and absorbable, VOCs in high concentrations and with repeated prolonged exposure can cause irritation and toxicity to various body parts, including the nose, mouth, eyes, liver, kidney, and respiratory and reproductive systems. Though in low levels that likely pose negligible health risks, research has found VOCs in all diaper products tested, even those labeled as "for sensitive skin" or "organic."[9] Given that young children with delicate skin wear diapers around the clock for years and covering their genitalia where skin has a particularly high absorption capacity, this is concerning.

Contemporary consumers are accustomed to pristine, bright-white disposable diapers, harkening back to when bleached diaper linens were associated with racial whiteness and affluence. Having been sold on diapers "as gentle as a mother's touch" for decades through disposable diaper advertising, consumers also expect diapers to be soft and gentle to babies' skin as well as supple enough to allow for comfortable movement and sturdy enough to prevent breakage and leaks. These taken-for-granted features of modern disposables have environmental impacts that, though smaller than before, still present risks. Using elemental chlorine that created carcinogenic dioxins to bleach and texturize diaper pulp was phased out by 1990, but contemporary bleaching processes still rely on chlorine derivatives that can irritate skin and respiratory systems. Moreover, phthalates used to make plastic diaper components more flexible and durable can detach as microparticles and be released into the surrounding environment, including air and skin. High concentrations of phthalates, which can disrupt hormonal systems, have been found in some infant diapers.[10] The US Consumer Product Safety Commission requires baby changing products, including diapers, to meet requirements for lead and phthalate content limits, registration cards, and tracking labels, but it doesn't require that diaper manufacturers disclose ingredients.[11] Even savvy diaper consumers who try to monitor and control the products they affix to their children's bodies may struggle to figure out exactly what is in their diapers.

In recent years many diaper lines have been developed to offer consumers chlorine- and phthalate-free diaper options, including Coterie, Hello Bello, Millie Moon, Huggies Special Delivery, and Pampers Pure. These lines are significantly more expensive—up to twice the price—than lines like Huggies Little Snugglers and Pampers Swaddlers and even higher compared with discount brands like Luvs and Parents' Choice. Not being able to afford eco-friendly diapers that risk less contact with chemicals may be one reason that children in poor families and families of color have greater exposure to phthalates and worse indoor air quality, in part due to higher VOC concentration.[12] Although they tend to be associated with less chemical exposure, even some cloth diapers have been found to contain VOCs and phthalates. Economic and racial privileges minimize diapering's chemical harms to some, while contributing to ill effects of diapering on others—namely, marginalized parents and their children.

Greater use of cloth and single-use diapers made with fewer or no VOCs or phthalates is likely the most effective way to reduce vulnerable young children's exposure to harmful chemicals via diapering. But both options are pricey. Recent efforts to create healthier, sustainable diapers have focused on nontoxic compostables, such as Dypers. Founded in 2019, Arizona entrepreneur and father Sergio Radovcic envisioned the Dyper brand as he routinely handled garbage cans full of his children's dirty diapers headed for landfills. The company's composting program ReDyper is a subscription-based service that sells bamboo diapers and offers pick-up services in select locations and mail-in services nationwide. Used Dypers are shipped to composting facilities where they are broken down into organic material for use in landscaping on highway medians. Alas, converting containers for infant excrement into fodder for beautifying roadways has a hefty cost. A 168-count box of size 3 Dypers costs $99; the packaging and postage to mail back those 168 diapers after use is an additional $39. Given that a typical six-month-old infant needs six to eight diapers per day, to use and compost Dypers would cost nearly $200 a month, more than double the cost of conventional disposables, resulting in a significant upcharge that only privileged families can afford.

Another problem is that most compostable diapers still contain plastic elements in fasteners and outer film, requiring sophisticated, expensive processes to break down. Caregivers typically roll a used diaper in on itself and refasten it to keep the waste inside, trapping biodegradable materials in the outer noncompostable shell, which becomes a barrier between oxygen and bacteria needed to biodegrade in landfills. Research on creating fully biodegradable diapers and industrial composting systems needed to process them is under way in many countries. Yet with almost no government regulation or economic incentive for corporate investment in developing fully biodegradable diapers, there is little hope for widespread use of biodegradables like Dypers that depend on families' desire to use them and their ability to afford them.[13] As earlier diaper-recycling programs revealed, breaking down modern disposables into component parts—consisting of a complex combination of wood pulp, cotton, viscose rayon, and several types of plastic—is as hard as establishing a market for the recycled outputs. Nevertheless, Procter & Gamble has pledged to recycle absorbent hygiene products, including diapers, in ten major US cities by 2030 with longer-term promises to make all products and packaging from 100 percent renewable or recycled materials. The company has partnered with the Italian healthcare group Angelini to create a recycling program that would convert dirty diapers into plastic bottle caps and viscose clothing.[14] Setting aside the aversion many might have to drinking from and wearing materials once infused with human excrement, and despite any technological challenges, families would need to be willing—and more importantly *able*—to pay a premium for diapers made of recyclable materials and dispose of them in recycling bins.

This raises an important question about who should bear the burden of reducing diapers' environmental impacts: individual families, diaper companies, governments, or a combination thereof? We must also consider who is most affected by those impacts as disposable diapers and resultant pollution accumulate. Most throwaway diapers now used globally consist of a polyethylene waterproof outer layer and a polypropylene inside layer, both of which require a lot of crude oil to produce and are virtually impossible to recycle or compost after use. Estimates indicate that more than a quarter of a million disposable diapers are sent to landfills every minute. That number continues to climb in areas with rising populations and a growing middle class, such as Indonesia where many of the six billion diapers used annually end up in rivers and other waterways where diapers break down into microplastics and leach chemicals that can contaminate drinking water and harm marine life. Lacking a waste infrastructure capable of safely handling that many diapers, local volunteer groups like the Indonesian Diaper Evacuation Brigade wade through rivers wearing hazmat suits to retrieve used diapers floating on water's surface.[15]

Disposable diapers have also become a huge environmental problem in many other parts of the world, like Zimbabwe, where a contentious national debate over single-use diapers led the Zimbabwean government to propose an outright nationwide ban on their use. The ban has yet to pass due to opposition from critics arguing that cloth diapers are old-fashioned and that disposables have become a permanent feature of childrearing, especially in urban areas. These criticisms echo those that prevented passage of disposable diaper bans in the United States in the late 1980s and early 1990s.[16] Ultimately a lot of experts claim that not creating disposable diaper waste in the first place is best.[17] Four decades after initial attempts to address the environmental impacts of disposables, most efforts to reduce diaper waste still narrowly focus on getting families to switch to cloth diapers. Despite money being a major limiting factor in families' abilities to use cloth, public subsidies that could offset upfront and cleaning costs have never been seriously considered in political discussions about curtailing the waste and financial burdens created by diapers. Yet controversies over the most eco-friendly diaper type have only ramped up in the ensuing decades as concerns over health hazards, pollution, limited landfill space, population growth, and climate change grow.

Infant diapers and their ecological impacts continue to play a unique role in these controversies, especially as some experts recommend having fewer children as one of the most effective individual-level strategies for reducing multigenerational environmental harms.[18] Debates over diapers and the environment tap into how parents choose to diaper their babies as well as shared notions of *waste* and *trash*. These social concepts signify not only which items end up in garbage bins, landfills, or waterways but also judgment categories for those labeled impure, unproductive, and irresponsible, as poor mothers often are.[19] How we grapple with waste and trash rests on ever-changing cultural ideas of filth, convenience, and affluence. The ability to buy newly invented disposable diapers was once associated with modern ideas of cleanliness, ease, and prosperity. The inability to choose reusable diapers now signals wasteful parents who fail to prioritize long-term environmental conservation over their own short-term convenience.

As past efforts to create and promote different diaper types and strategies reveal, diapering's environmental impacts are influenced by factors both big and seemingly small, ranging from national policies and global waste management infrastructure to the mundane ways that parents clean cloth and fold soiled disposables before tossing them in the trash. As with any technology, how we make, buy, use, and dispose of diapers unfolds within specific social, political, economic, and cultural contexts—all of which matter when contemplating how to increase diaper accessibility and affordability while decreasing diapering's ecological harms. To some, the obvious answer to both problems points to a simple question: Why can't parents just use cloth diapers?

ENVIRONMENTAL INEQUALITIES OF CLOTH DIAPERING AS A CLASS PRIVILEGE

Social awareness of diaper insecurity has increased in recent years, due in large part to journalistic accounts of families' struggles to get diapers and diaper banks' efforts to help them.[20] More than thirty years after Michael Decourcy Hinds wrote in the *New York Times* about how disposable diapers had come to symbolize toxic throwaway culture, *New York Times* parenting columnist Jessica Grose wrote in March 2021 about mothers' experiences of diaper deprivation and despair. Some commenters on the 2021 article asked what could be done to help diaper-insecure families, but others expressed beliefs about root causes of both diaper need and environmental harms of costly disposables:

> Oh, come on. In the 1950s all of our mothers used cloth diapers and laundered them, some with machines, some with scrub boards and wash tubs. Not only was this economically more sensible than store-bought plasticized diapers, it was better for the environment than putting billions of used plasticized nonbiodegradable diapers into landfills.

> Cloth diapers are work, granted, but my mom did it in the '50s and '60s and my dad was a low-paid blue collar with lots of kids, so it can be done. Better yet, don't have a lot of kids one cannot afford.

> Back in the day, there were these pieces of cloth called "diapers." The neat thing about them was that a baby would soil one, it was removed, washed, and could be put on again. . . . All this can be accomplished by hand. No expensive diaper service, not even regular access to a washing machine, though it helps. Is it smelly? Of course. Is it affordable? Absolutely. Though I seriously doubt someone who has a passel of kids cares one whit about the environment, cloth diapers won't pollute the planet.

> My mother raised six of us using cloth diapers and ran our boarding house all the while. Hand washing cloth diapers seems one of the least dangerous things one can do with our polluted environment. But with the perceived need to have both parents working to buy a McMansion or new car, priorities dictate.

> What did women do in the days before disposable diapers were ubiquitous? Plenty of women got by with lots of kids and no disposable diapers OR automatic in-home washers and dryers and it wasn't all that long ago.

> Cloth diapers are permanent, very comfortable, low cost, and effective. Also, they are not a huge source of wastepaper, ending up in landfills!!

> Cloth diapering is cheaper, plain and simple, as is breastfeeding. Sacrifices need to be made in life.

> If you use cloth and clean them yourself that would probably save a huge amount of money.

Several commenters referred to how, for centuries prior to the advent of disposables, parents simply used fabric for diapers, and that in the 1950s,

1960s, and 1970s their own mothers and wives used cloth washed by hand in a bucket and hung on a clothesline, no washing machine or dryer required. Comments emphasized that cloth diapering would be cheaper, feasible, and better for the environment than disposables mothers couldn't afford.

What did mothers do before disposable diapers were common? Chapter 2 provides the longer answer, but in short, they raised and diapered children in a culture and economy that no longer exist. Notably, most of the commenters telling mothers to use cloth didn't, by their own admission, do the work associated with cloth diapering when they or their children were young. Their mothers and wives did. During the 1950s through 1970s, most infants wore cloth diapers, relatively few mothers of young children worked outside the home, and those who did typically worked fewer hours than mothers do now. When cloth diapers were ubiquitous, they were also normal, meaning that others were unlikely to scoff when children wore pieces of cloth likely to leak and smell. As diapering types and practices changed, so too did the likelihood a soiled, stinky cloth diaper violated norms of social decorum.

Also long gone are the days when a "blue collar" single-family bread-winner could provide for an entire family, leaving less time for childcare, especially washing cloth diapers. Most mothers of young children are now in the paid labor market, not because they want a "McMansion" but because costs of living, including for basics like housing, have increased as real income has decreased. In 1960 the median annual income was around $5,600, while the median home cost about $11,900, a price-to-income ratio of two to one. Sixty years later, estimated median income is $74,580, while the median home cost $433,100, resulting in a home price-to-income ratio of almost six to one.[21] Rather than choosing to work to buy luxuries, families must work more to attain a modest middle-class lifestyle. Poor and low-income families must work more hours just to buy basics, which have increased in cost as wages adjusted for inflation have gone down.

Condescending advice for mothers to use cloth to prevent diaper need is rooted in erroneous presumptions about limited labor, lower costs, and fewer environmental impacts. And *New York Times* readers are not the only ones who make these mistaken assumptions. According to the diaper bankers and diaper policy advocates I interviewed, legislators who have the power to pass policies providing more public diaper support often share these views. Lucy, a thirty-year-old white diaper bank director, described to me her experience testifying to a legislative committee about a bill that would have provided unprecedented public funding for diapers in her state. "Disposable diapers are not deemed medically necessary because cloth diapers are available," she explained. "That was the issue they had with my testimony, and the question about the environment. . . . Legislators didn't even think about the laundry issue. . . . These parents are working multiple jobs. Who has time to wash ten diapers a day? But they still ask, 'Why don't they just use cloth?'" Lucy pointed to lack of understanding about low-income parents' lives and constraints leading to assumptions that parents simply need to work harder, such as by using purportedly cheaper and more eco-friendly cloth diapers.

Most diaper bankers I interviewed shared similar stories about policy-makers and community members who responded to requests for diaper support by asking, "Why don't they just use cloth?" Embedded within this seemingly simple question are sexist, classist, and racist assumptions about easy individual solutions to structural problems like diaper insecurity. Policymakers and *New York Times* readers are more likely to be white, affluent, older men who change few diapers, much less struggle with diaper need. Conversely, the parents I interviewed were mostly poor mothers of color who had already tried cloth diapering but found it to be *more* expensive, labor-intensive, and time-prohibitive. Cloth is the primary diaper type used by a very small proportion of American families, with the typical cloth diapering parent being a white stay-at-home, married, middle-class, home-owning mother with an in-house washer and dryer.[22]

It is no coincidence that the rising popularity of single-use diapers coincided with the influx of American mothers, especially those with children still in diapers, into the paid labor force in the 1960s, 1970s, and 1980s. As discussed in chapter 2, although disposable diapers have always been a convenience commodity that helped mothers manage dual demands of employment and raising children, diaper advertising highlighted disposables as a product that allowed mothers to provide optimal care.[23] Capitalizing on gendered norms of maternal domesticity, cloth diapers were discouraged through messages that soiled cloth diapers were unsanitary and irritated infants' delicate skin, and hence "good" mothers chose disposables. With disposables now universally available and normal, if not affordable, cloth diapering has struggled to regain popularity in the United States, where more than 95 percent of infants wear disposables most or all the time.[24]

Environmentalists, cloth diaper advocates, and cloth diaper bankers are working to reverse this trend. Supporters describe cloth diapering as a cost-saving measure that is better for babies due to reduced chemical exposure and better for the planet due to less of the 7.6 billion pounds of annual garbage generated by single-use diapers.[25] Hundreds of how-to books and websites on cloth diapering guide parents through choosing, buying, treating, washing, storing, and traveling with cloth diapers. Many also provide advice about how to convince family and childcare providers to use cloth diapers. Recognizing that many parents nowadays are unlikely to have mothers and friends who fully cloth-diapered their infants, these sources frame their advice as demystifying common misconceptions about cloth diapers. The popular site Babylist.com provides a "Cloth Diapering 101" tutorial claiming that "cloth diapers today aren't like they used to be. Your grandmother's pins and rubber pants have been replaced by easy-to-use all-in-ones with tons of prints and styles."[26] Outlining pros and cons of different cloth diapers systems, the site estimates that start-up costs range from $115 for the cheapest type, prefolded thick material pinned and covered with a waterproof shell, to $660 for the most expensive "all-in-ones" made of attached waterproof covers and inner-cloth lining. These estimates presume that parents will do laundry every two to three days and purchase more supplies as babies grow into larger sizes. They don't include the cost of accessories like wet travel bags, cloth diaper pails and liners, and toilet-attachable diaper sprayers, which can total around $200 or more. Most families that cloth diaper invest at least $500 in start-up supplies and accessories.[27]

Although the cloth diaper market has grown in recent years, cloth still accounts for fewer than 10 percent of diapers sold in the United States.[28] This, along with the relatively privileged circumstances of cloth-diapering families, casts doubt on cloth as a solution for diaper need. The push for cloth diapers also ignores the time pressures mothers of all economic groups face in balancing employment and childcare. Even most of the one in five parents in the United States who stay home full time don't use cloth.[29] Add costs and constraints to a carework infrastructure ill-equipped for cloth diapering, and one can see why most parents never even consider cloth as a diapering option. As mothers shared with me, the social, economic, and political conditions that create diaper need also prevent them from using cloth diapers to meet that need. Yet assuming that cloth is a cost-effective, feasible alternative to disposables fails to account for intersecting inequalities that limit marginalized parents' diapering choices specifically and constrict their carework options generally. As gender scholar Chikako Takeshita argued, beyond prohibitively expensive start-up costs, challenges of managing carework, housework, and paid work in poverty are not conducive to the demands of constantly cleaning dirty cloth diapers, making "eco-diapering" a class privilege.[30]

Nevertheless, just as women across all classes face gendered pressures to be hard-working intensive mothers who are child-centered and self-sacrificing, increasingly they are also expected to be "intensive green mothers" tasked with raising happy, healthy children while protecting the environment.[31] For evidence of this, look no further than advertisements for "green" baby products such as cloth diapers, "certified nontoxic" toys, and organic foods that center images of clean and serene infants. Although targeted at them, such ads rarely show the mothers held responsible for being eco-friendly parents who must compensate for the environmental degradation of childbearing through consumption choices that add labor and costs to caregiving. Directives and moral appeals for supposedly pro-environmental maternal behaviors—such as breastfeeding, organic home cooking, and cloth diapering—discount an already inequitable division of unpaid and devalued domestic labor that unevenly falls on women, especially low-income mothers of color who disproportionately manage their and others' household waste.[32] Expectations for mothers to reduce environmental burdens through labor-intensive and commodity-based practices represent an ever-growing sphere of green intensive parenting that pushes women without resources further to the margins of normative motherhood.[33] These expectations also ignore the lived experiences of poor mothers who often opt for single-use consumer goods to seem modern, to avoid the stigma of poverty, and to meet their children's basic needs.[34]

Ultimately, "Why don't they just use cloth?" is not just a question. It is an ideological tool that deliberately disguises that *they* are usually women and that to *just use cloth* diapers requires intensive and extensive physical, emotional, and cognitive gendered labor that presumes access to the supplies, support, and job schedules that allow for cloth diapering. Controversies over cloth versus disposable diapers epitomize ongoing conflicts between conservation and convenience. But for mothers I interviewed, considerations over choosing one diaper type over another really came down to two other factors: cost and constraints. There is a strong mismatch between eco-diapering ideology and the reality that nearly all US parents use disposable diapers. As disposables have become the near-universal diaper type of choice among families across the socioeconomic spectrum and increasingly around the globe, cloth diapering has indeed become a class privilege few families can afford. This is due not only to obvious costs of money and labor but also to the hidden costs of stress and stigma. Any hope for the development and widespread use of greener diaper options will depend on understanding and minimizing these costs.

"NOT EASIER OR CHEAPER": THE COSTS OF CLOTH DIAPERING

Low-income mothers are often shamed for not using cloth diapers when they struggle with diaper need. However, many mothers I interviewed had tried cloth diapering for a week or month, only to find it was *more* expensive than disposables. Their careful calculations didn't include the costs of diaper work associated with cloth diapering, including tracking diaper supplies; washing, drying, folding, and storing cloth diapers; traveling to and from laundry facilities; planning around washing and drying schedules; and worrying if cloth diapers leaked, smelled, or appeared dirty. Initially mothers encountered prohibitively expensive start-up costs. After pricing how much it would cost to buy enough cloth diaper sets to last a day or two, they discovered that to "save" money in the long run would take many months up to a year. To be an actual cost-saving measure, they explained, cloth diapering works more like a long-term investment strategy that requires upfront assets needed to buy diapers, accessories, and cleaning supplies as well as time to recoup initial monetary outlays.

These were assets and time mothers didn't have to spare. Joanna, an eighteen-year-old Afro-Latina mother of one, noted that she found a set of used cloth diapers in her child's size for $100 online, but that "immediately it was a no for me. Even if that would be saving me money in the future, I can't afford that giant chunk right now. And then what happens when he outgrows that one size?" Similarly, Molly, a thirty-one-year-old Black mother of two, shared that cloth wasn't an option for her family because both she and her husband were out of work when their son was born. "It just wasn't in the budget to even start with cloth, which would have been three hundred dollars. . . . How do you come up with three hundred dollars all at one? I just can't, not when we're both unemployed." Much like disposables are cheaper per unit when parents can use intertemporal savings strategies to buy in bulk and during sales, having enough money to get started with cloth can eventually reduce diapering costs over time. But, as with Joanna and Molly, low-income mothers rarely, if ever, have enough discretionary money on hand to spend a lot on diapers all at once.

Then there were other expenses beyond purchasing the diapers, including those for water, electricity, detergent, laundromat fees, travel, and diaper creams. Even for mothers who received free cloth diapers, cleaning costs quickly added up. Tracy, a twenty-five-year-old multiracial mother of three, qualified for a no-cost cloth diaper subscription through a former foster youth program. Yet she still couldn't afford laundry costs to clean them. "If you have to wash diapers," Tracy noted, "it's going to be the same amount of money you're going to spend on regular diapers, maybe more. . . . The social worker told me it would be easier and cheaper, but then I ended up spending like forty dollars just to wash the diapers. That's not easier or cheaper." Leslie, a twenty-eight-year-old Black pregnant mother of one, likewise explained, "Some think cloth are free. But then you have to spend on washing, detergent, water, electricity, and all the work and worry. You still have to pay for it in some way." Terri, a thirty-year-old white diaper banker, compared assumptions about the cost-effectiveness and convenience of cloth diapering and breastfeeding that discounted the value of mothers' labor. "People say, 'it's easy and free.'

Yeah, but only if a women's time and work aren't worth anything," she concluded.

These financial concerns were compounded by worries that even laundered cloth diapers weren't fully clean and presented health risks for babies and mothers. Justine, a thirty-eight-year-old white mother of three, described using cloth diapers as an "awful, expensive" experience that harmed her son. "Honestly, it's so much money because you're washing them all the time, using so much bleach, which bothers baby's skin, then you need more diaper cream. It's just more all around, more laundry, more time, more money on detergent, bleach, water. Between the money and the time, they're not cheaper, and they stink! The ammonia in the pee breaks down the plastic." Tia, a thirty-one-year-old Black mother of three, asked me, "How do you get them fully clean? My son has eczema real bad, and you can't put a lot of stuff on his skin. I couldn't scrub a cloth diaper enough to make sure it doesn't hurt him. And a laundry card alone is five dollars. I already spend twenty-five dollars a week on laundry. How is that not wasting my time and money on something you can't get fully clean?"

Because Sonia, a thirty-three-year-old Latina mother of two, couldn't afford more than a day's worth of cloth diapers, the "special baby detergent," or daily trips to a laundromat, she washed cloth diapers daily in a bathroom sink. She concluded that "two months of washing eight diapers by hand every day was starting to peel my skin. I had to stop because of the toll it took on my hands." Like Justine, Tia, and Sonia, many mothers worried that cloth diapers were unsanitary, inefficient, and irritating to infants' delicate skin when worn and mothers' skin when frequently washed, requiring pricey diaper and hand creams that further increased cloth diapering costs. Such time pressures, labor issues, and childcare problems prevented mothers from continuing with cloth diapering. Maria, a thirty-year-old Latina mother of four, told me, "I tried but couldn't keep up with it. I had to keep up with the kids, cooking, cleaning. It was overwhelming. I think if you have help, it's easier, but it's too hard if you're by yourself." Other mothers emphasized how adding cloth diapering to an already tightly calibrated juggling act of employment, housework, and care for young children was impracticable, if not impossible. Hannah, a forty-two-year-old white mother of one, lived on the eighth floor of an apartment building and had to find someone to watch her young son when she went down to the basement to wash cloth diapers in the laundry room. "I have no place to store them in my 450-square-foot apartment," she emphasized, "and it's not like I can open the windows wide because I don't want my son to go out the window."

Employed mothers and mothers going to school especially struggled to use cloth diapers because they spent more time out of their homes and utilized more out-of-home childcare. These mothers often reserved their limited disposable diaper supplies for outings and when others, usually those in daycare facilities that wouldn't accept cloth diapers or relatives who were reluctant to use cloth, cared for their children. Ramona, a twenty-one-year-old Latina mother of one, used cloth and makeshift diapers at home so she could manage to provide the forty disposables per week her son's daycare required. Alejandra, a twenty-eight-year-old Latina mother of two, shared, "My grandmother is watching him while I work, and she's in her seventies. I was just grateful she was watching him. I can't ask her to deal with cloth diapers and all that." Mothers believed that cloth diapers would have placed an undue burden on family already providing free or reduced-cost childcare.

Moreover, very few respondents received encouragement or support from family members or others within their social networks to use cloth diapers. Despite "just use cloth" commenters' references to grandmothers and mothers who faithfully cloth diapered their children during earlier eras, mothers I interviewed noted that their own grandmothers, mothers, aunts, and older sisters discouraged cloth diapering by telling them "horror stories" about times before disposables. While these older family members warned mothers about the expense, work, and mess of cloth diapering, many similarly aged peers were unfamiliar with cloth diapers and how to use them. Ten mothers I interviewed didn't know what I meant when I asked if they had considered or used cloth diapers. "You mean that thing I use as a burp cloth? The ones you have to pay for and still wash later for more money? No, just no," responded Juana, a twenty-nine-year-old Latina mother of two. Similar comments revealed how much cloth diapering has fallen out of favor as a normative, preferred, and feasible diapering option.

Despite this, diaper bankers frequently encountered comments like those from *New York Times* readers. Rosemary, a forty-eight-year-old

white family-services case manager, said about giving public presentations on diapers: "The older men say, 'Oh, I don't deal with diapers,' or 'My
wife does that,' or 'Why don't they use cloth?' We have that option, but it's
not as simple as 'Here's a cloth diaper. You can just use that.' You need
water, detergent, the right equipment. It could be an economical way to
diaper your child if you had the right resources, but that's where people
get stuck. They think everyone has the resources to cloth diaper, but they
don't. Some people don't even have water. What are they supposed to do?"
Coming from a point of privilege, commenters didn't consider the many
costs of cloth diapers. To further prove her point, Rosemary introduced
me to her colleague, Melissa, a thirty-two-year-old white mother of three,
who'd become their diaper bank's "cloth diapering expert."

Melissa described the process she used to clean cloth diapers, which
involved first using a toilet sprayer to remove feces, followed by a prewash
scrub in a bucket, and then a thorough machine wash with towels for the
right agitation. Melissa bought special detergent for hard water to prevent
"mineral burns" on her baby's skin and laundered at least every other day,
often daily, and occasionally did a third wash to remove ammonia stains
and "barnyard smells" from diapers. Her washer, dryer, special detergent,
water softener, bathroom sprayer, plunger, and bucket cost two thousand
dollars. Melissa admitted to buying disposables when she didn't have time
to wash cloth diapers: "Some weeks I fall behind and have to pick up some
disposable diapers. But I'm still trying to encourage families to use cloth
even if it's just supplementary, like 'Why don't you have a few on hand?
That way if you're running low on disposables, you could use that.' People
were always telling me, 'It's too much work. It's too much money. It's not
really cost-effective.' But I'm kind of an environmentalist. I don't like the
idea of just throwing away all these diapers that sit in the landfill forever."
After talking to Melissa for twenty minutes about all she did to cloth diaper, she paused and concluded, "But, yeah, it doesn't work for everyone,
not if you don't have privilege."

Other diaper bankers faced frequent questioning about why cloth diapers weren't a viable option for parents who couldn't afford disposables.
David, a sixty-three-year-old white founder of a diaper bank, was once
asked during a community meeting, "If swaddling cloth was good enough
for baby Jesus, why do *they* need disposables?" He replied, "Do they really

expect people who've worked all day and are trying to make it by on next to nothing to wash them in the toilet or shower? If you're working two jobs or even three jobs, do you really want to come home and spend the little bit of time you have doing laundry or with your baby? After all, Jesus's mother Mary was a stay-at-home mom."

Heidi, a forty-year-old white diaper bank founder and director, similarly described barriers to cloth diapering faced by families she served. "We have a big transient population staying with their aunt or cousins, staying at the shelter, or staying wherever, they're all over the place. People don't have consistent washing facilities, or money to pay for laundry." Heidi used cloth with her twins because she could afford to stay home and had easy access to a washer and dryer. She shared, "I always get the question, 'Why don't you do cloth diapers?' Well, because it's just not feasible at this point for these families. I wasn't trying to work, trying to buy groceries. I could sit at home and change them every hour. But that never even entered their mind."

Rachel, fifty-eight, white, and manager of a baby supply bank, likewise explained, "I've had a lot of people suggest that our families use cloth, but a majority live in temporary housing. A mom living in a hotel room would have to wash diapers out in a toilet, rinse in the sink, and hang them in the shower? How is that clean? It just doesn't work for the infant or mother." Expectations that poor families use cloth, many diaper bankers concluded, added another burden to already overworked families doing all they could to make ends meet. Veronia, a sixty-year-old Black diaper advocate, encountered similar questions rooted in privileged assumptions. She told me, "You get old ladies like me who write asking why these young girls won't wash diapers. 'Hold on, that's not what this is.' When you tell people that they can't be legally washed in a laundromat, they go, 'Oh, that makes a difference.' Even if I have a voucher for reduced daycare, even if I can go to school, if I don't have eight diapers a day, I can't do any of that." Indeed, several mothers who used cloth or makeshift diapers at home reported that they had missed work or school because they didn't have enough disposables, pointing to missed opportunities for wage-earning and upward mobility as another potential cost of cloth diapering.

As June, a seventy-year-old white diaper bank codirector, explained, "When people ask why not use cloth, the most significant issue from a child welfare and economic stability viewpoint is that you have to take disposable diapers to most daycare centers. If you can't, you can't get job training, can't work, can't go to school. How do you pull yourself up and out?" Mothers and diaper bankers stressed that what seemed like an obvious choice to "just use cloth" to fix diaper need only made sense when decontextualized from lived experiences and conditions of poverty, low-wage and long-hours work, unstable housing, and childcare demands. Commenters rarely recognized the "choice" to use cloth as rooted in privilege. But as mothers could attest, because many had already tried to use cloth, being poor also made cloth diapering cost more, and not just more money.

"WHAT'S WRONG WITH HER?": HIDDEN COSTS AND CLASS CONNOTATIONS OF CLOTH DIAPERS

Beyond the obvious financial expenses, cloth diapering came with its own kind of diaper work for mothers, including additional labor and hidden costs of anxiety and stress. Although Tracy qualified for free cloth diapers through a program for former foster youth, she found using them "so much more stressful than disposable diapers. They use them up so fast, and if you run out, you have to wash all of them. You have to constantly think if there's pee or poop and clean them out right away for poop." Aurelia, a twenty-five-year-old Latina mother of three, avoided using cloth diapers because washers and dryers in her apartment complex were often out of order. During the several days it took for the manager to fix them, she constantly worried about having enough clean diapers.

Another part of mothers' cloth diaper work was managing the emotional and psychological fear that using cloth diapers would signal deprivation, dirtiness, and negligent parenting. Mothers and diapers bankers both described a pivotal cultural and structural shift in the class dynamics of diapering. They emphasized how, only a few decades ago, cloth diapering was near universal before affluent mothers who could afford to regularly purchase throwaway diapers led the change to disposables. Now few parents opt for cloth, while those who do are likely to be more privileged parents who can afford the labor and expenses of cloth diapering. Mothers described cloth diapering for their children as a desperate last resort, one associated with despair, deprivation, and having no other diaper options. Despite disposables' origins as luxury items first available in high-end department stores, they are now part of "normal" parenting that transcends class lines. Cloth diapers—once associated with scarcity, rickety scrub boards, and wash buckets used among the poor—have become a marker of class privilege and affluence.

This shift shaped how mothers thought about distinctions between disposable and cloth diapers. Trinity, a forty-two-year-old Black mother of three, told me, "I used cloth with my son because I was at home when I was young, but I work now with her. I'm thankful I haven't been desperate enough for that, that I can use normal diapers." Audra, thirty-three, white, and a mother of five, described her brief time using cloth diapers as a "disaster, all those little buttons, and plastic on the outside. It's not easy, especially when you're working, worried about how you're going to get the next meal for your kids, put gas in the car, get back to work, and get the kids to school. Then you have to wash poop out in the middle of all that? No, I'll continue with the usual ones." Faith, a thirty-two-year-old Black mother of two, shared, "I use regular diapers, unless I can't afford them and have no choice but to use cloth." Tellingly, like Trinity, Audra, and Faith, many mothers used the language of "normal," "usual," and "regular" to describe disposables as synonymous with "diapers."

Connections between poverty and cloth diapering were most powerfully described by mother-of-two Estelle, thirty-six and Latina, whose early childhood memories of washing her siblings' cloth diapers in a bucket in her Mexican hometown brought her to tears:

> I still remember being nine years old washing diapers to help my mom, only wanting to go play with my friends, go to school. I wanted to cry. When I washed the diapers, I was imagining another kind of life, a good life. In Mexico we use cloth on babies. I imagined growing up in America, buying diapers in the store, not having to wash them when I grew up. But now I work in the field, I'm up at 6:00 in the morning, and I'm too tired to wash cloth, especially in a bucket. I buy diapers, but life isn't much better. I still have to work so hard.

As a child, Estelle associated disposable diapers with the American Dream and upward mobility. As an adult immigrant experiencing working poverty in the United States, she paid a significant portion of her low earnings for disposables because she was too exhausted to wash cloth diapers after long, laborious days spent picking produce.

Mothers' thoughts about cloth diapers pointed to structural and cultural changes that have profoundly reshaped diapering trends. Women's increased paid work hours and subsequent greater use of childcare facilities in an increasingly mobile society mean that most children are no longer cared for by full-time, stay-at-home family members. Rising social expectations of cleanliness combined with decades of advertising taught mothers to think of disposable diapers as an extension of maternal love and part of modern, middle-class childcare choices that "good" mothers make. Thus, to poor and low-income mothers, cloth diapering had two distinct class-based connotations. One was associated with the privileges of being able to afford fancy, expensive cloth diapers and supplies and to stay at home by choice with round-the-clock access to personal washers and dryers. The other, which captured the experiences of mothers I interviewed, was as a marker of poverty laden with stress, inadequate resources, and severely limited diaper options that risked their children developing diaper rash or being perceived as unclean and unloved.

Many mothers feared judgment as bad parents if, while in public, feces or urine soaked through cloth diapers or if children's cloth diapers were mistaken as "rags." Mothers were especially concerned about infants' skin irritation, lingering smells, and stains that could be interpreted as signs of parental neglect. These fears were especially acute among mothers of color who worried that publicly using cloth diapers could trigger involvement with the child welfare system. Given that mothers of color are more likely to be surveilled, cited, and punished by the child welfare system for parental "neglect" defined by the conditions of poverty, avoiding diaper methods that could invite suspicion of their parental fitness was a strategic and rational choice.[35]

Solange, a twenty-four-year-old Black mother of four, shared, "I find myself throwing them all away after. I don't think it's sanitary. Some of them get stained, and I just don't feel right reusing them, definitely not out of the house." Similarly, Natalie, a twenty-nine-year-old multiracial mother of three, described avoiding cloth because "when we're in public, I get so worried that other people think my son doesn't have a real diaper on. They'd likely say, 'That lady didn't put a diaper on her kid. What's wrong with her?'" Although Aurelia worried about whether her apartment complex's washing machines were working, her bigger concern was using cloth diapers in public, where "other people might see you changing him and think you're not taking care of him. People might make certain assumptions about you as a parent because it looks like you're using paper towels or something like that." Given intersecting racialized, classed, and gendered connotations of cloth diapering, beyond preventing leaks and rashes, mothers believed that disposables also protected them from unfounded concerns about their parenting abilities as poor women of color held to impossibly high caregiving standards and responsibilities.

EXPECTING MORE OF MOTHERS WHO ARE POOR

Beyond describing how cloth diapers were impracticable for their families, mothers expressed concerns about environmental impacts of disposables. Sonia, who tried cloth diapering until the skin on her hands started to peel due to frequent handwashing, shared with me her doubts about disposables. "I worry that they're not environmentally friendly because every time I've tossed a diaper, it's like where is the diaper going to end up?" Like Sonia, many mothers were interested in trying cloth diapering if they could find ways to offset start-up and cleaning costs and reduce the labor of using and washing them. They were also interested in biodegradables that came with the convenience of disposables and smaller environmental impact. Yet given that mothers struggled to afford the cheapest disposables, costly biodegradable diapers were prohibitively expensive. "I try to be conscious," Sonia concluded, "but someone needs to figure out the right way to be environmentally friendly in pushing diapers. . . . People can pass more disposables out, but where are they going in the end? Just creating more trash that never goes away?"

Many diaper bankers had thought carefully about this dilemma—getting more diapers to families in need while minimizing diapers' environmental impacts—and offered cloth diaper kits for families who could feasibly use cloth at least part of the time. Sierra, thirty-three and white, ran an all-cloth diaper bank that provided a "Cloth Diapering 101" class and a free start-up package of a day's worth of cloth diaper changes per child for income-eligible families. The goal, she explained, was to break down financial and conceptual barriers that make cloth diapering inaccessible. "We try to bust myths that make cloth seem scary, like that you have to use a special detergent or wash them in ten million steps. It's just dirty laundry. We give people a chance to touch and try the diapers, ask questions. Some people say, 'I can't imagine dealing with the poop.' But then you have a kid and realize you're dealing with poop all the time anyway." Sierra challenged "misconceptions" about low-income families' abilities to use cloth diapers:

> The messaging of disposable diapers banks is "Low-income people can't do it. Daycares don't take cloth. Working families don't have time for cloth." They often throw up these barriers. We found that there are only two states with laws restricting cloth use in daycares. Most laundromats don't have policies preventing people from using cloth. . . . And we teach people how to handwash, how to free them from the laundromat cycle. We do a lot of education around how it's not all or nothing. "You can use cloth part of the time or just at home. You're saving money and that's less disposables you have to buy," instead of saying "You're living in poverty, so you don't get to make that choice. It's not an option for you."

Sierra reached a similar conclusion about the shifting class and racial connotations of diapering. She noted that disposables were once a status symbol of how someone could afford to toss rather than wash diapers, but "now cloth diapers have been co-opted by this white elite with the method of a special detergent, all these steps, and it must be perfect. . . . It's been totally owned by the natural parenting movement that's frankly kind of elitist. We're fighting back against that. . . . We can't work to fix poverty through solutions that trash our planet. . . . We've got to fix those problems together."

Other diaper bankers noted that they provided cloth diapers, but families very rarely asked for them. "If anyone wants cloth, we'll do it. But no one is asking. I've had maybe two requests for cloth diapers in ten years. We did a pilot once with one agency because we had a donor who really wanted to do it. It went nowhere," explained Emily, a thirty-one-year-old white founder of a diaper bank. Still, most diaper bankers encountered criticisms and questions from donors, community members, and public officials about why diaper banks did not focus on distributing cloth diapers given the environmental ramifications and presumed higher costs of disposables. Jane, a thirty-year-old multiracial diaper bank manager, shared: "Some people yell at me while dropping off [cloth diaper] donations about how wasteful we are, that low-income families need to understand what they're doing to the environment. It's hard for me to educate someone like that, to talk about how privilege influences people's assumptions about families living under the burden of poverty. It would be great if that could influence actual social programs, but the media and mommy diaper blogs talk about how people need to have a smaller impact. It doesn't account for context, what some families are living through."

Melinda, a forty-eight-year-old white director of a diaper bank, told a similar story: "This guy walked in, said we're doing it all wrong, that we should be making our own diapers. He proceeded to go home and send me YouTube videos on how to make your own cloth diapers. . . . I have a cloth diaper program so I can do away with the naysayers. We're better in their eyes because we offer cloth, but I'll tell you, we gave out maybe one kit in two years. The fact is, if you're working three jobs, you can't afford your basic needs, and you don't have a washing machine, cloth diapering is hard." Likewise, Tina, a thirty-year-old white diaper banker, explained, "I want to ask those people, 'Have you ever used a cloth diaper?' . . . If someone donates them to us, we distribute them, but the requests and the donations are pretty infrequent. No one wants them. . . . I understand the environmental impact of a diaper. I'm not stupid. I've been paying attention, but the privilege ingrained in doing that is very stark." Most diaper bankers had encountered this kind of backlash about why they did not exclusively provide cloth diapers to address diaper need.

Having been involved in diaper banking for many years, they all knew that the families they served needed and wanted disposables, and that lacking them could perpetuate diaper insecurity by undermining parents' economic opportunities. Gail, a forty-six-year-old white founder of a diaper bank, described this dilemma: "I'm not sure what the solution is to helping people have babies in drier bottoms so they can work, support their families, and take into account sustainability. Our society is set up to keep the cycle of poverty going without diaper help because it impacts people's abilities to get themselves to work, to school, to get care for their children, which means you have to have disposable diapers to further your education. We need help so that families are sustainable, as much as a sustainable environment." Gail reasoned that any efforts to protect the environment also need to consider struggling families' circumstances as they raise their children while trying to raise themselves out of poverty. Promoting more sustainable diapering would be futile, she believed, if supposedly greener diaper options were always more expensive or labor intensive.

Encouraging cloth diapers specifically for poor families because they couldn't easily afford disposables was especially misguided, many diaper bankers claimed. Having been on the receiving end of comments like those expressed by *New York Times* readers, Janine, a white, fifty-year-old diaper bank founder, explained:

> The answer to the environmental issue can't be made on the backs of those in poverty. Sure, make it easy, make it possible, make a diaper that's environmentally positive, that's affordable. We expect so much more of poor mothers, so why not cloth? There are diaper banks that do both. We encourage both. For families for whom that works, great! People write to me all the time to say, "Wash your diapers in a bucket in the bathroom. It can be done, right?" But most people don't. This idea that somebody working a low-wage job, living in a building where there aren't washing facilities, which is most people who struggle financially. Really, how are they going to wash their diapers? That we would say, "Well, that's a way to save money." Is it? Why do we expect the poorest families to do the most work? . . . In many conversations services come up, but what doesn't is that most cloth diaper services only work in higher-income areas because they don't go into poor areas as a rule. Those services use a huge amount of water. We really do try to support both. I just want people to have what they need, and most of them need disposable diapers.

Both mothers and diaper bankers were acutely aware of environmental concerns and controversies over using and distributing disposables. Sadly, they also were intimately familiar with the challenges of cloth diapering amid constraints poor families face. Mothers' experiences of cloth diapering point to how "just use cloth" comments signal a profound lack of understanding about the structural conditions that create diaper need and economic inequities that stratify access to diapering options. Cloth diapering assumes and requires multiple forms of privilege, including money for start-up and cleaning expenses, housing with washer and dryer hook-ups and space to store, wash, and ventilate cloth diapers, and means to pay higher water and electricity bills.

Beyond this, using cloth diapers requires social support, both knowing how to do it efficiently and having social networks willing and available to help in the effort. It can also be a barrier to childcare, as nearly all day-cares in the United States require the use of disposables before children can enroll and get dropped off each day, if not as a matter of law and regulations against cloth, as a practice that helps manage the hard and underpaid labor of professional childcare. Diapering norms have also changed significantly because of marketing and advertising. Major diaper companies have positioned disposables as the cleaner and more comfortable choice that better parents make. Mothers in poverty, especially mothers of color, are understandably reluctant to use a type of diaper that might be perceived as inferior or otherwise deviating from mainstream diapering norms.

New York Times commenters are unlikely to have lived with fear of being judged an unfit mother because they don't use the "right" kind of diaper, the kind that nearly every other parent in the United States now uses. As a middle-class white mother who never considered using cloth, much less try to do so, I didn't worry about whether my daughter's diaper would be perceived as too full, leaky, stained, or smelly. Not all mothers are afforded that same privilege. Disposable diapers have become ubiquitous and normative in our society. So too have the surveillance and punitive policing of the parenting choices of poor mothers of color. Is it any wonder then that parents like Aisha, whom we met in the introduction, feared that using cloth diapers perceived "as rags" could cause others to question her parental fitness and put her at risk for losing her daughter to the child welfare system?

Studies of small-scale efforts to offset the costs of cloth diapering are promising but also point to persistent challenges. Anthropologist Sarah Renkert and sociologist Rachel Filippone studied families who used free cloth diaper kits distributed by a diaper bank. They found that not having to pay start-up expenses allowed low-income caregivers to reduce overall diapering costs and stress associated with diaper need.[36] Caregivers able to use cloth diapers the most lived with another adult who could provide cloth diaper support. Moreover, cloth diaper use happened mostly at home, and caregivers in the study continued to use disposables a lot of the time, especially while children were in public and daycare. Still, results suggest that offsetting initial expenses of cloth diapering through programs or policies could help address diaper insecurity by offering families an additional part-time diaper option.

Another effort to do so is the eco-friendly diaper brand Believe Diapers. Launched in 2021, the Believe brand uses renewable bamboo as a primary material but no chlorine, latex, or phthalates. At about sixty cents per size 3 diaper, Believe Diapers cost two to three times more than mainstream diaper brands. Yet there's a key difference between Believe Diapers and other similarly priced green brands. Believe uses a one-for-one matching charity model that donates one diaper to Baby2Baby, a nonprofit organization that coordinates one of the largest diaper banks in the United States, for every diaper sold. To date, it is the only diaper company that identifies a twofold mission to address diaper need while preventing the environmental harms of diapering as core to its brand. Claiming commitments to meet the needs of families and the planet—"Earth is a Mother, too!"—by fixing the economic inequities in diaper care, the Believe Diapers company donated 3.2 million diapers in its first two years.[37]

·   ·   ·   ·   ·

Despite condemnation of low-income mothers for not using cloth diapers, many mothers I spoke to did. Or at least they had tried. They did cloth diapering for a while, only to discover that it is more expensive than disposables after you add up initial expenses and transportation to laundromats, where washing diapers may be prohibited and can cost five dollars or more to wash and dry a full load. Disposable diapering is not always a matter of convenience. It is often a calculated, rational, and cost-effective choice. Moms struggling with diaper need already know how to create diapers out of any paper or cloth item found around a house—toilet paper, pillowcases, dish rags, T-shirts, paper towels, menstrual pads, and so many others. The public just doesn't see it. Mothers save their disposables for childcare and public outings, when they know their parenting choices will be on display and open to scrutiny.

The wholesale shift from universal cloth diapering to nearly all families using disposables can only be understood if one considers the class, race, and gender dynamics of diapering. The earliest disposable diapers were created as a convenience commodity, one intended to help middle-class mothers manage the dual demands of childcare and paid work, while lower-income mothers who couldn't afford disposables' costs continued with cloth. Now more affluent mothers are more likely to use cloth given the time, labor, and upfront financial investments required. Despite once being stereotypically associated with poverty, cloth diapering is now most practically feasible among the privileged.

Moreover, any additional childcare and household labor associated with cloth diapering still falls mostly on the shoulders of mothers. The suggestion that cloth diapering is somehow free or cheaper only makes sense if one assumes that women's time and work have no value. Families most likely to use cloth diapers are those who include a full-time, stay-at-home parent. Growing inequality, wages that have not kept pace with inflation, and rising costs of living have made it nearly impossible for most parents, including mothers of very young children, to stay at home full time. Because family policies in the United States fail to offer universal paid leave to care for new children and do not mandate that employers offer family accommodations, many mothers are back to work mere weeks after giving birth. Mothers compelled to work for pay when their children are very young are more likely to rely on childcare facilities and social networks of care that require or prefer disposables. These conditions force mothers into a perpetual bind when it comes to work and the costs of caregiving.

These are also the very conditions with which we must grapple if we are ever to make progress on developing truly environmentally sustainable diapering products and methods. Inventing a "greener" diaper that most parents will actually use won't likely come down to the materials used to construct it or the processes used to recycle it. What will likely matter most is who is buying and using it and how eco-friendly diapering fits within their budgets and daily lives, including purchasing, changing, and disposing of diapers, as well as the equally important matter of how they will be judged for doing it. The blithe "cheap and easy" refrain often used to describe cloth diapering as a solution to diaper need not only ignores the realities of poor mothers' parenting experience. It also reflects unspoken gendered ideologies of parental responsibility that task women with devalued feminized care labor, including diapering, as well as the work of sustaining families and the natural environment.

As mothers and diaper bankers described to me, modern US society is not cloth diaper friendly, culturally, politically, or economically. There are still no tax incentives or large-scale public programs for cloth diapers, and any additional costs associated with cloth diapering must be absorbed by individual families. Asking why more families don't use cloth dismisses diaper need as the result of individual failures—having too many kids, being ignorant of family planning and conservation efforts, or being too lazy to do the work of cleaning reuseable diapers. This rationalizes larger structural failures to devise systemic solutions to both diaper scarcity and the environmental harms of diapering. Narratives of individual responsibility for preventing pollution and environmental degradation often blame marginalized women for making destructive environmental choices, while ignoring how economic and political elites deliberately fail to pass policies allowing for more sustainable consumption and childrearing practices.[38]

Ultimately it's easier to shift the burden of solving enormous and complex environmental problems onto individuals, especially low-income mothers who just need to make "better" decisions to use cloth diapers. Ignoring money and time constraints, discounting class and race stigma, and framing the issue as one of ignorance or indifference also allows us to blame mothers who use disposables as failed parents who deliberately refuse to do their part to protect their children and the planet. Only by understanding why most mothers—especially very low-income mothers—don't use cloth diapers can we start to envision more feasible sustainable diaper options and the larger social supports and policies required to solve the problems of diaper need and the waste and environmental harms diapers create.

5. Pampers Politics

A LASTING LEAK IN THE US SOCIAL SAFETY NET

All the pain inside amplified by the fact that
I can't get by with my 9:00 to 5:00, and
I can't provide the right type of life for my family.
'Cause, man, these goddamn food stamps don't buy diapers.

—Eminem "Lose Yourself" (2002)

Widely thought to be one of the best hip-hop songs of all time, Eminem's semiautobiographical "Lose Yourself" portrays the struggles of low-income father and aspiring rapper B-Rabbit, the fictional protagonist in the movie *8 Mile*. Likely the most famous pop cultural reference to diaper insecurity, Eminem's lyrics speak to a single parent's anguish over his inability to make ends meet and get everything his child needs, despite working full-time and receiving government assistance. With the song's urgent narrative delivery woven through a tense midtempo track, referencing how someone can't buy diapers with food stamps may seem an unlikely touchpoint about overcoming destitution to become a famous rap musician. That the nod to diapers comes in as the song builds to its ultimate crescendo suggests its importance in the narrator's life as a parent in pain just trying to "provide the right type of life" for his family. Why does it matter so much that B-Rabbit can't use food stamps to buy diapers for his young daughter?

Embedded within these lyrics is a larger story that reflects the harsh realities of working poverty, insufficiencies of our social safety net, and hardships parents face due to both. The movie's title was a reference to 8 Mile Road, a real-life highway separating the predominantly Black and poor neighborhoods of Detroit from the city's mostly white, more affluent areas. As one of the poorest cities in the United States, Detroit has long been a focus of antipoverty political initiatives, including the War on Poverty—the unofficial name for a set of policies and programs created in the mid-1960s intended to eliminate poverty and improve low-income Americans' living conditions, health, and economic opportunities. When President Lyndon B. Johnson first declared "war on poverty" in his 1964 State of the Union address, researchers in Procter & Gamble's Exploratory Division were working to create the world's first mass-produced disposable diaper—Pampers—about 150 miles outside Detroit in Miami Valley, Ohio.

As policymakers and diaper developers stood on the horizon of an era that would see an unprecedented expansion of the social safety net and profound changes in how families diapered their babies, one in four children in the United States lived in poverty.[1] As part of Johnson's Great Society programs aimed at increasing Americans' access to basic needs and services, including housing, food, healthcare, and education, Congress expanded cash aid programs and housing subsidies, passed the Food Stamp Act, and created Medicaid, Medicare, and Head Start.[2] Pampers hit the market around the same time in 1966 and shortly thereafter became available on store shelves nationwide.

Johnson's War on Poverty certainly won a key battle in the struggle to reduce childhood deprivation. In the ensuing years, expanded safety net programs contributed to a steady decline in national child poverty rates and ensured that more children had access to housing, food, and other basic needs.[3] Although government transfers and tax credits played a relatively small role in calculating poverty rates in the late 1960s, they became increasingly important during the following decades. Based on the historical Supplemental Poverty Measure, which accounts for income and payroll taxes and tax credits and noncash benefits like food stamps, childhood poverty rates in the United States fell by more than one-third from 20 percent in 1967 to 13.7 percent in 2021.[4] This decrease was driven almost entirely by government policies that increased how much cash and in-kind aid families received and how much of their income they were able to keep when credits for work and raising children reduced their tax bills.

Yet the larger war against poverty, and childhood poverty specifically, has yet to be won. By the time Eminem wrote and recorded "Lose Yourself" in the early 2000s, many safety net policies had been curtailed, significantly impacting the more than 50 percent of Detroit children living in poverty at the time.[5] Unrestricted cash aid was on the wane, while in-kind programs like SNAP and WIC limited what families could buy, and tax credits almost exclusively benefited those who were employed. When you live in a city where children are more likely to be poor than not, it matters a lot that food stamps don't buy diapers. This gap around diapers in the social safety net is an important case of how our policies, though certainly better than they once were at providing what children need, are neither as efficient nor effective as we need them to be for our country's youngest residents. Interviews with mothers and diaper bankers and advocates suggest how we might fix the lasting leak around diapers in our social safety net. First, we must understand how the leak started.

THE GREAT DIAPER (POLICY) GAP IN THE GREAT SOCIETY

During the latter decades of the twentieth century, just as more people needed a social safety net to get by, the net got weaker and started to fray, undermining Johnson's vision of the Great Society. Inflation-adjusted or "real" wages declined, and employment rates decreased during the backlash to War on Poverty policies, especially growth in direct cash assistance or "welfare."[6] Stagnant wages, significant growth in low-wage sectors of the labor market, and rising costs of living all contributed to higher rates of working poverty (when full-time work doesn't make enough to keep a family from being poor). These labor market changes collided with significant changes in welfare policy that further reduced low-income families' access to resources.

Prior to the 1980s, most American families with children in poverty could rely on the primary federal cash aid program, Aid to Families with Dependent Children (AFDC), which provided guaranteed direct cash benefits to all eligible families as an entitlement. During the Reagan administration, AFDC was criticized for encouraging single parenthood, laziness and unemployment, and dependency on government. Growing dissatisfaction with AFDC and rising caseloads, especially among families of color, hastened the push for overhauling the welfare system and Clinton's campaign promise to "end welfare as we know it," resulting in strong bipartisan support for welfare reform, which replaced AFDC with Temporary Assistance for Needy Families (TANF). TANF provided block grants to states, which could set stricter eligibility rules, impose job requirements and lifetime limits on aid, and use discretion to put welfare money toward programs other than direct cash aid.[7] The evolution of AFDC to TANF— which took a primarily cash-based assistance welfare program and turned it into a series of service-based programs, including job training, parenting skills education, childcare, and transportation—exemplified the growing tendency in US antipoverty programs to provide services rather than goods or cash. For many families on welfare, TANF was their only unrestricted cash income they could spend as they chose. Yet, overall, states continued to reduce the amount of TANF funding spent on direct cash assistance, such that only one dollar of every five dollars allocated to TANF went to cash aid by 2022.[8]

Replacing AFDC with TANF was disastrous for millions of American families who relied on government cash aid to buy basic needs, such as diapers, that were explicitly prohibited in other aid programs like the Supplemental Nutrition Assistance Program (food stamps). In 1995, the year prior to TANF's passage, AFDC helped move 2.9 million children out of deep poverty, defined as having a household income less than 50 percent of the official poverty threshold. In 2017, TANF did the same for only 260,000 children, fewer than 10 percent of those moved above the deep poverty threshold two decades earlier.[9] Now, only about one in four poor families receives any cash assistance through TANF, and those who do receive inflation-adjusted benefits worth far less with much lower buying power than what families received through AFDC. Negative effects are particularly pronounced among Latine and Black children, who are still more likely to live in poverty than white children and more likely to live in states with more restrictive cash aid programs with lower benefit levels.[10]

The late 1980s and early 1990s also marked a pivotal period of change in diapering habits. More American families opted exclusively for disposables over cloth diapers, making disposable diapers normative and expected.

Disposable diapers became a common, ongoing, and pricey household expense for families with infants and toddlers just as government cash assistance was on the decline and women's earnings increased very little in real dollars, especially among those on the lower end of the income spectrum and those of peak childbearing ages.[11] More mothers of young children in diapers entered the paid labor force to compensate for fathers' falling real wages. Mothers also increasingly relied on childcare centers that required disposables while using more disposables at home to manage the time crunch between paid work and household labor. Employed mothers had less time and energy to wash cloth diapers, while childcare providers were unlikely to accept them in any case.

At no point during the six decades after the Great Society's unprecedented expansion of the safety net were diapers ever targeted for inclusion in aid programs. No doubt policies for housing, food, and healthcare—what economist Janet Currie referred to as the "invisible safety net"—passed during this time were crucial for meeting poor families' basic needs.[12] Yet there is still no program for essential items needed to clean the homes that housing subsidies allowed families to rent or the bodies that food stamps allowed them to feed. Food stamp programs in the mid-1960s and WIC in the 1970s were designed to reduce food insecurity and families' financial contributions to their food bill, thereby freeing up income to buy items like household cleaning supplies and hygiene products. With an explicit focus on hunger relief and strict limits on buying nonfood items, food assistance programs were never intended to cover other basic needs. But they were created during large-scale expansion of all safety net programs, including cash aid for buying basics not allowed under housing, food, healthcare, and education programs.

For decades, Medicaid has provided access to healthcare and medicine for low-income families but has otherwise been extremely limited in coverage of nonprescription hygiene items (such as diapers, menstrual supplies, and toilet paper) that are equally necessary for physical cleanliness and health, mental well-being, and emotional dignity. Medicaid will cover some diapers for children with disabilities diagnosed as medically incontinent but not until they are three to five years old, depending on the state. To qualify for diaper coverage as a medical supply, in most states families must submit a doctor's prescription for diapers, prior authorization documentation, and/

or proof that parents have already tried to toilet train their children. Head Start, an early childhood education program, has promoted school readiness for generations of low-income children from birth to age five, including formula, diapers, and wipes for time children spend in program activities. Head Start families, however, have always been on their own when it comes to providing these necessities while young children are at home.

Since the 1990s when cash aid was restricted, other direct cash benefits in the form of tax credits, namely the Earned Income Tax Credit (EITC) and the Child Tax Credit (CTC), have increased working-poor families' incomes. Yet a key difference between welfare and these tax credits is that the credits come to families as a once-yearly lump-sum after tax filings based on job earnings. Low-income families tend to spend this annual tax refund windfall on stockpiling nonperishable essentials like diapers as well as expenses like paying off debt and buying durable goods such as cars.[13] These funds tend to be spent quickly, relieving financial stress for cash-strapped families for only a few months of the year. Because tax credits phase in as earnings increase, the lowest-income families benefit the least from the EITC and CTC because many of them do not make enough money in a year to qualify for the full credit. Other cash assistance programs like Unemployment Insurance and Supplemental Security Income have similar specific eligibility requirements that disqualify most poor families with young children from receiving aid.[14] The safety net shift from one based on need to one based on work significantly disadvantages parents who stay home to care for their children, as they are largely excluded from tax credits and government benefits premised on employment.

This all created the perfect storm of diaper despair. Families needed to purchase disposable diapers regularly and out-of-pocket just as a restrictive and dwindling TANF became the crucial year-round safety net program for most poor families with very young children. One can then understand how a working-poor, cash-strapped parent like Eminem's B-Rabbit would sing about the pain of not being able to provide for his family by lamenting a welfare system in which "———damn food stamps don't buy diapers." Among high-income countries the United States has the highest child poverty rate, with one in three children living in relative poverty, where their families do not make enough to maintain an average standard of living.[15] Perhaps the most damning thing about the US system and the diaper poverty it creates is how truly exceptional it is compared with public safety nets for young children in all other wealthy nations.

THE EXCEPTIONALISM OF US (DIAPER) POVERTY

Before Johnson's declaration of war on poverty, the government did not systematically collect reliable poverty statistics, nor was there general agreement about what "being poor" meant. In 1965, Johnson tasked the Social Security Administration with developing an Official Poverty Measure (OPM), ultimately adopting a definition based on the US Department of Agriculture's Economy Food Plan. Presuming that those who share households also share resources and that the average family of two or more people spent about one-third of their after-tax income on food, the government poverty threshold was defined as three times the subsistence food budget. Updated annually, the OPM is tied to the consumer price index, a cost-of-living measure based on the price of a basket of goods and services purchased by urban consumers.[16] The OPM has long been critiqued for undercounting those in poverty based as it is on an absolute income level tied to household size, which may not capture relative factors, such as geographic differences in cost of living and varying needs based on family members' ages. The Supplemental Poverty Measure is widely considered to be a better measure of poverty than the outdated and flawed OPM because it more accurately captures families' access to money and resources by accounting for tax credits and government transfers.[17] Including taxes and transfers in poverty measurements definitively shows a marked reduction in child poverty in the United States over the past five decades.

There is another way of measuring poverty that tells a somewhat different story. The relative poverty measure, which gauges the proportion of people whose incomes are not keeping up with the typical household's despite making enough to afford basic necessities, shows gradually rising poverty rates.[18] Tax credits and transfers have certainly slowed the rise, but when compared to a median level of household resources, nearly 18 percent of people in the United States had less than half that level in 2023.

In short, US poverty is on the decline in large part thanks to safety net policies, but that net could be stronger to prevent more low-income households from falling further behind.

Using a relative poverty measure, the United States has historically had higher rates of child poverty than other advanced economies. The European Union adopted a very different approach to defining and measuring poverty based instead on deprivation indicators, which go beyond absolute income or monetary thresholds to account for goods and services deemed necessary based on where a person lives and their family and individual life circumstances.[19] The European Union conceptualizes poverty along three distinct dimensions: monetary poverty, low work intensity, and material and social deprivation.[20] European definitions of monetary poverty—which align most with US definitions and include those families who live on less than half of median income—would categorize more than 20 percent of American children as poor.[21] Deprivation—defined as not being able to afford goods, services, or social activities deemed essential for an adequate standard of living—is a more holistic and accurate assessment of what many mean when they think about poverty as lacking things necessary for a decent and dignified life.[22] It also aligns with how poverty shapes parents' lived experiences. Very low-income mothers do not talk about their financial situations as "poverty" or being "poor," but rather as difficulties providing their children's basic needs like housing, food, and diapers and how deprivation negatively affects their parenting practices.[23]

Diaper need exists at the nexus of material and social deprivation. Lacking diapers denies young children something needed for health, comfort, and happiness, while also denying families opportunities for work, education, socialization, and well-being. Much like poverty, basic needs can be defined in both absolute and relative terms. Absolute basic needs, such as food and clean water, are necessary for physical survival, while relative basic needs reflect perceptions of what is needed to maintain a basic standard of living, which differs across places, time periods, and cultures. The disposable diaper is a quintessential example of how something that is not absolutely necessary for subsistence becomes relatively essential in context. A baby will not perish if they don't wear a disposable diaper, as evidenced by humanity's existence during the many millennia prior to the advent of disposables during the twentieth century. However, given modern hygiene standards, childcare requirements, and parents' need to work for wages, not having sufficient disposables can seriously compromise contemporary families' standard of living and children's health and development.

Another important difference between the United States and many other countries, including Australia, Canada, and most in the European Union, is that they have much more robust and generous social policies for children, especially when it comes to providing cash assistance to support childrearing. Variously referred to as child or family allowances, child benefits, baby bonuses, or baby bounties, these cash payments are universal (every family with children receives them, though some are income based); unrestricted (governments don't dictate how parents can spend them); and highly effective (they significantly reduce poverty and deprivation among children). More than half of countries worldwide have a child or family allowance.[24] Yet, as the wealthiest country in the world, the United States is not among them. The US policy most like a child allowance is the Child Tax Credit. But it differs in key ways in that not every child receives it (one in three children don't receive the full benefit of $2,000 per child because their families don't earn enough to qualify); it is work based (tax credits allow families to keep more earned income, while child allowances are free government money regardless of employment status); and they aren't as generous (the US tax credit is up to $2,000 per qualifying child, while the Canadian child allowance for those age five and younger is more than double at nearly $5,500 in US currency).[25] Countries with child allowances also tend to have paid parental leave policies that cover a significant portion of parents' income for part or all of a child's first year of life.

At the height of the COVID-19 pandemic in late 2020 and throughout 2021 following the passage of the American Rescue Plan Act, low-income families in the United States received monthly payments through an expanded CTC regardless of earnings or taxes owed. This effectively provided an unconditional child allowance and enabled families to count on a recurring influx of cash to cover persistent purchases like diapers. Along with other income supports, this policy change contributed to a historic 75 percent drop in child poverty to its lowest level since 1967.[26] This drop put the United States on par with other high-income countries with universal child allowances like Norway and Germany.[27] Sadly, this success was only temporary. After the expanded CTC expired at the end of 2021, US child poverty measured according to the SPM doubled, rebounding to 12.4 percent in 2022—a significantly higher rate than in most other high-income countries. This short-term expansion of the social safety net provided additional evidence of what other countries' child-focused income support policies have long proven: child poverty is amenable to targeted policies that seek to reduce childhood hardship and deprivation.

Child allowances enable families around the world to buy essentials their infants and toddlers need, and when combined with paid parental leave, allow parents to focus on caring for and bonding with them without having to choose between working to buy diapers and being at home with their children to use diapers.[28] In the absence of these family supports, many American parents struggle to afford new expenses that come with an infant, contributing to a form of rarely acknowledged deprivation: hygiene poverty. Diapers are one among many basic nonfood household goods—including soap, toilet paper, toothpaste, deodorant, laundry detergent, shampoo, and menstrual products—that families of all economic backgrounds deem essential. Those who can't afford them often feel embarrassed for fear that not having such products signals to others that they don't care about their health, hygiene, and appearance and that they are not "good" parents or a "respectable" family.

Given how important these items are for one's social standing and self-respect, families will often cut back on or forgo buying other essentials like food, rent, and utilities to buy them. Families experiencing hygiene poverty skimp on or stretch necessities, such as by watering down detergent and shampoo, bathing without soap, washing dishes and clothes with water only, and delaying diaper changes.[29] When families must do without or make do with less, they often avoid social settings, including school and work, where others may judge them as dirty or smelly. Diaper need specifically and hygiene poverty generally reveal how being poor is not just about lacking income and living with material deprivation. It also has emotional and relational dimensions, notably lacking dignity and living with social shame. Social policies—or their absence—have the power to mitigate or reinforce this shame through ideological and discursive framings of poverty, how public programs are structured, and administrative requirements for accessing support. Public programs can contribute to stigma and denial of dignity, or they can support self-respect, pointing to the practical and symbolic significance of public food and housing assistance. Practically, WIC, SNAP, and housing programs provide need-based aid to cover some, if not all, families' food and shelter requirements. Symbolically they reflect that food and housing are basic human needs to which all should have access regardless of families' abilities to pay.

The absence of any similar systematic policy or program for diapers contributes to experiences of diaper need as a particularly damning parenting failure. Diapers are taken for granted as parents' responsibility, but politically they are a "discretionary" expense. This policy oversight is misaligned with how parents understand their young children's specific basic needs, which for most mothers I interviewed came down to milk and diapers. Food stamps and WIC offered some support for one. No comparable acknowledgment or assistance for the other meant that mothers struggled even more to access an essential need policy didn't even officially recognize their children have. Mothers astutely suspected that their diaper struggles were shaped by a larger political climate that prioritized individual parental responsibility, scrutinized parents' work behaviors and spending habits, and stigmatized childbearing among poor families.

Calls to "end welfare as we know it" were motivated by presumptions that poor women deliberately have children they cannot afford and become dependent on entitlement programs that reward bad work and family-formation choices.[30] Almost half of states at one point after welfare reform passed family cap policies intended to limit additional childbearing among welfare recipients.[31] These policies were rooted in racist ideas that women of color especially had more children to collect additional benefits.[32] Government support for diapers—a need created by having (more) children—could be seen as rewarding behaviors welfare reform was intended to prevent. In the decades after welfare reform, parents in the United States experienced exceptionally high levels of diaper need due to a specific confluence of social, economic, and political factors. Social norms called for disposables and parental self-sufficiency, low-income families were making less through work, and narrow political definitions of poverty failed to codify hygiene items as basic needs. At the same time, low-income families received little support from workplaces and the government after having children, while welfare changes minimized public aid families could use to buy diapers. In this fraught sociopolitical environment, mothers struggled to afford and access diapers.

WHEN NEITHER WELFARE NOR WORK ARE ENOUGH

Although most mothers I interviewed received government assistance (including WIC, food stamps, housing assistance, and/or TANF), aid was usually insufficient to buy all the diapers their children needed. Solange, a twenty-four-year-old Black mother of five, received WIC for her one-year-old daughter and recently discovered she was twenty weeks pregnant with her sixth child. Describing how difficult it was to qualify for cash aid and how little it bought, she wondered why case managers never asked about diapers:

> I have to get everything kids need. Being low-income, it isn't the easiest to survive. There's this old saying, "If you have clothes on your back, food in your mouth, and the house lights on, you're okay." Nobody cares about the other stuff, like does your baby have diapers? They think people like me are ungrateful because we need more resources, but there's more to life than just clothes, food, and electricity. They're like, "You get WIC? You get this service? You should be okay. You should be able to afford everything." But no one cares about diapers, the under stuff of life.

Some mothers asked case managers for diaper assistance, only to receive condescending responses about why they didn't use cash aid. Aisha, a twenty-year-old Black mother of one, responded, "It doesn't cover everything, and you have to figure it out on your own. People almost act like we don't want to get her diapers, or we just like spending money. But when it comes down to making sure that the bills are all paid, it just doesn't always work in our favor." Many mothers echoed Solange's and Aisha's concerns about how welfare didn't stretch far enough to cover diapers on top of other household expenses.

Others refuted stereotypes about poor mothers' spending habits, especially the belief that if children don't have everything they need, it is because their parents don't effectively manage welfare aid. Brenda, twenty-five, Asian, and a mother of three, said: "If you get any government assistance and you need more because it's not enough, people wonder where are you putting your money? They just think, 'You're buying this, you're buying that, you're not buying shit for your kid.' I do whatever needs to be done for my kid, and my kids come first. But cash aid, it's never enough for the gas, the bills, keeping the lights on. . . . They think it's not enough for the diapers because we screw it up. But it's not enough because it's not enough." The problem with cash aid, mothers explained, was that benefit levels didn't fully account for real costs-of-living expenses like rent and utilities, much less hygiene items including diapers. Mothers refuted mistaken ideas that they deliberately mismanaged lavish government handouts and called out lawmakers who had the luxury of overlooking how little meager benefits could actually buy. As Brenda concluded, "We get only about $260 a month, but then $100 of that goes for diapers. That doesn't leave much for everything else. Food stamps are for the kids, but they need diapers too."

The falling value of cash benefits combined with purchasing restrictions on other aid forced mothers into a perpetual bind when it came to work, welfare, and diapers. Many mothers couldn't afford to work due to the prohibitively high cost of childcare and lack of lower-cost options such as family-based care. When they could access childcare, daycare center requirements for disposables that had to be changed at least once every two hours increased the cost of mothers' employment. In California in 2019 a family of four could earn monthly gross income up to $3,970 before losing WIC benefits. Yet a similarly sized family could earn only $1,724 before their TANF benefits were reduced. Even low-wage work could earn just enough to disqualify them or reduce the value of mothers' cash aid. Ramona, twenty-one, Latina, and a mother of one, noted, "When you work on CalWORKS, they cut your benefits. Once you start working full time, you're barely making it. That's why a lot of people don't want to receive welfare because it really doesn't cover everything you need, not even half, realistically speaking."

Mothers in households with an employed adult underscored the stresses of the working poor whose jobs didn't necessarily protect them from diaper scarcity. Petra, a twenty-nine-year-old Latina mother of three, described how her husband's low-wage job didn't earn enough to afford diapers yet made it harder to ask for diaper support:

> I'm embarrassed to ask people for help because they'll say, "Well, your husband works so you should be able to afford them." But, no, there's more things I have to pay for besides diapers. . . . I think it's even more of a problem because a lot of the working class, we don't get a lot of extras. I barely get WIC, barely any financial support, and it took my husband getting deducted in hours for us to possibly get food stamps back. It's harder because everything has to come out of his paycheck, and we literally have to pinch and dime every single thing for the diapers.

Employed mothers, especially those who worked full time or had employed partners, questioned how parents could work and still not be able to pay for their children's essentials. Like Petra, most of the twenty-four mothers I spoke with who worked for pay emphasized the strains of living paycheck to paycheck, especially when their income levels disqualified them from receiving government assistance that could offset diaper costs. Working families have it harder in some ways, Yazmin, twenty-eight, Latina, and a mother of three, reasoned because their diaper struggles were invisible or seemed unjustified. "Both me and my husband have full-time jobs," she said. "But we're in a lot of debt, we don't qualify for anything, and we have to rely just on our income. I'm working. He's working. There should be no reason why she shouldn't have diapers, why I should struggle getting diapers." That two married, full-time employed parents struggled with diapers challenged assumptions that "doing everything right," to use Yazmin's words, protected families from diaper deprivation.

Other employed and married mothers questioned how they could play by all the rules of a welfare system that promotes individual responsibility and economic self-sufficiency, yet still can't afford to raise children with a sense of financial security. Alexis, a twenty-three-year-old Asian mother of two, earned $1,000 a month in take-home pay working full time at Walmart, while her husband earned slightly more doing seasonal farm work. The exceedingly high cost of living, especially with children, made it impossible for them to make ends meet on two incomes:

> They used to say it takes a village to raise a child. Now that means it takes a village to fund a child, like paying for the diapers. . . . I work, I go to school,

he works, but not everything's peaches and cream. If you do get a job, you get cut off from everything. And I knew I could never be a stay-at-home mom because nowadays it takes two working. I've looked at my paycheck. On minimum wage, you work, say, five days out of the week, and out of those five days you get paid, taxes take out about two of those days. You work hard, you do all these things, and still you're going to struggle because you don't make enough for diapers.

Yazmin and Alexis felt stigmatized when asking for diaper help because they were employed. In their experiences people assumed that a dual-earner household "should have it all together" enough to cover all the bills, including formula and especially diapers. Yet low-wage work, much like welfare, was insufficient to meet diaper needs.

The reason for this, mothers speculated, was because legislators' economic, gender, and racial privileges prevented them from understanding diaper deprivation. Leslie, a twenty-eight-year-old biracial mother of two, described policymakers' lack of awareness about how little cash aid would buy given low benefit amounts and high diaper costs. "Government expects people on cash aid to somehow manage that money for diapers and everything else. But it's not a lot of money. . . . Mostly people in Congress who run the laws are white men, so they appeal to their own needs." Similarly, Rachel, a twenty-one-year-old Latina mother of one, speculated that there was limited public support for diapers because among lawmakers "the number of men outweigh the number of women. It's not their life. It's not what's important to them. It's not what's going to get them elected. They have the resources to buy diapers. It's not something they have to deal with on a daily basis."

Mothers felt that diapers' connection to children they were ostensibly too poor to have also undermined political will for diaper support. Natalie, a twenty-nine-year-old mixed-race mother of three, believed there wasn't a program like WIC for diapers because: "Policymakers just think, well, 'They had a choice to have that child. There are all these other programs out there. They should be able to provide at least this one thing if they choose to have the baby. Nutrition, we're not going to take that away. That's definitely a necessity. Housing, people need housing, so we'll help with that. But diapers, that parent can figure that out on their own. There are programs for everything else, come on, you can do diapers if you decide to have that baby.'" Several respondents noted the hypocrisy of this stance given some lawmakers' staunch opposition to abortion. Lack of official recognition of diapers as a basic need of infancy was ironic, many mothers believed, when women were compelled to complete pregnancies leading to infants for whom diapering was a necessity. This contradiction became even more severe after the 2022 *Dobbs* Supreme Court decision, which effectively limited access to abortion by shuttering most or all abortion clinics in many states and compelling more women to travel long distances across state lines to obtain abortions.[33]

Maria, thirty, Latina, and a mother of four, wondered if excluding diapers from safety net policies was an effort to punish or penalize poor families for childbearing. "Maybe it's one of their ways to control the population of people having babies. Maybe they figure, 'We give you cash that you should use to buy diapers. You should make them last and stretch until you get your next check. We're not going to give you everything on a silver platter when you should be working and supporting these babies you chose to make.'" Believing parents should live with the consequences of their deliberate choices, Maria elaborated, ignored the harsh realities of low-income families' constrained circumstances. "We didn't plan for another baby. Our daughter was already potty training. She was in school. I was going back to school. My husband was working. I was on birth control. It failed us. . . . We almost aborted him, but I couldn't, and sometimes things are out of our control. People shouldn't be like, 'Oh well, you shouldn't have a baby if you can't provide diapers.'" Maria's husband, a fieldworker, lost work hours due to extreme heat and wildfire smoke that ravaged the California Central Valley during the summer of 2018, while Maria had to cut back work hours because they couldn't afford childcare. She criticized lack of support for millions of families like hers that did their best to live responsibly on low wages combined with exceedingly limited government aid that didn't account for diapers.

Mothers suggested how public aid could cover diapers, including allowing diaper purchases using food stamps. Alicia, twenty-two, Latina, and a mother of two, recommended changing food stamp restrictions so families could buy other basics like diapers. "People should be able to buy whatever they need with food stamps. They can go a long way if you use them correctly. We used to get food stamps, and then I started working, so we don't get them anymore. They should give a monthly allowance for diapers. Some people kind of mess it up for everybody, though, because who knows if they're really using it to get other stuff." Melissa, a thirty-two-year-old Asian American mother of three, also described the value of being able to use food stamps for diapers. "I would be willing to cut my food stamps in half if the other half could go for diapers. I don't need the full $500; $300 is enough to cover food. If I could use the other $200 for diapers, I would be in heaven because I would put that $200 on rent. Because many people cheat the system, you don't get to decide how to spend the money you get." Rather than faulting the welfare system for being miserly or mistrustful, Alicia and Melissa blamed those who didn't use government aid as intended, ruining it for families that did.

Other mothers thought WIC was a more appropriate program for diaper aid than SNAP, especially if WIC offices could provide diapers directly or offer diaper vouchers. Joanna, an eighteen-year-old Latina mother of one, worried that food stamps would be insufficient to cover both food and diapers. "It would be good if I can buy diapers with food stamps, but then I would have to give up thirty, forty, sixty dollars a month. WIC would be the perfect place to put the [diaper] resources because they have so many moms with little kids who go there." Ciara, a thirty-eight-year-old Latina mother of two, said that "because not everybody can qualify for cash aid, it would be nice if diapers were part of WIC. A voucher under WIC would be best. . . . I'm working, doing everything I can to find a full-time job, but I need that extra help so I can get out of this mess."

Six mothers received thirty-dollar monthly diaper vouchers as part of their CalWORKs (California TANF) cases. Vouchers didn't buy all the diapers they needed, but they offset diaper costs and reduced diaper-stretching strategies. Molly, a thirty-one-year-old Black mother of two, shopped at a supermarket that gave twenty-dollar gift cards if customers spent one hundred dollars on infant items. Molly added her first month's thirty-dollar diaper voucher to seventy dollars in cash and bought four large boxes of diapers that lasted two months. Adding the twenty-dollar gift card to the second month's voucher gave her fifty dollars to spend on groceries and toiletries. Before the voucher she purchased diapers in smaller quantities due to limited funds and spent twice as much. Beyond halving her diaper costs, the voucher came as a cashable check with no tracking or receipts required, making Molly feel trusted to spend the money based on her family's needs.

Emphasizing the voucher's value and flexibility, Diana, a twenty-five-year-old white mother of five, noted that the voucher "lets me stretch my dollar in other places on stuff we need. It's just like a regular check from your job. I put it in my bank account and buy diapers or what you need the next day." The voucher allowed Kelly, thirty-two, white, and a mother of three, to buy a second box of diapers toward the end of the month when she usually changed diapers less often. Buying a second box not only covered her diaper gap, but it also prevented Kelly's embarrassment when she needed to get diapers from a local church, where "the people were nice about it, but . . . I kind of felt like they were thinking, 'Well, why do you have a baby if you can't afford to pay for diapers?'"

Unfortunately, three of the six mothers who received the voucher quickly lost eligibility, pointing to drawbacks of voucher programs. Molly received vouchers for only two months before her household income barely surpassed the $2,100 income limit for a family of four, disqualifying her for CalWORKS and redoubling her diaper costs. Aurelia, twenty-five, Latina, and a mother of three, also received vouchers only twice before sustaining life-threatening injuries in a car accident that kept her from fulfilling her work-plan requirements. She reverted to stretching diapers after becoming ineligible for the voucher. Yadira, a twenty-five-year-old Latina pregnant mother of three, received a letter about her eligibility for vouchers contingent on finalizing her work plan. Diagnosed with a high-risk pregnancy requiring bed rest, she explained, "It's a great benefit, but you have to do a particular work program to get diapers, and I just can't work right now. I need the diapers, but not if it's going to hurt the new baby." Offering public diaper aid as a work support reduced the stigma and shame of receiving it, but also meant that many mothers who desperately needed it didn't qualify.

PROMOTING BETTER DIAPER POLICIES FOR THE "DESERVING" POOR

Many diaper bankers advocated for better policies to include diapers in the social safety net. They often came up against misconceptions that federal and state programs already covered diapers. According to Emily, a white thirty-one-year-old diaper bank founder, "A lot of people . . . don't understand that SNAP and WIC don't cover anything for personal hygiene, diapers, or bottles even, just formula and regular groceries." She emphasized how designating diapers as a "discretionary" expense increased their cost for consumers, mostly mothers. Similarly, Moira, a white thirty-two-year-old diaper bank founder, noted, "I would say 85 percent of people have no idea what's covered by food stamps and WIC. Like me, they thought you just walk into a grocery store and use your card to get anything you need. But you can't get anything that makes you a clean, decent human being—soap, toilet paper, cleaning supplies, paper towels, shampoo, none of it's covered."

Many diaper bankers critiqued how not only did government not provide diaper support, but it also taxed diapers to increase revenue on the backs of struggling families. Jamie, a white forty-eight-year-old diaper bank executive director, spoke of the "pink tax," the additional economic burden laid on menstruators and infants' caregivers, mostly women, who purchased period supplies and diapers to meet their and their children's bodily needs. Like mothers, several diaper bankers noted how legislator demographics that skewed toward older white privileged men meant those in positions of power lacked lived experience to understand the importance of diapers as a basic need. Gail, a white forty-six-year-old diaper bank director, noted:

> I testified on behalf of [a state] bill. Most of the Ways and Means Committee, there were a few women, maybe two young men. The rest were all old men, who perhaps because of their age and the time when they were probably having children, a lot of families back then had wives who stayed home and could do cloth. One gentleman did say, "In light of equality between men and women, you guys realize that Viagra is tax exempt, but diapers and tampons are not?" But it's usually an older generation that grew up with their babies in cloth diapers because they had stay-at-home wives and never worried about buying or cleaning diapers.

Controlled by elites who never needed diapers, legislative processes were bound to result in a void around diaper need, advocates reasoned. Paula, a white sixty-eight-year-old diaper bank founder, simply concluded, "How many legislators have ever even changed a diaper?"

Diaper bankers emphasized how policymakers' stereotypical and stigmatizing views of poverty limited public diaper support. Brianne, a white thirty-five-year-old diaper bank founder, explained, "It often comes down to stigma against certain families, assumptions that they just want welfare, they're lazy, don't want to work. Maybe that's a one-in-a-million person. But it's hard to imagine a mother who doesn't want to be able to provide diapers for their child and just waits until the government hands it to them." Kristi, a white sixty-two-year-old founder of a baby supplies organization, similarly noted: "When we put this bill into the legislature this year, we got an opportunity to talk during a committee meeting when an assembly member presented it. Some comments out of mouths of our lawmakers were, 'Eww, I don't want to talk about it,' and 'Why don't these people line their babies' diapers with newspapers or use cloth?' People can be really out of touch. 'Why do we have to give them disposable diapers? It's an entitlement.' They don't look at it as a safety net. They see poverty as a character flaw." Diaper bankers and policy advocates like Kristi realized they faced an uphill political battle in trying to expand political conceptions of need, especially to include an item practically and symbolically connected to childbearing among those in poverty.

Diaper advocates called out racist subtext of opposition to public diaper support based on individualized notions of personal responsibility and self-sufficiency, two key themes of welfare reform that substantially shrunk the social safety net. Those most likely to report diaper need—poor single mothers of color—are the demographic most stigmatized as undeserving recipients of public aid through gendered and racially coded references to promiscuous, fecund, and lazy women who have children to collect additional welfare benefits. Rochelle, a Black thirty-seven-year-old diaper bank founder, described highly stigmatizing assumptions she encountered in her advocacy work:

> I've talked to county officials, legislators who ask, "Aren't you worried that they're going to take the diaper and sell it?" These are the people we put in place to help wrap our mind around budgets and programming, and they're worried about people stealing, but not wondering why people would need to steal or repurpose twenty diapers? . . . There are so many scenarios that lead to struggle that we don't even think about because we've convinced ourselves that people put themselves in the struggle. It's so gendered and racist

to conclude, "Well, why did these women have these kids if they can't afford them? Why don't they get a job?" . . . Diapers are a small part of a big puzzle of most people disassociating themselves from poverty because they're not personally experiencing it.

Darren, a white fifty-year-old diaper bank director, described facing similar stereotypes. "Federal and state programs are almost designed to make it difficult to use cash aid. . . . Diapers don't really come up because a lot of the undercurrent of thinking about welfare is, 'Why make it easier for poor people to have babies they can't afford? Emphasize work and self-sufficiency, not dependency.'" Changes in welfare policy, specifically transitioning cash aid as an entitlement for those in poverty to get what they need to a "benefit" one must earn through proper work habits and responsible family decision-making, reflected such stereotypes.

Diaper bankers learned to frame their appeals for diaper support in terms more amendable to these political ideologies. David, a white sixty-three-year-old diaper bank founder, noted, "If you're talking to a conservative audience, you point out that not having enough diapers is a barrier to work. That's a strong conservative value, that people should work. What about people who want to work, are trying to work, but can't afford day-care because of diapers?" Melissa, a white forty-eight-year-old diaper bank founder and executive director, took a similar approach. "For a conservative audience, I immediately talk about how 78 percent of the families who receive our diapers are working one to three jobs."

Advocates tended to framed appeals for diaper aid in terms of support for young children in poverty and working parents, two "deserving" populations. June, a white seventy-year-old diaper bank founder and director, shared with me that "when you talk to certain people, say, 'We need to pass diaper laws because it's the right thing to do, and this is a basic need that contributes to health and welfare of children and families.' When you're talking to other people, you might say, 'You need to get this passed so that people can get off welfare and get back to work.'" Other advocates cited statistics about working parents struggling with diaper need, learning to couch their messaging in a work-first theme of individual responsibility. Kristi, a white sixty-two-year-old diaper bank founder, often told policymakers and potential donors that "a single mother working full time at the minimum wage will spend 6 percent of their annual gross income just on diapers. . . . This is not an entitlement; it's a safety net to make them self-sufficient."

The role of diapers in the development and education of very young children, a particularly sympathetic demographic, was another common advocacy message. Tracy, a white thirty-year-old diaper bank director, explained:

> Right now, I'm focused on diapers in relation to childcare and early learning because that's a hot topic for elected officials. I use economic impact studies when I talk to Republicans. "Listen, you have to support children and their parents going to work and school because that is the best thing for our economy." . . . I still frequently hear the rhetoric of "If you can't afford them, don't have them," so for those people I have to say, "Well, do you care about people going to school? Do you care about neurological development in the first three years of a baby's life?" That's an easier sell than people should simply have what they need.

Rosemary, a white forty-eight-year-old diaper bank founder, also foregrounded messages that diapers helped children rather than parents. "Someone just asked the other day, 'Isn't it really those poverty-stricken families that don't use birth control?' That took me aback. I had to keep it professional and told her, 'It's the baby we're putting diapers on.' People take it differently when you say you're 'helping families.' That terminology is more welcomed because people assume babies don't have a choice." Strategically focusing on diapers as necessary for infants and toddlers, a social group too young to be irresponsible and not old enough to be self-sufficient, generated more support for diaper aid across the political spectrum. Although that support took time to gather political momentum, the trajectory of diaper policy proposals indicated a rapidly opening window for public diaper aid.

A BRIEF HISTORY OF DIAPER POLICIES

Diaper policies initially faced a steep uphill battle. In 2011, Representative Rosa DeLauro (D-CT) first introduced the Diaper Investment and Aid to

Promote Economic Recovery (DIAPER) Act, which would have amended the Child Care and Development Block Grants to require use of state funds to cover diapers. In 2015 and 2016, federal lawmakers proposed the Hygiene Assistance for Families of Infants and Toddlers Act to create a funding stream for pilot projects that provide diapers or diaper subsidies. None of these bills made it past congressional committees. Before leaving office in 2016, President Barack Obama proposed a $10 million federal initiative to test projects for increasing diaper access.[34] Although this funding was never administered, the White House facilitated the Community Diaper Program, a partnership between online retailer Jet.com and First Quality, manufacturer of the Cuties discount diaper brand. Within a year thirteen hundred community benefit organizations were part of the program.

By 2017 diaper policies were gaining traction when eighteen states introduced diaper legislation, including diaper tax repeals and state funding for diapers or diaper banks.[35] The 2017 version of the federal Lee-DeLauro End Diaper Need Act proposed expanding TANF to allow states to create their own diaper distribution programs using federal grants, a model inspired by the San Francisco Diaper Bank funded by county and federal TANF money. While few of these state bills passed and the End Diaper Need Act didn't progress, diaper policy proposals made inroads as more states repealed diaper taxes and California started the first state diaper voucher program. In 2017, California passed A.B. 480, the Diaper Assistance for CalWORKS and Cal-Learn Families Act, which provided thirty-dollar monthly vouchers for diapers as a welfare-to-work supportive service. "Supportive services" under the California Work Opportunity and Responsibility to Kids (CalWORKS) welfare-to-work program enable participation in work and school activities by covering costs for transportation, childcare, books, tools, work clothing, and fees. Adding diapers to this list was the outcome of a multiyear effort by California Assembly member Lorena Gonzalez Fletcher, who first proposed the voucher program in 2014 as a $165 monthly cash benefit for all children covered by CalWORKS (state TANF) and MediCal (state Medicaid). Coverage was increasingly restricted as the bill made its way through the California legislative process. The State Assembly removed children covered by Medicaid and limited vouchers to children three years old and younger whose parents had a qualified CalWORKS work or education plan.

The voucher value was also whittled down with each version of the bill, first to $80, then $50, and finally to $30, when it ultimately passed the Assembly and governor's desk in 2017. At the time, to be eligible for CalWORKS, a family of three could make no more than $1,282 per month, and the average monthly CalWORKS grant was $514, or about $17 daily. Adding $1 per day was enough to buy three to four diapers, the number needed for an eight-hour work shift. The legislative trajectory of the California diaper voucher was telling about which political justifications would be most effective for weaving public diaper support into a work-based safety net. The California Women's Caucus that lobbied for the state diaper voucher bill primarily framed diaper need as a contributing factor to reliance on public assistance when parents miss work or school. California lawmakers also emphasized how insufficient access to diapers can lead to severe rashes and urinary tract infections, which increase publicly funded pediatric office visits and emergency rooms trips. The country's first statewide diaper law passed only when framed as an investment in the success of welfare-to-work programs, a way to promote parental self-sufficiency, and a strategy for reducing public healthcare costs.

Also in 2017, California designated $10 million—an unprecedented amount of state funding at the time—for the California Department of Social Services Diaper Bank Program to fund diaper purchases and distribution to community partners via food banks throughout the state. The first five years of funding enabled the purchase and distribution of more than 160 million diapers to more than 1 million families with 1.6 million infants and toddlers, at a cost of about a quarter per diaper.[36] During this time federal lawmakers persisted in introducing diaper legislation annually. In 2019, legislators proposed the federal Lee-DeLauro End Diaper Need Act, which designated diapers as "medically necessary" and would have appropriated $100 million a year for state pilot programs testing innovative approaches to providing diapers or integrating diaper programs into other need-based government services. Like its antecedents, it failed to make it past initial congressional committee deliberations, with critics citing potential lost tax revenue. Leading up to the COVID-19 pandemic, state-level diaper tax exemptions and budgetary line items for public diaper funding met more success, as diaper advocates discovered

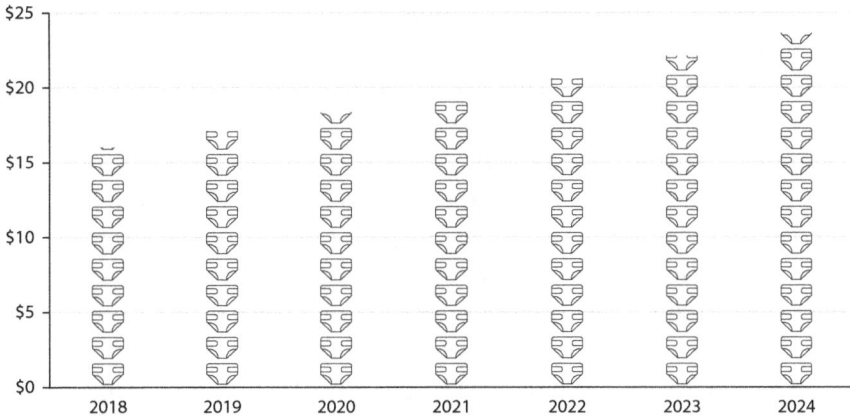

Figure 3. Average cost of a package of diapers in the United States, 2018–2024. *Source*: Eifrig (2024).

that generating fiscal support through piecemeal funding was easier than pushing systematic diaper policies through legislatures.

As federal and state governments responded to social and economic crises during the pandemic—when diapers prices, diaper need, and requests to diaper banks increased significantly—potential for public diaper support seemed especially promising.[37] Diaper costs in the United States rose at unprecedented levels due to inflation, higher demand and input material costs, supply-chain disruptions, and shipping cost surges, imposing an especially heavy economic burden on already cash-strapped families.[38]

The Heroes Act, a relief bill passed in May 2020 by the House of Representatives, included a provision for $200 million in direct diaper assistance. Shortly thereafter, in September 2020, lawmakers in the House introduced the Improving Diaper Affordability Act, which would have made diapers federal tax-free and reimbursable through health savings accounts. In February 2021 a Senate bill, the COVID-19 Diaper Assistance Act, proposed spending $200 million through the Social Services Block Grant to states to provide diapers, wipes, and supplies to families. Although these proposals never passed, they signified growing recognition of diaper need and government efforts to address it. The first major federal success for diaper support came in 2022, when the Office of

Community Services within the Administration for Children and Families initiated the Diaper Distribution Demonstration and Research Pilot (DDDRP). The goal of the DDDRP was to evaluate operations and expansion of diaper distribution for low-income families in partnership with community agencies that provide wraparound services, such as housing, early childhood education and childcare, food and nutrition, and employment and job training services. In the pilot's first three years the federal government allocated $40.2 million to grantees in twenty-four states and four tribal communities to support, expand, and study diaper distribution programs and participants' experiences and outcomes.[39]

Also in 2023, House and Senate legislators reintroduced diaper bills, including the Diaper Need Act, which would have appropriated $200 million per year for distributing diapers to low-income families, and the Improving Diaper Affordability Act, which proposed removing sales taxes on diapers, wipes, and other infant care items. Though neither bill passed, more states joined the growing list of those that provided funding for diapers, including California, Colorado, Connecticut, Delaware, Georgia, Hawaii, Indiana, Iowa, Michigan, Minnesota, New York, Tennessee, Vermont, and Washington.

Modeled on long-standing maternity package and baby box programs in other countries, in 2023 the US Department of Health and Human Services partnered with the Baby2Baby diaper bank to pilot the Newborn Supply Kit Program in three states with high maternal mortality rates.[40] Compared with those in other high-income countries, women in the United States are significantly more likely to die in childbirth or as a result of pregnancy or postpartum complications, with mental health conditions being among the top causes of pregnancy-related deaths.[41] Goals of the newborn kits are to provide items that aid in postpartum recovery, breastfeeding, and newborn care, distribute information about community resources, and reduce stigma associated with seeking government services. Valued at $300, the kits include, among other items, a grocery delivery voucher, nursing pads, an infant carrier, blankets, lotion, wipes, diaper cream, and a month's supply of diapers. Parents reported in an evaluation that diapers were the most helpful item.[42]

The reversal of *Roe* v. *Wade* in 2022 also inspired a new push for diaper legislation, especially in more conservative Republican-leaning states.

With the *Dobbs* v. *Jackson Women's Health Organization* decision, which ruled on the constitutionality of Mississippi's Gestational Age Act—a law that banned most abortions after fifteen weeks of pregnancy—individual states regained the power to regulate abortion access. Prior to *Dobbs*, the twenty-one states that had passed laws reducing or repealing sales taxes on diapers were those with the most expansive abortion access, while states with the most restrictive abortion laws were more likely to have diaper taxes and the highest diaper taxes. Shortly before and after the June 2022 *Dobbs* decision, more states with majority-Republican legislatures passed diaper policies as efforts to be "family friendly" and "pro-life" rather than just "pro-birth."

Four states—Florida, Iowa, North Dakota, and Texas—repealed state diaper taxes immediately after *Dobbs* substantially limited abortion access via state trigger laws. In Texas, a state with restrictive abortion access prohibiting all abortions outright except in cases where the pregnant parent's life is at risk, the immediate post-*Dobbs* diaper tax repeal finally passed after seven previous annual attempts.[43] Although Texas Democratic lawmakers advocated for legislation to repeal taxes on diapers, baby wipes, menstrual products, bottles, and breastfeeding products for nearly a decade prior, the repeal didn't gain bipartisan support until the near-total abortion ban went into effect in 2022.[44] In a post-*Dobbs* abortion access environment, Democrats promoted policies increasing diaper affordability and accessibility to reduce financial burdens of forced childbearing. In Tennessee, where preforming abortions is a felony punishable by up to fifteen years in prison, Republican governor Bill Lee proposed a program allowing poor families to receive up to 100 diapers per month until the child's second birthday at TennCare (state Medicaid) pharmacies.[45] Utilizing part of the $330 million in savings from Tennessee's Medicaid federal block grant funding—money previously declined by the state that could have supported resources for families in need—the law went into effect in summer 2024. It marked the first time a state Medicaid program provided free diapers to children younger than three years not diagnosed as medically incontinent.[46]

Diaper brands with political missions, including pro-nuclear family and antiabortion appeals, as core parts of their brands have also recently sprung up. Founded in July 2023, EveryLife is an explicitly "pro-life" diaper company founded to "inspire a new generation of parents to choose and celebrate life."[47] Promising the "highest-quality, clean diapering products on the market at an accessible price point," a 150-count box of size 3 diapers cost $69.99 in 2025 ($0.47 per diaper), about 40 percent more than Huggies and Pampers. Claiming that the abortion industry profits off women, EveryLife donates part of its proceeds to "pro-life" organizations as a direct response to Kimberly-Clark's philanthropic efforts, including donations to the Association of Women's Health, Obstetric and Neonatal Nurses, which was publicly critical of the *Dobbs* decision.

INEQUALITIES OF DIAPER TAXES

The most successful diaper policy by far has been tax repeals, which have not only reduced diaper costs but also politically recategorized diapers as essential. As of 2025, twenty-five states have sales taxes on diapers, down from forty states in 2017. These taxes have been as high as 9.6 percent, with states with larger proportions of children of color having higher diaper taxes than states with larger proportions of white children.[48] Sales taxes of less than 10 percent may seem negligible, but even a 5 percent tax can add up to an entire month's worth of diapers over a year, affecting families' abilities to buy diapers.

In economics terms diapers have traditionally been viewed as an inelastic good, meaning that as prices go up or down, consumers' spending habits remain relatively unchanged. This is based on the logic that when families with infants need diapers, they will pay even as prices increase. Although this seems true for higher-income families, low-income families are particularly sensitive to diaper tax changes given limited income. Research finds that in low-income areas parents bought more diapers when taxes as low as 5.4 percent were removed, while tax changes didn't affect diaper-purchasing trends in higher-income areas.[49] Notably, when diaper taxes were repealed, spending on children's pain medications *decreased* by 6.2 percent, perhaps because as families can buy more diapers, children are less likely to experience painful health problems linked to diaper need.

Diaper tax rates for which everyone, regardless of income, pays the same amount mask other inequalities. A 5 percent tax on a $25 box of

diapers will cost a mother in poverty the same $1.25 as it would an afflu-
ent mother. Yet flat taxes operate as regressive taxes because lower-income
families must pay a larger share of their overall income to cover them. For
a mother whose monthly household income is $797, the average among
those I interviewed, that tax represents 0.16 percent of their monthly
income. But for a mother whose monthly income is $5,725.25 (the
national median in 2019, the year I conducted interviews with mothers),
that amount is only 0.02 percent.[50] As a portion of their income, that
$1.25 tax on a box of diapers will cost a poor mother eight times more and
have a much larger impact on their ability to buy enough diapers. Mothers
told me that diaper taxes cost them up to $5 per box, which is a lot of
money for families who account for every cent spent.

An argument against tax repeals is that because diaper demand is inelastic, removing diaper taxes would have a large fiscal impact on state and
local budgets due to lost revenue. Yet as mothers' experiences of diaper
stretching suggest, low-income families often buy fewer diapers or forgo
buying diapers when they can't afford them. Moreover, state budget
impacts are relatively small. A legislative analysis in Michigan estimated
that repealing the state diaper tax would cost $18–20 million annually.
This may seem like a lot, but in fiscal year 2021 the state of Michigan
spent a total of $68.4 billion; diaper tax revenue accounted for a mere
penny of every $3,800.[51]

Opponents of diaper tax exemptions also contend that cutting sales
taxes specifically on diapers is unfair to struggling families that don't need
diapers but would benefit from a tax break.[52] This is akin to arguing that
exempting taxes on menstrual products is unfair to men because they
don't have periods. It points to perhaps the biggest problem with taxing
diapers. Tax policies reflect social norms about which goods and services
are necessary, which are detrimental, and whether they have a positive or
negative social impact, as evidenced by so-called "sin taxes" on cigarettes,
alcohol, and gambling. Goods and services deemed essential in the tax
code like groceries, food, and medicine are tax-exempt because they are
necessary and have a positive social impact. Taxing diapers signals that
they are discretionary and, by extension, that having and raising children
negatively impacts society. Not only do diaper taxes directly increase the
cost of raising children, but they also send the message that childbearing

is optional and harmful. This is why most efforts to repeal diaper taxes have recategorized diapers as a tax-exempt hygiene or healthcare product or clothing, goods deemed necessary and beneficial. Many states have successfully repealed diaper taxes through this route.

.   .   .   .   .

Diaper politics are wrapped up in ongoing struggles over the role of government in providing basic needs, addressing public health concerns, and passing poverty-alleviation policies. Debates over public diaper provision reveal how difficult it can be to expand political notions of need when welfare is no longer an entitlement, the social safety net promotes work over care, and policy fails to recognize hygiene items as essential. This is especially true when the item at stake is highly privatized due to its association with taboo bodily functions and parents' personal responsibility to provide. In the United States public aid is framed as a "benefit" not a "basic need." Political discussions of diapers raise questions about what humans require to survive and thrive and issues of what we, as a society, have a collective responsibility to provide for everyone, despite individual families' abilities to pay. Like menstrual hygiene products, diapers offer a solution to a bodily function the wearer can't control and are thus inextricably linked to political, economic, and social rights to health, sanitation, education, dignity, and freedom from discrimination and stigma.[53] How we politically define diapers—as a benefit, a work support, a basic need, or something else—has significant implications for how we devise dignified solutions to diaper need.

6. Handing Out Huggies and Hope

Before visiting the Happy Baby Diaper Bank in 2018, I couldn't imagine what a million diapers packed together looked like. They were in a large warehouse with polished concrete floors, industrial forklifts, and rows of massive metal shelves holding tightly bound, plastic-wrapped pallets of boxed diapers stacked over fifty feet high to a vaulted ceiling. A single diaper pallet holds 100 to 250 boxes of diapers, with the average pallet containing five thousand to ten thousand individual diapers. Families who received diapers through organizations that partnered with the Happy Baby Diaper Bank got thirty to sixty diapers per month. Chapter 3 described mothers' diaper math as part of inventive diaper work—the tracking, budgeting, and stretching to manage diaper need. My visit to Happy Baby taught me about another type of diaper math—the stocking, storing, and supplying of diapers for thousands of families struggling with diaper despair.

Just past the pallet shelving were hundreds of unopened boxes of diapers awaiting delivery to diaper pantries that would distribute diaper packs to families. The work of converting pallets, each holding thousands of diapers, to single thirty-diaper packs was no small task. In a pristine, moisture- and temperature-controlled room just off the warehouse, ten volunteers in hairnets and rubber gloves opened boxes to prepare for repackaging diapers into smaller allotments through a process called *diaper wrapping*. A common practice among diaper banks trying to serve more families, diaper wrapping started with dismantling boxes containing eighty to two hundred diapers. Diaper wrappers then counted out thirty diapers, secured the bundle with a rubber band, and attached a size label. The next step involved firmly encasing the diapers with foodservice-grade plastic wrap while rotating the bundle to tightly compress the diapers. After stretching one final rubber band around the plastic, a volunteer secured the pack corners in more plastic to ensure an air- and watertight seal before passing it down the wrap line. Another volunteer then inspected the wrapping and size label for quality assurance and tallied it on an inventory sheet before passing it to yet another volunteer for placement on a shelf with hundreds of other bundles of the same size. Every diaper was accounted for, loose bundles were repackaged, and original diaper boxes compressed for recycling.

A sterile procedure—both literally in that the goal is to keep all diapers dry and germ-free, and figuratively in the sense that the whole operation appears unsentimental and monotonously dull—diaper wrapping is a popular volunteer activity, with waitlists and appointments stretching out months. I understood why after I participated in my first diaper wrapping session. Although diapers don't expire in the same way food does, they can, as one diaper banker told me, become "pest pockets" for insects or sponges for ambient moisture if stored or packaged inappropriately, rendering them unsanitary and unusable. Wrapping diapers is also, according to diaper bankers, a remarkably tangible way to grasp invisible effects of poverty. One senses viscerally that each diaper touched, wrapped, and logged is one less diaper that babies must do without—and perhaps fewer missed meals, unpaid bills, or anxiety attacks for parents. One starts to understand why diaper bankers see their work as handing out hope as much as distributing diapers.

Yet that hope can be dashed when considering the larger diaper math equation unfolding every day across the United States in the hundreds of diaper banks that serve thousands of diaper pantries spread across the country. If any sight brings into sharp relief the large and growing problem of American families' diaper despair, it is the massive stocks of diapers housed within our nation's rising number of diaper banks like Happy Baby. There is a thriving community diaper distribution infrastructure encompassing hundreds of millions of diapers, thousands of staff and volunteers, and diaper drives in nearly every community in the United States. Yet these vast efforts meet less than 5 percent of diaper need among diaper-desperate families.[1]

A group of people dedicated to increasing capacity to meet a larger portion of that need have convened each October for more than a decade at the annual National Diaper Bank Network (NDBN) conference sponsored by Kimberly-Clark, maker of Huggies brand diapers. I attended these diaper banking conferences for five years from 2018 to 2022.[2] Having already visited Happy Baby and several other diaper banks, I expected to learn about diaper bank operations, such as fundraising, warehousing, volunteer management, and working with partner organizations. The kickoff keynote address for the 2018 NDBN conference didn't address these topics. Nor was the speaker involved in diaper banking. A white man in his late sixties and founding director of one of the nation's largest and oldest food banks, which had been in operation for nearly forty years, shared with us that "lacking food or diapers is only the presenting problem. If you're struggling with diapers, it's likely you're paying too much rent, didn't have access to an education, and are working in a job that doesn't pay a living wage."

To a captivated audience of hundreds of diaper bankers consisting mostly of white women, he concluded, "There is enough of everything. There is enough food. There are enough diapers. It's just not in the right places, and the right people are not in control of it. We've got to reshape the conversation and consciousness around why people are poor and the structure that creates poverty. . . . For us, food was the tool. Diapers are your tool." The message had nothing to do with collecting, packaging, or handing out diapers. Rather, it was about diaper need as a symptom of larger economic inequities, social exclusion of marginalized groups, and fundamental unfairness in access to and control over basic needs. In other words, it was that diaper banking can be a tool of social justice.

Subsequent keynotes, panel discussions, and workshops I attended covered various topics, including distributing diapers as natural disaster response; working with corporate donors; studying economic impacts;

managing inventory; developing nonprofit boards; building volunteer programs; fundraising; using Census data; and getting involved in diaper advocacy. These session topics, among others, pointed to just some of the many hats diaper bankers wear, and all centered around another type of diaper math: righting injustice of an unequal, exclusive economy that makes enough diapers to meet the needs of all but doesn't ensure that everyone who needs them can get them. Hence my surprise when, later that same night at a social event for conference attendees, I overheard a conversation among three diaper bankers discussing how many diapers their respective pantries distributed to clients each month. A white woman in her thirties said, "We would never give out fewer than fifty. Our families usually need more than that, but for most this fills their gap." A Black woman in her forties responded, "We'd like to give that many, but we can really only afford twenty-five per child per month, or else we'd have to accept fewer families." A third woman, a Latina in her thirties, concluded, "We give them ten. We want to help them make it to the next payday, have enough to get to work, but we want to encourage self-sufficiency, not dependency on our diapers."

As the three women chatted about the pros and cons of limiting diaper allotments, I thought of Aisha, the mother we met in chapter 1 who once received fifteen diapers from a pantry. Aisha decided that diapers that wouldn't even last three days wasn't worth the bus pass fee, the hassle of taking her infant daughter to verify eligibility, and two hours spent on the roundtrip, not to mention the humiliation of asking for a rationed handout. The pantry's location and limits, and the shame Aisha felt, prevented her from becoming dependent on the pantry. But they also kept her from returning for the diapers she desperately needed to keep working and caring for her daughter. Yet for every mother I met who struggled with difficult logistics and indignity, I met another for whom diaper assistance was a supportive and even empowering experience. This chapter explores what shapes those distinct experiences by focusing on the history, motivations, and constraints shaping diaper distribution as a relatively new but exponentially growing source of community support for families with young children. It draws on diaper bankers' and mothers' stories to reveal the benefits and burdens of diaper banking as a solution for diaper need.

Distributing diapers can be a tool in the arsenal of combatting oppression and preventing poverty. But receiving those diapers can evoke an array of feelings, ranging from frustration of navigating diaper bank logistics and dejection associated with proving need, to liberation from stress of diaper despair and validation of knowing that others understand diapers' importance and want to help. As I started to learn during that visit to Happy Baby, where committed volunteers meticulously wrapped diapers into packages that would make their way to families, diaper distribution via a large and growing network of diaper banks is a well-intentioned, if labor- and time-intensive, way of trying to ensure that more diapers get to the right people in the right places. For both diaper bankers and mothers like Aisha, that means in the hands of parents and on the bottoms of babies who desperately need them. But as with food banking, diaper banking raises a lot of questions about the logistics and ethics of relying on philanthropic efforts to meet families' fundamental needs.

THE PROMISES AND PITFALLS OF
BANKING ON BASIC NEEDS

The US diaper bank movement can trace its origins to 1994, when Resolve, Inc., a small consulting firm in Tucson, Arizona, organized a winter holiday event to collect disposable diapers for a local children's crisis center. The December Diaper Drive became an annual tradition, with Resolve volunteers collecting three hundred thousand diapers each year to distribute to thirty family-serving agencies. By 2000 that event became the Diaper Bank of Southern Arizona, considered by many to be the United States' first diaper bank, as it provided ongoing emergency diaper assistance to families in the Tucson area.[3] Inspired by the Southern Arizona model, Joanne Samuel Goldblum, a social worker who had worked with families experiencing diaper need, founded what is now known as the Diaper Bank of Connecticut in 2004 in her own home. By 2011 the Diaper Bank of Connecticut had become the nation's largest diaper bank, and diaper banks, pantries, and organized diaper drives had sprung up in most states. Goldblum started the National Diaper Bank Network (NDBN) that same year to raise awareness of diaper need and connect diaper collection and distribution organizations throughout the country.[4] Much of what is now known about diaper banking comes from data collected by the NDBN, which sponsors research on diaper need and diaper banks, an annual conference, grants to support diaper bank operations, and bulk-purchasing of Huggies diapers.[5]

Diaper banks are a specific type of basic needs banks, which are nonprofit charitable organizations that collect and purchase necessities like food, clothing, and hygiene items for direct distribution or through intermediary partner organizations that serve those who can't access and purchase essentials. Many other basic needs banks, including food banks and clothing closets, distribute other childcare, hygiene, and household goods, such as baby wipes, diaper barrier creams, formula, infants' and children's underwear and shoes, school supplies, menstrual and adult incontinence products, and laundry and cleaning supplies. About half of NDBN member diaper banks distributed products other than diapers in 2021. Arizona was also home to the nation's first food bank, the most common type of basic needs bank in the United States. In 1967, upon discovering grocery stores discarded a lot of edible food, Jon van Hengel founded the St. Mary's Food Bank Alliance in Phoenix, Arizona, by collecting unused food items from stores and manufacturers. A decade later there were food banks in eighteen US cities, followed by the creation in 1979 of America's Second Harvest (now Feeding America), an umbrella organization for food banks.

As suggested by the 2018 NDBN conference keynote speaker, there are many important similarities, as well as differences, between food banking and diaper banking; these comparisons are illustrative for understanding how and why diaper banks typically operate as they do. Whereas diaper banks existed before state or federal policies provided public diaper support, policies for which diaper bankers were primary advocates, food banks emerged in response to curtailment and defunding of public food assistance programs. Food banks in the United States can be traced back to Great Depression soup kitchens and food pantries, both forms of emergency food assistance intended as temporary measures to address food insecurity during a severe economic downturn that left millions hungry. Along with school food programs, the Supplemental Nutrition Assistance Program (SNAP, familiarly known as food stamps) was first piloted during the late 1930s and made permanent in 1964, followed by the Special

Supplemental Nutrition Program for Women, Infants, and Children (WIC) in 1974. Data from this time showed that food assistance programs were effective at reducing hunger and malnutrition.[6]

In the 1970s growing costs of living and inflation combined with stagnating wages and high unemployment increased food insecurity at rates that didn't keep pace with changes to food assistance programs. In the 1980s the Reagan administration made drastic cuts to federal food assistance programs, especially food stamps, resulting in more people needing food assistance just as fewer people were eligible for it. Food banks and pantries privately funded by corporations, foundations, and individual donors proliferated across the United States as the public food safety net was dismantled. Growth of the charitable food system marked a pivotal shift away from basic needs assistance from public entities and government programs to a greater reliance on nonprofit community organizations. Every major city in the United States now has a food bank, with food pantries available in most smaller communities. Public support for food banking is usually secondary and only available if advocates can secure grants or line-item budget funding from local, state, and federal programs. Intended to be short-term support for those experiencing food insecurity in the face of economic recession and government cutbacks, the food-banking system was institutionalized as a permanent feature of the country's highly unequal national landscape.[7]

Within the system itself there are inequities in size, variety, and frequency of offerings, with some areas, especially underserved rural communities, having significantly less access to food aid. As part of that landscape, the antihunger movement in the United States consists largely of two main groups—those who seek to address root causes of food insecurity through more rigorous government food programs and policies, and those who believe that hunger should be solved through charitable food distribution organized by the private philanthropic sector.[8] As antihunger advocate Andrew Fischer argued, the latter approach focused on food charity, which tends to individualize and depoliticize food insecurity and differentiate the "deserving" and "undeserving" poor, has been dominant in the United States since the 1980s. This is why so many charitable food programs highlight food insecurity among children, the ultimate demographic of the "deserving" poor viewed as least powerful and responsible for their hunger. With no control over the circumstances of their birth or the families into which they are born, children haven't yet made mistakes and bad choices that deem them "unworthy" of basic needs assistance. Consequently, antihunger programs that target kids are more readily fundable.[9]

Yet there are systematic limitations to food banks specifically and basic needs banks generally. The national charitable food system expanded tremendously in the past fifty years and distributed billions of pounds of food via millions of meals, and yet hunger and food insecurity remain high. Similarly, diaper banks have distributed more than a billion diapers since that first diaper drive in Arizona. As the NDBN conference speaker told our audience, food insecurity and hunger are not intractable problems.[10] Both are preventable given the availability of enough food to feed everyone, especially in the United States, the world's wealthiest country and one that wastes 40 percent of food it produces. Food insecurity is not a matter of lacking resources to meet the need, but rather the inequities and power differentials that stratify access to those resources. Food banking expert Katie Martin explained, "If we define hunger as a lack of food, then the solution seems quite simple: grow, collect, and provide more food to those in need. . . . If we define hunger as a symptom of poverty caused by a broken system, and rooted in social inequalities, then the solution becomes quite different. . . . We are doing very good work to distribute food in our communities, but it is a short-term Band-Aid to a much larger problem."[11]

Many diaper bankers define *diaper need* in the same way, not as lacking diapers but as symptomatic of poverty in a broken social system shaped by capitalist exploitation, racism, and misogyny. This understanding profoundly shapes many diaper bankers' goals, which include promoting awareness of diaper need as a structural problem and advocating for policy solutions in addition to the work of collecting, packaging, and distributing diapers. Goldblum put it this way: "The NDBN's mission is not to apply a Band-Aid to a problem but to provide a long-term solution to a chronic issue. Just as food banks are a reliable source of support for families in need, diaper banks provide a basic need for families in crisis."[12] Goldblum later said at an NDBN conference that while some criticize the "Band-Aid approach" to basic needs banking that purportedly does little to uproot the structural conditions of food insecurity and diaper need, "to a bleeding person, a Band-Aid sounds pretty good." Shifting the structure that denies necessities to some is a crucial part of the work basic needs banks do. In the meantime families need food and diapers, which basic needs banks can help provide.

But families' needs go beyond material essentials. Those who use basic needs banks also have social and psychological needs for connection and dignity, without which many refuse to seek support. Sociologist Jennifer Sherman found that shame and stigma of dependency keep people in need from fully utilizing available social safety nets.[13] Like food banks, many diaper banks operate on a scarcity model that rations what clients receive by setting eligibility criteria, enforcing time limits, and limiting items distributed (hence the need to wrap diapers into smaller-quantity packages). One rationale typically offered for this is that, if given unlimited free items, clients will engage in fraud and abuse by taking more than they really need, lying about how many people live in their households, and selling excess items to get money for vices. Despite stereotypes that those in poverty prefer handouts over hard work, recipients of basic needs banks tend to use them as a last resort, and doing so often takes a negative toll on their identity, self-esteem, and emotional well-being.[14] Clients of basic needs banks also feel they must show gratitude and deference to staff and that they have little right to complain, despite what and how much they receive and how they are treated.[15]

No one *wants* to use a food or diaper bank. People only come to basic needs pantries after having faced various dehumanizing and demoralizing situations, including unemployment or working in jobs that fail to provide a living wage, lack of education and affordable housing, violence, hunger and other forms of deprivation.[16] Research consistently shows that to manage the stigma associated with seeking basic needs support, people avoid utilizing both public assistance programs and charitable organizations.[17] Recipients are well aware of the culture of suspicion surrounding those who use government and community aid programs, leading to feelings of anxiety, shame, and guilt. For this reason many food and diaper bankers use the language of justice, equity, and rights in hopes that it will displace common narratives of hard work, self-sufficiency, and personal responsibility that infuse charity models.[18]

Yet using basic needs banks can feel anything but just and equitable. Those who rely on basic needs charity must often navigate burdensome logistics and jump through administrative hoops to prove they are poor enough to deserve help from others who have never experienced poverty. Especially for those pantries that rely on in-kind donations and volunteer labor, item quality can vary widely, stock can be inconsistent, and hours of operation can be severely limited.[19] Limited hours and long wait lines add bureaucratic burdens that contribute to stress, stigma, and exclusion. Given that economic insecurity is associated with less flexible schedules, those who rely on basic needs banks tend to have shorter and less frequent windows of time when they can access what they need. This is especially true compared to those who have means to travel to and purchase necessary items from stores with large and diverse inventory, round-the-clock open hours, and ample checkout lines that require little wait time, if any at all.

Clients of basic needs banks face eligibility rules that require verification of need, including proof of identity, address, household composition, and/or eligibility for other means-tested programs, which can be hard to provide for those in poverty whose lives and living situations are often highly unstable and not officially documented. These requirements create a heavy burden of proof and carve out a notion of deservingness based on proven need rather than fundamental right, erecting barriers to worthiness that exacerbate feelings of humiliation and shame. Relational aspects of basic needs assistance can form additional barriers rooted in interpersonal interaction characterized by significant emotional labor for recipients that go beyond managing shame and stigma. When basic needs assistance occurs within a framework of charity, clients feel obligated to outwardly express appreciation for anything they get.[20]

Moreover, relationships between staff, volunteers, and clients tend to be highly stratified, structured by class and race inequalities and shaped by organizational policies that reinforce social asymmetry, distance, and hierarchy.[21] Exchanges of basic needs for grateful reverence often unfold between paid staff and unpaid volunteers who tend to be white and middle class—and for volunteers, older, retired or semiretired, and lacking lived experience in poverty—and clients who are more likely to be people of color, poor or low-income, younger, and unemployed. The ability to volunteer usually depends on having the time, energy, and other resources, such as transportation, to devote to charitable causes rather than to navigating need and daily deprivation.[22] Staff and volunteers carry out intrusive intake procedures that involve asking for private information, including clients' income, employment status, aid received, and household members. Some of the volunteer population consists of people who have utilized the services and want to give back, structure their days, and engage with others in ways that increase their self-esteem. Yet these volunteers can also be prone to judgment and symbolic boundary drawing between themselves and current clients in need.[23]

No doubt many basic needs banks staff and volunteers work hard to forge connections with clients that make these administrative procedures feel more humane and comfortable. Many diaper bankers and diaper bank volunteers directly rejected an us-versus-them mentality when it came to interacting with clients, which helped build connections and generate empathy while providing diaper aid. Yet limits on how much clients can receive often evoke resentment and set up an antagonistic relationship between volunteers tasked with restricting charitable distributions and clients who need more than volunteers can distribute. This is the context in which many diaper bankers I met decided they wanted to start or staff a diaper bank.

FROM PARTNER AGENCIES AND DIAPER PANTRIES TO PARENTS: GETTING DIAPERS TO FAMILIES

The Golden State Food Bank was the largest diaper provision organization I visited. The director, Valentina, a Latina in her thirties, gave me a tour of the expansive fifty-thousand-square-foot warehouse that held five hundred thousand diapers stacked three pallets high in sections arranged by size. The tour ended at a delivery dock where staff of nearly one hundred partner agencies, including prenatal health programs, shelters, and colleges, picked up weekly diaper orders. Despite holding half a million diapers, Valentina told me, the Golden State Food Bank didn't give diapers directly to families. Later that day, I had a chance to visit Sunny Starts, one of their many partner agencies that did. It was a women's and children's health clinic housed in a fifteen-hundred-square-foot office space where Gertrude, a white volunteer in her seventies, asked me to sign in before taking a tour of the office. As I did, I exchanged smiles with the four pregnant mothers and their six children as they played in the waiting room. According to Gertrude, all four mothers—one Black, one Latina, and two Hmong—were there to receive diapers after getting a prenatal checkup. Around the corner from the waiting area leading into a narrow hallway were three rooms with exam tables, a set of tidy bathrooms, and two small consultation rooms that doubled as staff offices and counseling centers.

At the end of the hallway was the diaper pantry, a tight closet containing diapers in five sizes packed in sleeves each holding twenty units, all of which Sunny Starts recently received through the Golden State Food Bank's diaper program. Hanging from the diaper closet door was a daily sign-in sheet with three columns for listing names of who had received diapers that day, sizes of the diapers received, and how many individual diapers were distributed to each client. At barely 11:00 a.m., the day's sheet had already recorded twenty names of those who had collectively received more than five hundred diapers. Many of those same mothers, Gertrude told me, would be back as soon as they were eligible to receive their next pack of diapers after a medical checkup or counseling session. The partnership between the Golden State Food Bank diaper program and the Sunny Starts diaper pantry represents one end of the continuum in how diaper distribution organizations work. Large banks like Golden State are led by numerous paid staff under the supervision of a Board of Directors, located in large warehouse spaces with adjacent offices, and procure diapers through a continuous bulk-purchasing program before they are distributed to partner agencies like Sunny Starts, which are responsible for direct provision to parents. As did Golden State, most large diaper banks have official IRS 501c(3) nonprofit status and paid staff members who manage complex operations, including programming, infrastructure, communications, human relations, community development initiatives, and interagency relations with partner organizations.

On the other end of that continuum, less formal, smaller diaper pantries tend to be primarily or completely volunteer-run, operate from a personal residence, community agency, or religious center, and make purchases on an as-needed (or as-affordable) basis using money collected via

ad hoc fundraising efforts. They rely heavily on individual monetary donations and receive much of their inventory from diaper drives and individuals who donate diapers after retail purchase or closet cleanouts.
Occasionally, they also receive diapers from stores and diaper manufacturers that donate imperfectly packaged items in dented boxes or previously opened plastic sleeves. The few paid staff are usually part time, and
volunteers sort, organize, and prepare diapers for direct distribution to
parents and community organizations with diaper pantries.

All along this continuum, just as food banks typically measure their
success and impact in terms of pounds of food distributed or individual
meals provided, diaper banks and pantries report individual diapers distributed. As one diaper banker told me, "What gets counted counts," and
number of diapers distributed is discrete, measurable, and crucial for
describing the full extent of diaper need to attract funders and advocate
for diaper policies. Diaper bankers often report measurable impacts of
receiving diapers, such as increases in the number of days worked and
childcare utilized and reduced incidence of health problems linked to
inadequate diapers (e.g., diaper rash). Diaper bankers hope to highlight
the human elements behind the numbers through personal firsthand
accounts of parents' experiences of receiving diapers and related impacts
on their and their children's lives—impacts that are harder to quantify but
no less important.

Though not all US diaper banks are affiliated with the National Diaper
Bank Network, their annual survey is the best source of information about
trends in diaper bank funding, acquisition, purchasing, and distribution.
According to the 2022 NDBN member survey, most diaper banks received
support from a mix of private individual donors (94 percent), corporate
donations (66 percent), and public funding (25 percent). More than half
(56 percent) acquired diapers primarily through direct purchase, while 33
percent received most diapers via donations. Two in three diaper banks
used an NDBN bulk-purchasing program. Despite diaper banking's small-
scale beginnings through diaper drives, relatively few diapers are now collected this way, as the nearly ten million diapers donated through more
than twenty-five hundred diaper drives in 2021 were less than 5 percent
of total diapers distributed by the network. That year, member diaper
banks distributed almost 188 million diapers (worth about $54.5 million)

to 3.2 million children.[24] All NDBN member diaper banks distributed disposable infant diapers, and 16 percent distributed cloth diapers. Only about 7 percent distributed incontinence products for adults.

Based on the 2010 "Every Little Bottom" study commissioned by Huggies, which found that families experiencing diaper need tended to be short about eleven to twelve diapers each week, the NDBN recommends that diaper banks distribute no fewer than fifty diapers per month per child.[25] In 2021, 65 percent of NDBN members reported meeting or exceeding this recommendation by providing fifty to two hundred diapers monthly per eligible child.[26] Cloth diapers typically come as kits with materials for ten to fifteen diaper changes, including wet bags, diaper covers, diaper liners, and fasteners. Determining who is eligible to receive diapers usually involves gathering information about children's ages and diaper sizes, parents' income and employment status, and/or eligibility for means-tested programs. About one-quarter of diaper banks use three years as the age cutoff for when children can receive diapers, while another third use a cutoff of four years, and 23 percent have no age limit. In many cases diaper banks let partner agencies determine income or other eligibility requirements (45 percent), while 34 percent rely on self-reporting of need, and 19 percent use enrollment in WIC, SNAP, Medicaid, and/or TANF to determine eligibility.

These differences and the wide continuum on which US diaper banks and pantries exist mean that "diaper bankers" are not a monolithic group. Rather, they are a growing contingent representing a variety of roles, ranging from directors of large community-based basic needs organizations and healthcare providers to antipoverty advocates and educators. Many collect and distribute diapers as their primary full-time jobs allow. They are motivated to start diaper banking for various reasons, including lived experience, philanthropic goals, religious beliefs, and political inclinations. Personal experience of diaper need was a common motivation for becoming a diaper banker. Rickie, thirty-seven and white, struggled to get diapers for her three children:

> One day I found myself in a grocery store, standing in the aisle. I had to buy diapers and milk and realized I didn't have enough money for both. I just stood there, eventually put the milk back, grabbed the diapers, and walked

out. It didn't hit me until I got in my car how much having to make that decision impacted me. When those diapers ran out, I called every nonprofit in the city asking for help, but I couldn't find an inkling of support for diapers. Now I have a degree in human services and run a diaper bank with seventeen partner organizations and forty more on a waitlist.

Faced with making that impossible decision between diapers and milk over a decade earlier, Rickie founded a diaper bank as soon as her life circumstances allowed so that other parents wouldn't face the same unbearable choice between food and diapers.

Rochelle, thirty-seven and Black, also created a diaper pantry due to her own struggles with diaper need when her son was an infant. Initially she paid out of her own pocket for most diapers she distributed, working at a financial bank during the day and running a diaper pantry at night. She single-handedly served up to three hundred families a month, offering each twenty diapers. Reflecting on what inspired her to become a diaper banker, Rochelle told me:

> I remember leaving the diaper on a little too long, not being able to take him to daycare because I didn't have enough diapers for the day. Spending money I didn't really have because he needed diapers, scraping together change, literally down to pennies, just to get store brand diapers so he would be covered. . . . I didn't see myself being in a low-income single parent situation, but who really does honestly? I didn't see my path as being one of poverty. . . . I know it's not a lot. I want to give out more. But I limit it to twenty so I don't have to turn people away.

Rochelle wanted to prevent other families from resorting to diaper stretching and scraping together change for diapers. Most of all, she empathized with the stigma and shame parents feel when their babies lack diapers. Even if it meant giving fewer diapers per family, she wanted them to have diaper support they could trust and count on. Gale, forty-six and white, vividly recalled a morning when she had only two diapers and two dollars and couldn't take her infant to daycare, which required six diapers. "I had no way to buy diapers. A friend told me about a place, and I ended up getting some emergency help with diapers. . . . Now my grown kids, including the one I couldn't take to daycare that day, don't remember a time before diaper drives and a wall of diapers in our house."

Religious beliefs, desires to do charity work, and social justice commitments inspired diaper banking among others. Many felt indignation upon learning that no safety net policy provided diapers and disappointment when discovering that no diaper-support programs existed in their local communities. Paula, a white sixty-eight-year-old retired Presbyterian pastor, ran an entirely volunteer-led diaper bank that started as part of a church ministry focused on providing infant diapers and adult incontinence products. Guided by the belief that providing basic hygiene needs for the young, old, and sick was a way to serve God and practice her spiritual faith, Paula partnered with fifteen organizations and delivered directly to homebound older adults and children with unique needs. These populations, she noted, were often excluded from diaper distribution services because larger diapers and incontinence products were more expensive.

Moira, thirty-two and white, first learned of diaper need when she read an article on social media while she was eight months pregnant with her second child. She looked for diaper support in her community and found only "a church that was starting to give out diapers. But it was one of those third Tuesday of the month, if you're the tenth person in line, and have these seventeen documents, you might get five diapers, if they have the size you need type of situation." Internet research led Moira to the NDBN's how-to guide for starting a diaper bank. After her maternity leave, Moira began to collect diapers and donations, which quickly led to the first diaper bank in her midsized city and another full-time job for her. When I interviewed Moira a year later, the diaper bank was working with fourteen partner organizations and had a long waiting list of others hoping to join them.

Micheline, forty-one and white, shared a similar origin story and talked about the "growing pains of being a diaper bank" and needing to "be prepared to explode because of the huge unmet need." Like others, Micheline started by distributing donated supplies directly to families and moved to bulk purchasing and distributing through partners when word about her diaper bank spread and diaper requests exponentially increased. She purchased diapers through Jet.com, which contracted with diaper manufacturer Cuties to produce diapers without expensive inked graphics and packaged in larger quantities to reduce retail costs from the typical thirty to fifty cents a diaper to only thirteen cents. Like Micheline eventually did, most diaper bankers associated with larger banks utilized a partner distribution model with the goal to connect families in need of diapers to other services partners provided. Jane, thirty and multiracial, worked for an infant support organization that had more than 150 partner agencies serving nearly four thousand families daily. "We know it doesn't matter if we provided families with thousands more diapers," Jane said, "we wouldn't meet the need. To be more equitable, we work with community-based organizations working with families directly that have a better understanding of how to provide safety nets for low-income families."

Other diaper bankers used a partner distribution model to outsource determining eligibility. Brianne, thirty-five and white, ran a bank using a partner model because "we were never comfortable with trying to vet anybody to make sure that they were really in need. For a while, we just didn't do it. It was trust-based. But as you grow bigger, you must have certain things in place procedurally." Leaders of larger banks that used a partner model emphasized other benefits, especially being able to devote more resources to building infrastructure and reducing diaper costs. Kira, thirty-nine and white, led a diaper bank that started with a $40,000 grant for forklift and warehouse rentals. "If you can receive them," Kira explained, "you can buy 250,000 diapers for an administrative fee of $6,000. . . . This one diaper that costs us potentially just a few cents could end up costing parents 75 cents or a dollar." Kira's diaper math was correct. Diaper banks that used the Huggies purchasing program through the NDBN spent around two pennies per diaper. At retail, parents could expect to pay nearly twenty times as much. For those struggling with diaper despair who tend to pay surge prices for smaller diaper packs because that's all they can afford, it could be up to seventy-five times the amount per diaper that large diaper banks spend through bulk purchasing.[27]

This ability to buy in bulk well below wholesale costs was the primary reason bankers encouraged cash donations over donating diapers after retail purchase. Just as food banks tend to receive donated canned foods that clients may not prefer or be able to use, diaper banks typically receive in-kind diaper donations in small sizes that are ill-suited for most families' needs. Moira explained, "When people want to donate and they go shopping for diapers, they want to bring me the largest number of diapers to make the biggest impact for their money. Or they think, 'Oh, it's a little baby,' so they get newborn or size 1. But that's not what we need. They don't choose size 3, 4, or 5, or Pull-Ups [Huggies brand disposable training pants], even though that's what we need the most." Focusing fundraising efforts on large monetary contributions from corporations and governments, building up large stocks of bulk-purchased diapers in various sizes, and utilizing a partner distribution model were all primary strategies for maximizing capacity.

Many diaper bankers maintained small-scale operations to personally connect with families. Patti, eighty and white, founded a diaper program with her husband in their small town and personally paid for fifty families' diapers. Going on their tenth year, Patti noted, "We give out diapers and kindness. We remind ourselves that we're not just standing there handing them a box. Without getting bogged down, we try to find out how things are going, if the supply has been enough, how the baby is." Similarly, Rachel, fifty-eight and white, ran a pantry that prioritized giving diapers to "people that just really need a hand up or just a hand, not a handout. We emphasize, 'We're here to help you. There's no shame in you being here.' We give people a bit of hope and encouragement."

Concerned that unused packaged diapers could be sold or bartered on the "black diaper market," some bankers distributed a limited number to discourage fraud. However, most criticized this practice as unjust and unbefitting the purpose of diaper banking, which was to distribute diapers to families in need to use as they saw fit. Otherwise, they claimed, limiting diapers or requiring intrusive eligibility procedures risked demeaning parents who might miss out on necessary diaper support. Many of those who led smaller direct-distribution pantries avoided asking for documentation or proof of need so as not to compromise trust and rapport with parents. Esther, sixty-eight and Black, explained how "some families are embarrassed that they need our help, so we don't ask for proof. If I had a family I thought was selling my diapers, if I know a child in need is getting the diapers on their bottom, it's not my place to judge." Ruth, sixty-seven and white, likewise noted, "We saw on Facebook people were selling a bag of our diapers with our logo for twenty dollars. But what can you do with a diaper, you know? You put it on a baby's bottom somewhere. We're okay with that. If they want to sell it, somebody is going to get the benefit of these diapers." Emily, thirty-one and white, concluded, "I would rather have somebody take advantage of the system than somebody in need not get help because of the documentation requirement."

Considering how using basic needs banks can be emotionally fraught, many bankers avoided invasive questioning and onerous documentation requirements so that pantries could be spaces of empowerment and dignity, rather than stigma and shame. Although diaper bankers saw the value of impact stories for promotional materials, donors, and evaluation reports, many felt that asking for details about families' personal and economic circumstances was extractive and exploitative. Other strategies for creating positive diaper bank experiences included setting up pantries as storelike settings where parents could "shop" by choosing diapers and other items they needed and keeping diapers in their original commercial packaging rather than repackaging them to signal they were from diaper banks. Viewing parents as customers with some semblance of choice and referring to them as "clients" were deliberate practices intended to dignify diaper distribution by treating recipients like those who can afford to buy diapers.

Other diaper bankers were uncomfortable treating diaper distribution as an impersonal transaction because they felt it undermined their ability to know families, their situations, and their other needs for assistance. Many of these bankers preferred a relational approach whereby diapers became a tool to recruit parents into other programs and services. Karen, a white forty-five-year-old outreach coordinator for a family service organization, noted, "Diapers are what draws our families. We try to provide for families' social as well as material needs, to serve through relationships. . . . Diapers get their feet in the door and allow us to serve families better." Yet using diapers as an incentive for other programming was one of the most controversial practices in diaper banking.

DRAWING THEM IN WITH DIAPERS

I took a guided tour of the Baby Boutique with Gina, a forty-two-year-old Latina who served as parent education coordinator for a large community center with a diaper bank. Set off from staff offices, classrooms, and warehouse space for storing nearly a quarter of a million diapers, the fifty-by-thirty-foot boutique was painted in pastel shades of green, blue, and yellow, decorated with cartoon characters from famous nursery rhymes, and organized in sections for clothing, bath items, toys, and books. The boutique even had a small storefront-like window with toddler manne-quins adorned in beautifully matched, slightly used, color-coordinated outfits. Except a vague musty smell, the space was just like any baby goods store. Yet items in this store could not be bought with money. Gina explained how parents could "purchase" three clothes items, books, or toys or one large item like an infant tub for each point earned attending the center's parenting classes. Nearly all parents "bought" diapers for half a point each and picked other items only if they had leftover points. Each class hour was worth twenty points or double points if both parents came. Classes consisted mostly of women, were offered in English and Spanish, and focused on what Gina described as "basic parenting tips." She said, "We don't tell them how to parent, but it's important to have an incentive-based program so we can be a one-stop shop for parents' needs and con-nect them to other services."

This common practice of using diapers as an incentive—what some critically call "bait"—for parents to participate in other programs and ser-vices is contentious among diaper bankers. Some like Gina believe that in addition to allowing families to access a basic need, free diapers created opportunities to learn about topics like infant safety, child development, and toilet training, as well as the chance to reflect on their parenting styles and practices with educators and fellow parents. Some diaper bankers emphasized how diapers provide an outreach opportunity to connect fam-ilies to additional services for which they qualify. Advocates of incentiviz-ing diapers believed that diaper provision can help build trusting relation-ships with parents because giving out diapers shows that service providers "get it."[28] Some research has indeed found that diapers can be a good ice breaker for clinical conversations with parents and an effective engage-ment tool when working with families who are hard to reach and track, as low-income families often are.[29]

All told, advocates claim, diaper programs operate as "entry points" for access to case management, child development resources, healthcare and mental health services, and housing and food support; partner agencies also use diapers to increase client engagement and retention in other programs, noting that parents are more likely to attend programs and meet with staff members if the parents know they will receive diapers.[30] Fifty-eight-year-old Norma, a Latina and family resource center coordinator, described how her organization:

> used diapers as a recruitment tool to connect with families, a way to engender trust with parents to help them more. . . . In fact, we don't really identify as a diaper pantry but a more comprehensive program. Diapers help us deliver the information that we have to make a better future for the child. Our program teaches about early childhood development, which is a big preventative piece. . . . Diapers are little incentives that empower them. It does bring them in, and they say, "Hey these people even care about diapers" because it means a lot to them to keep their children clean and dry. . . . Giving the diapers shows that you get parents' struggles.

Many bankers described using diapers as a tool for education, prevention, and empathy. Janet, a white forty-eight-year-old diaper bank director, shared this perspective: "Yes, it's an incentive, but it's more than that. It's a way to say, 'I get it.' Not that you're going to have that same experience, but I at least understand this is important to you, something you need for your child, so we have that. I've heard it characterized as incentivization. To me that's very transactional. I really think it's more relational." Esther, a Black sixty-eight-year-old diaper bank founder, shared, "It's all about parenting and how to teach them how to parent. To do that, the child must have a safe, clean, dry environment. Diapers are a point of connection." Esther meant that diapers were crucial for parent-child bonding as well as forging trusting bonds between parents and services providers who offered both diapers and knowledge about children's physical, emotional, and social needs.

However, critics believed that using diapers as an incentive can have the opposite effect by undermining trust and respect when parents feel compelled to jump through bureaucratic hoops and share stigmatizing personal details with strangers. Drawing them in with diapers can be coercive, critics claimed, if it compels parents to participate in programs and interact with service providers when they otherwise wouldn't if "free" diapers they needed weren't at stake. Victoria, sixty-seven and Black, strongly opposed using diapers as an incentive through the midsize urban diaper bank she founded. "They don't go for parenting classes. They go for the diapers. To get anything, they're wiggling diapers in front of their faces. I'm really upset about that. Some agencies require you to come and sit for an hour and a half for a class, and they'll give you twelve diapers. They don't even give you a package." Jaime, a white thirty-six-year-old diaper bank founder, shared:

> "Just give us the damn diapers!" was our first mission statement. Someone suggested we wordsmith that a bit. . . . Our partner organizations can never use diapers as an incentive to participate in programming, and they have to sign off on our antiracism, antioppression tenets. We've pulled out of other organizations that used diapers as an incentive. Incentives are such a paternalistic way of helping. Even if people are participating in whatever programming in order to get the—you name it, diapers, car seat, crib, whatever—they are not self-selecting to be in that educational experience. That means they are not getting out of the program what the aim is.

Debates about distributing diapers as incentives resemble controversies over safety net programs. The US welfare state has increasingly provided services that purportedly help people in poverty improve their behaviors leading to self-sufficiency, while reducing unrestricted cash transfers and in-kind goods families can use at their discretion.[31] "Just give us the damn diapers" refers to distributing needed items without strings attached.

At best, critics of incentivization argue, requiring parents to do something in exchange for diapers creates additional burdens for already busy and stressed families. At worst, it assumes that parents need to learn to parent better and suggests that service providers know better than parents themselves what their children need—that is, that lacking diapers results from limited parental know-how rather than economic constraints rooted in systemic inequalities. "Wiggling diapers in front of their faces," to use Victoria's words, perpetuates these stigmatizing ideas and inequities that harm poor families. Melissa, a white forty-eight-year-old diaper banker, spoke directly to this problem:

> We recognize that if families are struggling with diapers, they're likely struggling with something else. If they want more info or services, great, but don't require it. There's a difference between offering an incentive and imposing a

barrier. For example, the clinic that we give diapers to that uses them to increase immunizations, we still give diapers if the families show up and don't want the shot but need the diapers. We will not give diapers to programs that require a Bible study, church service, immunizations, parenting classes, anything to get the diapers, because it's a basic human need, and there should be no barrier between babies and diapers. . . . These families are stressed and busy in so many ways, forced to wait in long lines, forced to do other things to get something simple that we take for granted, right? We can go to the store and just get things. They have to travel, wait in two-hour lines to get a pack of diapers, and then you want them to take a class on top of that? It sends the wrong message about what they really need and our responsibility to help them get it.

Melissa explained how requirements for basic needs support add insult to the injury of the need itself, whereas privileged families can buy what they need without obligation.

This insult often kept mothers from accessing support, even when diaper distributors were kind, compassionate, and nonjudgmental. Tia, a thirty-one-year-old Black mother of three, lived in a shelter for victims of domestic violence with her toddler and newborn after a traumatic birth. While dealing with delivery complications, she was afraid to leave the hospital because she became unhoused when she left her abusive boyfriend, who was incarcerated for the violence perpetrated against Tia. Because he was her primary source of economic support, Tia was also at risk of losing her car because of overdue payments. Amid these extreme stressors, she was particularly worried about getting to a class at a women's health center so she could get diapers. Tia explained: "Sometimes I can go to a class, and they give you a pack or half a pack of diapers, and that's about it, but that's my life. Once a month I can get twenty-four or twenty-nine in a pack, but that will only last about three days. No one there makes you feel like you don't need or deserve the diapers, and they teach you about parenting, how to manage with a child. It takes me out of my actual element, the day-to-day mess I'm dealing with. You get to hear about other people's situations and good advice." Though Tia said many positive things about classes she took in exchange for diapers, situations like hers call into question the value of imposing requirements, especially parenting education, for economically and socially vulnerable families to get diapers.

Despite how Tia appreciated the information and connecting with other mothers, travel and time constraints often prevented her from getting to classes. She doubted that she would be able to do it again if her car was repossessed. More than lessons on stages of healthy child development, Tia needed a safe place to live with her children, a reliable form of transportation, and medical care to recover from childbirth. Ultimately, along with diaper need, Tia identified a need for connection with others, something that the parenting classes provided along with diapers, thereby meeting both her material and socioemotional needs for empathy and dignity. However, the element of coercion embedded in the classes, and especially Tia's worries about missing classes because she wouldn't get the diapers, points to a need for distributing diapers using a no-strings-attached approach that doesn't condition diaper aid on unrelated requirements.

Many mothers I interviewed had to take mandatory parenting classes to get diapers. Despite how they often they found information and social support in the classes useful, such requirements created an additional barrier to diaper aid. Ramona, twenty-one and Latina, earned "mommy money" for diapers by "taking parenting classes that were pretty helpful, with topics on cash and speakers talking about how they handle their money." Ramona credited the healthcare organization with "saving me" when she was unemployed and about to give birth to her daughter. Staff were respectful and "didn't make you feel absolute crazy because you don't have enough diapers for your kids. They don't treat you differently because of your money situation." Yet once Ramona picked up more hours at her job as a restaurant server, it was harder for her to attend classes. Because her expanded work hours conflicted with class times, she couldn't earn "mommy money" and instead had to use a significant portion of her low wages to buy diapers out of pocket.

Other mothers shared similar stories. Mary, a twenty-eight-year-old Latina mother of three, received diapers from an organization that required parents to watch "1980s videos about fathers. It's all mothers there, and they make you sit there for thirty to forty-five minutes of your time. It's pointless. 'Just give me some Pampers, or that's not really helping.' The video they made us watch says to get fathers involved, but my kid's dad already helps with Pampers when he can." This requirement made little sense to Mary, who needed diapers not messages about fathers. Other mothers reported having to take classes, or watch videos about family dynamics, infant cold and flu symptoms, and breastfeeding, and some were even quizzed to prove they were paying attention. Audra, a thirty-three-year-old white mother of five, had to "watch videos on eating right, the kind of videos they make you watch at WIC to get food." She only went to diaper giveaways when she got "really desperate because who wants to sit out there and say, 'Give me diapers'? It's sad and embarrassing to be like, 'I'm struggling.' The videos they make you watch just rub it in."

Every three months, Jessica, thirty-seven, white, and a mother of five, watched a twenty-minute video on securing car seats and preventing choking hazards to get diapers from a church pantry. She called the videos "helpful" and the diapers "generous, enough for two weeks" but wondered why she had to rewatch videos that hospitals showed parents before they left with newborns. After all, she had been safely securing her daughter's car seat for two years. Jackie, a thirty-five-year-old Black-Latina mother of three, also questioned requirements: "You get thirty diapers a month only after you go to class for an hour. I guess things that cost cash money people are less willing to give out without making you prove or earn it somehow. They want you to have a child of a certain age, bring them to class, or at least come to their classes on healthy eating, discipline, dealing with tantrums. I've had to go to every class just to keep up with her diapers." Jessica and Jackie concluded that diapers weren't "free" if they had to pay for them with their presence, time, and attention.

While most mothers said the information from classes was helpful, none told me they would have taken classes if they didn't get diapers for doing so. Solange, a twenty-four-year-old Black mother of four, attended classes for diapers through a prenatal health program. Before each class, she called the program to confirm they had her daughter's diaper size. "I go there to get a little bit of learning, but I mainly go there to get diapers. I don't miss any class if they have her size. You never know who is going to help you out, so I just try to be as nice as I can." Diaper bankers said that parents expressed appreciation for classes along with diapers. However, as Solange shared, mothers often engaged in performative gratitude in the hope that it would help them access diapers they desperately needed.

SUCCESSES AND SETBACKS OF SEEKING DIAPER SUPPORT

About two-thirds of the mothers I interviewed used or tried to use diaper assistance services at least once. Half of these mothers had generally positive experiences seeking and receiving diapers and interacting with diaper bank staff. Sonia, a thirty-three-year-old Latina mother of two, described it as "one thing in my life I knew I could count on, which gave me a sense of peace. If I run out or have a problem, I can go over there and ask and probably get another set of diapers." Alejandra, a twenty-eight-year-old Latina mother of two, received diapers from a university pantry that required her only to scan her student ID and note the needed size to a student staffing the pantry. Describing why her experience was positive, she emphasized how "other students were running it, and they probably had a tight budget too and would understand." Sensing empathy over shared financial struggles reduced potential shame and stigma associated with diaper need for Alejandra.

Mothers emphasized the importance of respectful anonymity, or when staff were courteous and treated mothers with kindness and dignity without otherwise prying into their lives' challenging circumstances. Trinity, forty-two, Black, and a mother of three, was grateful for the six packs of diapers she received monthly through a municipal diaper bank that served all TANF recipients in her city. "I just show up with my government issued [electronic benefit transfer] card and say, 'I'm here for diapers.' They just give them to you. At first I was embarrassed to go get them, but I had to work through that. I put in my share of time. I've worked and paid taxes my whole life. I'm just in a unique situation right now. I don't know what I would do without this program." Trinity felt justified in accessing diapers as a tax-supported service because she saw it as a benefit earned through work rather than a charitable handout. She appreciated that there were no additional intake processes or burdensome eligibility requirements for diapers.

These experiences align with those reported via diaper bank evaluation studies, which find connections between receiving diapers from a pantry and positive changes in parental mood, child health and happiness, and increased opportunities for work, school attendance, and childcare.[32] Recipient families reported reduced stress, due not only to having access to a full diaper supply but the reliability of that access and being able to plan accordingly, rather than facing the uncertainty of diaper need. Mothers noted that receiving diapers increased parenting self-efficacy, specifically confidence in their abilities to meet their children's immediate basic needs, leading to better child health outcomes, including greater comfort, better sleep, less crying, and fewer rashes.[33] As mothers told me, positive effects linked to diapers lasted longer than the diapers themselves.

The other half of mothers who received diapers described negative experiences of using diaper assistance as inconvenient or uncomfortable. These mothers invested significant time and energy in tracking pantry schedules, planning to get there, and ensuring they had proof of need, which often included their children's presence. Gina, a sixteen-year-old Latina mother of one, received diapers from a church pantry that required an adult guardian, government-issued ID, and Social Security card. Yet because her mother's work hours conflicted with distribution times and Gina lived many miles from the church, Gina rarely got diapers. Transportation presented similar challenges for others, especially when diaper giveaways happened only during narrow time windows on specific days.

Several mothers shared about traveling long bus routes with young kids, only to arrive at pantries that gave few diapers or had run out. The number of diapers received varied widely from as few as five to full two-hundred-count boxes. Most got thirty-five to fifty diapers monthly, which aligns with recommendations for filling families' typical diaper gaps. Some pantries distributed a certain number of diapers per child but others did so per household, meaning fewer diapers per child for families with diapered children. As part of diaper math, mothers considered if diapers they received outweighed the costs of getting to pantries, including concerns about traveling with children in unfamiliar places. Molly, a thirty-one-year-old Black mother of two, wouldn't go to a church that gave out diapers because "it didn't feel safe. People warned me about the location. I have two little ones and don't feel comfortable going down there with them, especially for how many you get."

Mothers also worried about pantries running out of their children's sizes. Jackie, a thirty-five-year-old multiracial mother of three, was nearing the end of her diaper supply because the organization from which she received diapers ran out of the larger sizes her son wore. As many mothers and bankers reported, smaller diaper sizes (newborn, size 1, and size 2) were in greater supply, while demand for sizes 3, 4, and 5 was higher. Jackie explained, "many places have smaller sizes because they're more supportive toward the newer babies versus the older ones." The standard weight range for size 2 diapers is twelve to eighteen pounds, with the typical infant outgrowing size 2 by six months. This made it hard for mothers to get sizes they needed for most of the time their children were in diapers. Only two mothers ever received disposable training pants intended for older toddlers. Mothers described the challenges of receiving poor-quality diapers that were minimally absorbent or irritated their children's skin. Jackie shared with me why she didn't want to use the diapers another nearby pantry distributed: "I haven't been going because they're not good diapers. My daughter sleeps through the night unless she's sick, and she keeps the same diaper on. I don't want to wake her up to change her. I'd rather use a good brand of diapers so I don't have to do that. Parents need a better choice, more variety of quality diapers. Not all kids can use all diapers."

Most organizations mothers used had a child age limit for diapers, which mothers reasoned was based on assumptions about when children should already be toilet trained. Yazmin, a twenty-eight-year-old Latina mother of three, once tried to use a diaper pantry, "but they said the baby was too big. I think she was like a year and half, and they're like, 'No, she needs to be in the bathroom by now.'" Mothers reported that twenty-four months was a typical age cutoff for receiving diapers, despite how toddlers in the United States typically do not start toilet training until at least two years old, with many initiating it after thirty months and needing several more months to learn to use the toilet throughout the day and night.[34] Age cutoffs messaged to mothers that they weren't potty training their children when they should. Cutoffs also defied decades of messages from child development experts, pediatricians, and diaper corporations about child-initiated and child-directed toilet training.[35]

For these reasons many mothers told me they did everything they could to get diapers on their own before resorting to "begging." Ciara, a twenty-eight-year-old Latina mother of two, asked family, bartered for diapers via social media, and sold other items for diaper money. She felt especially anxious asking people she didn't know for diapers because it made her feel like a failed parent. Moreover, because she lived in a rural area twenty miles away from the closest place she knew that gave out diapers, seeking diaper support was not merely inconvenient but also cost-prohibitive. "I know that [diaper pantry] gives out donations, but it's way out there," Ciara said. "My car doesn't always have gas to get that far. For 'free' diapers, I would be spending the money on gas." Aurelia, a twenty-five-year-old Latina mother of two, described the inconvenience of seeking diaper support: "I know [organization] provides diapers, but I haven't done that because they make you go to the office and register new. You have to take all kinds of paperwork. It's a bunch of errands and hours of work to get it from them. After all that, you don't get that many diapers." Fear of stigma prevented mothers from utilizing diaper assistance. Jamie, a thirty-eight-year-old white mother of one, said about using a diaper pantry:

> You have to provide a lot of information about why you need diapers that people wouldn't share if you weren't in that situation. It's humiliating and humbling. Some of them are understanding. Some are just judgmental. If you have a lot of energy or stutter, they think you're on drugs and look at you like, "What's wrong with you?" Like you can't provide, or my baby's dad can't provide. . . . All that for only fifteen diapers, which is fine, maybe that will last him three days if I'm lucky and he doesn't have diarrhea, but it's a lot of effort when you're in the car. Sometimes it's not even worth it.

For Jamie the costs of diaper assistance included gas money, travel time, and shame of interacting with diaper pantry staff she feared would judge her behavior and family.

Other mothers faced similar judgment when seeking diapers, especially mothers of color who experienced racial prejudice and dependency stigma. Faith, forty-three and multiracial, was guardian of four young children, including three-month-old twins, whose mother had recently died of cancer. The twins' mother had passed, not Faith's. Diagnosed herself with lung and cervical cancer and undergoing radiation and chemotherapy treatments, Faith tried once to get diapers from a charity. A white woman there asked Faith if she had a car, implying that if Faith had a valuable asset, she could sell it and wasn't yet needy enough to get free diapers:

> I took off my wig. "I'm going through chemotherapy. I'm not going to put my car up for sale. It's paid off. I don't want a lien where I may not be able to get it back. I don't have time when I have to raise these four babies because their mama died." I shouldn't have to explain why they should help me. It's so

humiliating because I'm used to doing things on my own. It's hard to explain why you need diapers to a stranger. They're looking at you like, "Why don't you get a job?" You feel judged. I'm not asking you to give me money for them. I just need a little help with diapers. She told me ways to get money, like pawn my ring. If you have anything worth a certain amount, they'll question you. Never went back there again.

Faith later received full boxes of diapers from a church group that offered support until the twins were toilet trained, helping dull the sting of humiliation she still felt after her first attempt to get diapers. Other mothers felt that requiring personal information to access diapers was an invasion of their privacy and reflected lack of trust that they were truthful about their financial situations. Alexis, a twenty-three-year-old Asian mother of two, said, "I shouldn't have to tell them my life story for them to help me with diapers."

Some mothers saw proving diaper need through a compelling story or poor-enough presentation of self as taken-for-granted requirements of diaper support. Alicia, a twenty-two-year-old Latina mother of two, said, "Some people mess it up for everybody, so I guess that's why they don't want to give us more [diapers] because who knows if they're really using it to get other stuff. It ruins a lot for people who actually need it. I'd be willing to take a drug test for diapers." Alicia was resigned to being suspected of fraud. Other mothers, especially Black mothers, often didn't know whom to trust and questioned whether diaper pantry staff would view their efforts to get more diapers as good mothering or as evidence of potential abuse or neglect. Specifically, they feared that asking for diaper support would trigger accusations of negligent parenting that could lead to involvement with the child welfare system. Several had prior experiences with child removal through Child Protective Services based on citations of unfit living conditions, including lack of diapers. Mothers who had or feared involvement with the child welfare system were careful about where they sought support and avoided it entirely if they suspected that asking for assistance could lead to doubts about their parental fitness.[36]

Child welfare wasn't the only government system mothers worried about. Undocumented immigrants and those with undocumented family were reluctant to seek diaper support from agencies that required proof of residency, identification, or a Social Security card, fearing that staff might disclose their status and put them at risk of deportation. Several expressed concerns that diaper pantries could be undercover immigration enforcement checkpoints. Though there were no known cases of this, mothers' fears nevertheless kept them from seeking diaper aid when documentation was required.

All told, mothers encountered various challenges in seeking diaper support. To receive a limited number of diapers, they often had to leave their homes and travel with children at specific times to distant locations and provide evidence and personal information they were reluctant to share. Natasha, a thirty-five-year-old Black mother of four, described diapers as a "daily struggle, but I don't want to put my business out there. People look down on us and start talking bad because we can't afford good Pampers. Some of us can afford to get out of the ghetto. Some of us can't. We need programs to help with the Pampers, but just don't look down on us for needing help." Trina, a twenty-nine-year-old white mother of two, confided that "getting diapers was quick and easy. After ten minutes of showing up, I just asked, and they gave me a full sleeve, no questions asked. But it still kills me to ask. It makes my stomach hurt. It just makes me feel like I didn't try hard enough at supporting them, making sure they had everything they need." Kelly, thirty-two, white, and mother of two, similarly shared that although she didn't feel judged by respectful and kind diaper bank staff, asking for diapers was still emotionally difficult. She confided, "I kind of felt like, 'Well, why do you have a baby if you can't afford to pay for diapers, you know?' The people were nice about it, but it was embarrassing."

Even in the absence of enacted stigma, discrimination or unfair treatment from others, those struggling with diaper need often experienced felt stigma, the internalized shame and expectation of discrimination that prevent people from seeking help.[37] Mothers' stories reveal how requirements that people share personal details of their life circumstances or provide documentation of need or proof of having children under a certain age may contribute to anxiety and depression experienced as part of diaper need and despair. Yet mothers' stories also point to how getting diapers can be a dignified and empowering experience, as many diaper bankers hoped it would be.

·   ·   ·   ·   ·

Sociologist Janet Poppendieck argued that basic needs banking seeks to manage poverty through damage control rather than structural change.[38] From this perspective food and diaper banks are part of a culture of charity that normalizes systematic deprivation; legitimates limited personal generosity and corporate philanthropy as responses to destitution; and serves as a moral safety valve relieving societal pressure to create more fundamental, long-lasting solutions. For evidence of this one could look at how the National Diaper Bank Network operates as a philanthropic arm of Kimberly-Clark by overseeing donations of millions of diapers each year to diaper banks across the country.

At the 2018 NDBN conference, where opening keynote speakers talked about the crucial role of basic needs banks, there was a panel on getting corporate donations during which an audience member stood up and said, "I'm having trouble with this conversation. The whole problem with the nonprofit model is asking for money from corporations that perpetuate the poverty that creates diaper need. How much diaper need exists because of high markups on Huggies diapers?" It was a fair question. In 2021, Kimberly-Clark donated seventeen million diapers through the NDBN. It costs about twenty cents to manufacture a diaper, around $3.4 million for seventeen million diapers. Kimberly-Clark reported $19.4 billion in net sales in 2021, with the cost of its diaper donations being equivalent to around 0.0175 percent of the company's net revenue that year.[39] Still, these seventeen million diapers, along with millions more purchased and distributed by diaper banks for a fraction of retail cost, were lifelines for untold thousands of families struggling with diaper need.

Diaper banks and pantries have little to no control over many reasons mothers had negative experiences accessing diaper aid, including transportation barriers and running out of diaper sizes due to limited donations. Inflexible schedules, inability to travel, and insufficient childcare are structural constraints diaper-desperate families face. No matter how hard they tried, diaper bankers don't have means to overcome the myriad obstacles that characterize the lives of poor families. This is especially true given their limited funding, reliance on in-kind donations, and mostly volunteer and lower-paid staff who have their own families, jobs, and needs. Yet other impediments mothers described—such as age limits, documentation and class requirements, restricted distribution hours, and limited aid rooted in assumptions of dependency—are within the immediate control of those who work hard to run diaper banks and pantries.

Diapers distributed through community diaper banks and pantries might be a Band-Aid solution, but they offered hope to many of the mothers I interviewed. Mothers described how a no-questions-asked, no-strings-attached approach that didn't require more of their limited time, energy, and resources mitigated negative effects of getting diapers. They felt respected when staff gave them the benefit of any doubt that they deserved diapers because of legitimate need without being required to jump through additional programmatic hoops. This trust felt more empowering than classes or services for which mothers never asked but were nevertheless required to complete in exchange for diapers. This trust was a key factor in whether mothers experienced diaper aid as a successful strategy for managing diaper need with dignity.

When it comes to the basic goal of diaper banking—to paraphrase diaper bankers, getting diapers on the butts of babies who need them—diaper banking undoubtedly works for the small portion of diaper-insecure families who know about and can access them. Despite accomplishing this, diapers banks, like all charitable organizations that distribute in-kind aid, tend to do so in exceedingly expensive and inefficient ways. This is neither the fault of those who run diaper banks nor those who use them. It's a design flaw inherent in any system that gives people things rather than money to buy them. This flaw is rooted in the paternalistic idea that families in need can't be trusted to use cash appropriately or that giving money encourages laziness. Although few diaper bankers personally believed this, the idea infuses diaper banking nonetheless.

Giving families cash for diapers, a strategy many diaper bankers supported through their advocacy work around vouchers and similar policies, would be far more efficient and effective for fixing diaper need. Distributing cash would require much less overhead and cut out the need for transporting and storing diapers as well as the in-person delivery, pick-up, or transfer of diapers. Ask any diaper banker, getting and giving away diapers is expensive. And the costs of doing so are not just financial. My interviews with those who ran diaper banks, often on top of other jobs and raising families, were telling. Between fundraising, getting nonprofit status, recruiting and working with boards and volunteers, setting up offices, warehouses, and websites, procuring, tracking, and transferring diaper stock, and managing ever-growing lists of partner organizations and parents, diaper banking is a significant investment of time, energy, money, and undeterred commitment to the cause. Some diaper bankers even told me about negative effects on their mental and physical health, marriages, and children.

Compared to buying it at a store, a diaper from a diaper bank requires purchasing, shipping, moving, unpacking, organizing, storing, repacking, locating, loading, unloading, distributing, and tracking by diaper bank staff or volunteers, not to mention the planning, traveling, asking, and qualifying for families. After all that, parents may not get the size, quantity, or kind of diapers their children need. Other strategies for getting diapers on babies' butts would likely prove as or even more effective. One such strategy, unconditional cash transfers, seems especially promising, as research finds that money with no strings attached increases parents' investments in basic needs and activities that enhance children's development.[40] Especially when cash transfers are framed as "babies' money," such as in the "Baby's First Years" study, mothers focus on investing the money in child-specific expenditures like diapers.[41]

Diaper banks can buy diapers in bulk at tremendously discounted prices, raising the question of why not just give families the option to buy diapers at that much cheaper rate instead, effectively cutting out diaper banks as intermediaries? But no one really ever asks this question because it's at odds with dominant ideas about poverty and how to address it—ideas that are deeply entrenched in the very structure of policy, aid to the poor, and community benefit organizations.[42] Diaper bankers are deeply committed people who profoundly care about children and families and are doing their best to work within this structure. But this doesn't change how diaper banking works on a tacit assumption that it's better to distribute diapers to the deserving children who wear them rather than cash to the potentially undeserving parents who might not use the money for diapers.

Of course, as I learned, diaper banks don't just distribute diapers. Many provide wraparound services and case management, connect families to other in-kind aid programs, promote awareness of diaper need and related problems, and advocate for diaper funding, policies, tax exemptions, and much more. Some families find value in these other services and goods, and the few programs that provide cash for diapers exist largely due to the work of these fierce advocates. But we must ensure that other services and goods are actually wanted and helpful, not hoops to jump through by already struggling parents. When it comes to efficient and effective basic needs support, we should always prioritize strategies that empower families to procure their most pressing needs rather than having to rely on someone else's assumptions about what and how much they should receive and deserve. Ultimately, beyond handing out diapers, this may be the most hopeful strategy for addressing diaper need.

7. Conclusion

A diaper is more than a diaper. I heard this statement from mothers, diaper bankers, and policymakers alike during the years I studied diaper need, the diaper bank movement, and diaper policies. The first time a diaper bank founder told me this shortly after I started this research, I thought it meant that diapers are more than mere pieces of cloth or paper and plastic that contain infant waste. They are a work support, an educational tool, and a medical product important for children's health. Not until I talked with mothers living through diaper need did I really start to grasp how inequities in diaper supplies and costs reflect and reinforce deeply entrenched inequalities with profound effects on family life.

Economically, *diaper need* is an illustrative case of how expensive it is to be poor in the United States and how we've created a society where childrearing has become unaffordable for so many families. As a leader in the diaper bank movement aptly put it, "It's really much bigger than a diaper. It's about the fact that people are so poor in America that they don't have a clean diaper for their kid. That's the problem. This isn't just about diaper rash. It's that we don't adequately care for each other and provide people with what they need. There are certainly other problems, too, but you can't get to those problems without taking care of people's basic needs first." Politically, *diaper need* reflects important assumptions about who is ultimately responsible for providing the most vulnerable among us what they need. The US social welfare system emphasizes *personal responsibility* for meeting children's needs and *self-sufficiency* among parents who must provide for the children they presumably chose to have. Struggles to get more diapers into the hands of parents who need them reveal the larger implications of our social safety net's failure to recognize hygiene items as basic human needs and to trust families to make their own decisions about how to use public aid.

As another diaper banker astutely explained, "How do we get more cash to more families? And how do we shift our narrative, our structure, to not demonize poor families, but to get more money to more families when they need it? . . . Ultimately, a lot of this comes down to how many of those in powerful positions have never once had to think, 'Am I going to be able to afford diapers for my baby tomorrow?'" Putting a real dent in diaper need will require us to expand official definitions of *need* to include diapers. That will force us to rethink how need-based policies stigmatize poor families and their childbearing choices and spending habits. Most of those with the power to do so have never lived diaper to diaper. The first major step in fixing diaper need is developing a deeper understanding of and true empathy for those who have. That was the main goal of this book. I sought to provide a clear window onto the lived experiences of diaper poverty, diaper work, diaper distribution, and the social, economic, and political forces that shape them.

Children across the class spectrum require diapering, but the labor required to meet that universal need is significantly stratified. Although all parents must attend to their children's elimination needs, diaper work more broadly accounts for the physical, cognitive, and emotional labor of coping with diaper poverty. As a case of inventive mothering, diaper work goes beyond being self-sacrificial, time-consuming, and child-centered to include strategies that are necessarily resource-stretching, dignity-protecting, and stigma-deflecting. It is therefore crucial that we understand care labor like diaper work as reasonable, responsible, and resourceful tactics shaped by the precarious and perilous conditions of marginalized mothers' parenting. This involves reframing how we understand parenting tactics developed in response to deprivation, not as survival strategies

but as rigorous, innovative, and productive practices ingeniously cultivated to address inequities like diaper need.

Lifting the veil on diaper work shows how limited public support for
care labor can have disastrous social, economic, and psychological ripple
effects through entire families. Although in most cases diapering applies
to a limited period of a child's life, diaper work reveals an overlooked
human toll of the decades-long dismantling of the US social safety net. It
also shows how the core components of *inventive mothering*—the physical, cognitive, and emotional labor involved in accessing key resources,
protecting children's dignity, and constructing a positive and valued
maternal identity in the face of gender, class, and race stigma—become
deeply entwined in a sociopolitical context that stigmatizes anyone, but
especially poor mothers of color, for needing public aid. This is especially
true when mothers silently struggle to meet a need that policy has only
just begun to recognize their children have.

We must acknowledge the exceptionalism of US diaper poverty and
diaper work. Mothers' inventive diaper work is a necessary response to the
distinctively American confluence of strict hygiene norms in a culture of
disposability, limited public support for childcare in a low-wage labor
market, and a shrinking and porous social safety net. These factors combined with exceedingly high rates of racialized childhood poverty and a
child welfare system that defines conditions of that poverty as parental
neglect lay a particularly heavy burden on families struggling to meet
their children's diapering needs. While other prosperous countries have
created family-supportive public policies, including child allowances that
provide unrestricted cash for purchasing early childhood items like diapers, the United States instead relies on intensive—and inventive—mothering to meet high expectations of childrearing amid heightened scrutiny
of poor parents. Sociologist Jessica Calarco described how American
women, especially mothers, hold society together.[1] As a clear case of this,
diaper work reflects how marginalized mothers sacrifice, stretch, and
strategize through ingenuity, initiative, and inventiveness to create private
safety nets for children when meager public safety nets fail them.

When it comes to diaper insecurity and diaper support, some things
have gotten better while others have become much worse since I conducted interviews for this book. I spoke with mothers and diaper bankers

from 2018 to 2021, when there were fewer diaper banks and pantries and less public support for diapers through state vouchers, public funding for diapers, and tax breaks. Diaper need is more visible, openly discussed, and a common focus of policy discussions and legislative bills intended to help struggling families with young children. However, two important numbers on the rise suggest that diaper need is worse, not better, than when I conducted interviews. Due to pandemic supply-change disruptions contributing to higher diaper costs and rising inflation, diapers are significantly more expensive, with some sources finding that families pay 32 percent to 48 percent more for diapers than they did just a few years ago.[2] Moreover, families are increasingly likely to report to researchers that they experience diaper need, with some studies indicating that nearly one in two families are diaper-insecure.[3] This is up from one in three a decade earlier.[4]

The good news is that compared to when I interviewed mothers, families now have more places, programs, and policies to turn to if they need diapers, in part because of the fierce advocacy of the diaper bankers I interviewed. But the bad news is that more families need that support, and diaper-insecure families are likely to struggle more. As those with firsthand knowledge of diaper need, one of the final questions I asked mothers was which diaper policies they would create if they could. Based on lived experience expertise, their answers were illustrative for thinking about how to design dignified policies and diaper provision so that years from now no family is forced to live diaper to diaper.

IF MOTHERS COULD DESIGN DIAPER POLICIES

Mothers emphasized the importance of diaper support policies and programs that are equitable, easily accessible, efficient, and didn't leave them feeling shamed or stigmatized. They also stressed that diaper support should be *enough*, meaning that it would allow them to get sufficient diapers to meet their children's needs and make it worth any efforts on their part to jump through logistical and administrative hoops required to get diapers or diaper money. Most mothers also noted how existing aid programs simply aren't sufficient to cover diaper costs or needs. TANF or cash aid is the most flexible form of public support for basic needs, and many families use part of their TANF benefits to buy diapers. However, that flexibility also means that families are more likely to use TANF to cover other household expenses not covered by other aid programs, thereby reducing its availability for diapers. Relatively few families receive TANF compared with other more restricted aid programs, and benefit levels are often too low to cover diaper costs along with other household expenses. Expecting parents to buy diapers with cash aid as it is currently structured will only exacerbate diaper need. Given all this, mothers offered several smart suggestions for what might work better.

1. A Program Like WIC for Diapers

The first most common recommendation from mothers was for a program like WIC for diapers. This was not surprising, as most of the mothers I interviewed had received WIC at some point and thus had experience with a government program targeted to provide a basic need to help pregnant women, mothers, and young children. In mothers' minds, food/infant formula and diapers were so closely entwined when it came to babies' most basic needs, it almost seemed odd to have a government program particularly for one but not the other.

Another advantage of a government program like WIC is the ability to purchase items in bulk at contractually agreed-upon prices at drastically reduced rates compared with retail costs. WIC provides nutrition support for 40 percent of US infants and buys at competitive prices more than half of formula consumed in the United States. A proven policy model for addressing basic needs gaps among mothers and young children, WIC has been a particularly successful part of the US safety net for nearly half a century. Mothers who participate in WIC tend to give birth to healthier babies that are more likely to live to celebrate their first birthday. Children served by WIC are more likely to have access to medical care, eat nutritious foods, and do better in school.[5] Using a legislatively approved competitive-bidding process, infant formula manufacturers offer significant discounts to state-based WIC programs if they are selected as the sole formula provider to WIC participants. This saves the federal government $1 billion to $2 billion annually and allows WIC to serve all eligible applicants without putting anyone on a waiting list because of lack of funding. This also benefits manufacturers because winning a WIC contract is associated with substantially more purchases of that formula brand among both WIC and non-WIC participants. Consequently, formula manufacturers tend to compete assertively on WIC contracts and offer substantial rebates because it benefits their bottom line to do so.[6]

To benefit babies' bottoms as well as family diaper budget bottom lines, a similar competitive-bidding process could be used among diaper manufacturers to provide diapers for state distribution programs at prices significantly lower than retail. It would likely have the same financial benefits for diaper companies, as families develop brand loyalty for diapers that work well for their children, just as they do with formula. We know that meeting the nutritional needs of pregnant parents and infants lays an important foundation for preventing the toxic and lifelong effects of maternal and early childhood deprivation and adversity, including physical, mental, and emotional challenges. The more we learn about diaper need, the more the evidence suggests that meeting the diapering needs of families has similar effects.

In addition to creating a WIC-like program specifically for diapers, some mothers suggested changing diapers to an allowable expense under WIC or SNAP (food stamps) guidelines. Although some noted that changing WIC and SNAP restrictions to allow for the purchase of diapers with current benefit levels would help, most of the mothers I interviewed already struggled to stretch the value of their allowances to cover formula and food. Because expecting very low-income parents to afford adequate food and diapers on the same allotted amounts would be counterproductive, mothers advocated increasing benefit levels to account for the typical monthly cost of diapers. They noted that even if monthly cash aid allowances could be increased by around thirty-five to forty dollars—just under half of the average monthly diaper bill—it would go a long way in helping families fill their diaper gaps.

Increasing both the funds and flexibility of existing safety net programs that many low-income families with young children already use would allow more parents to acquire an adequate supply of diapers in the same way that they provide food for their children. Unfortunately, this would entail using eligibility for other means-tested programs to determine eligibility for diaper support, potentially excluding groups most likely to struggle with diaper need, including undocumented immigrants, those struggling with unemployment, and the working poor. Although undocumented immigrants can be eligible for WIC, which does not have work requirements, those who lack documentation or authorization and those who don't meet income or work requirements for SNAP would be excluded. Similarly, some have suggested funding diapers through state-supported childcare programs. Yet only a small portion of those who qualify for publicly subsidized childcare receive it, and those who do are subject to government work requirements.

2. Public Funding for Diaper Banks

The second most common recommendation among mothers was for more publicly funded diaper banks. There will always be diaper need among families who don't qualify for other need-based programs like WIC and TANF. Those who run diaper banks and pantries and other organizations that distribute diapers work tirelessly to serve families, and yet with existing infrastructure and reliance on direct donations of diapers and private and corporate monetary donations used to purchase diapers, they are only able to meet a small fraction of the need. Still, my interviews with mothers suggested that the very existence of diaper banks and pantries destigmatized diaper need by normalizing diaper aid and recognizing diapers as a necessity for which struggling families deserve support.

As with food banks, accessing diaper banks can come with costs, some obvious like transportation and others hidden such as fears of being labeled a failed provider and reported to the child welfare system. Yet accessing banks and pantries can also reduce feelings of isolation by connecting parents in need to welcoming and supportive staff and others who struggle with similar needs.[7] Mothers' different experiences accessing diaper aid through community organizations reveal the importance of well-designed diaper distribution programs that, in addition to providing diapers, reduce the shame, stigma, and invisibility surrounding diaper need. From a scarcity perspective, the most effective diaper support programs are ones that don't require parents to invest additional resources—money, time, physical labor, or emotional energy—into planning, traveling, negotiating, or providing proof to get diapers. Diaper support programs or policies that fail to address the psychological aspects of diaper scarcity will be minimally helpful to families. Thus programs and policies must be designed to not only fill families' diaper gaps but also offer a dependable and unconditional source of diaper support that doesn't impose an even greater bandwidth burden on parents.[8]

Although mothers' experiences suggest that diaper banks are less efficient and effective than direct parental acquisition of diapers, those experiences indicate that diaper banks and pantries play a crucial role in ensuring continuity of diaper access. For that reason significant and systematic public funding for diaper distribution services is gravely needed. Ongoing local, state, and federal funding would increase the reach of these important community resources that are all too often reliant on piecemeal private funding and donations. Moreover, mothers suggested that receiving diapers funded by a public system into which they have paid taxes and contributed to in other ways could alleviate some of the shame associated with needing to seek diaper assistance. As a taxpayer-supported initiative, publicly funded diaper banks would likely increase the dignity of parents who must use them when they see it as an earned reward for work rather than a charitable handout. If we could ensure that diaper aid wasn't only justified as a work support or conditioned on employment, parents would likely feel valorized, rather than stigmatized, for using diaper distribution services that their labor and taxes helped fund, enhancing feelings of public responsibility, social inclusion, and equity.

Mothers had several useful recommendations for diaper banks and pantries, many of which accord with what diaper banking experts advocate as best practices for need-based diaper distribution. Mothers emphasized how important it is to provide each recipient at least a week's worth of diapers, to carry sufficient supplies of diapers in each size—including larger sizes for toddlers and older children with unique toileting needs—and to not require extensive documentation or that children be present. Although half of the parents who received diapers as incentives for classes or other wraparound services said that the information and resources were useful, even these mothers admitted that such requirements could be another obstacle to getting necessary diapers. Using diapers as incentives was especially prohibitive for mothers who lived in rural or remote areas far from diaper pantries and bus routes, those with multiple children, mothers without access to childcare, and those whose work hours conflicted with class or service times.

Diaper giveaways tend to be most beneficial for those with the documents, flexibility, geographic access, and money to travel to specific locations at designated times with required proof of need. Working parents, those in more isolated geographic areas, and those without adequate transportation or documentation are less likely to benefit from these services. This, of course, assumes that parents even know such services exist. Without systematic support, a patchwork collection of diaper banks and pantries reach only those who are lucky enough to learn through social service agencies or word-of-mouth that there are places they can go to get diapers. Even if they do, unfortunately, many mothers never return after a first visit because of other obstacles.

Diaper bankers had heard these recommendations before and strove to implement them. They tried to distribute as many diapers as possible per child, both to ensure that children had access to sufficient diapers and to make it worth parents' efforts to seek diaper support. The problem they often ran into on their end was limited diaper supplies, forcing a choice between giving more families fewer diapers or fewer families more diapers. In a system where there will always be many more families who need diapers than diapers available, this will continue to be a common dilemma for diaper banks. Diaper bankers were also aware of the importance of sufficient supplies based on sizing, which they tried to address by carefully tracking demand for each size and ordering accordingly or asking for specifically sized diaper donations.

As for documentation or other proof of eligibility, many diaper bankers told me they were only complying with requirements of their funding sources to collect and confirm this information. Some tried to circumvent such requirements by relying on parents' existing eligibility for other programs like WIC or Medicaid. Programs that allowed parents to show up and get diapers with an electronic benefits card reduced the administrative and logistical burdens of getting diapers for some. For others, however, it meant that because they didn't receive other forms of aid, they didn't get diapers either. Requirements for accessing diapers can reinforce stigmatizing deficit perspectives about the parenting choices and abilities of those who struggle with diaper need and despair. Just because a mother needs diapers does not mean that she lacks the information and initiative to properly care for her children. Diaper need is not due to lacking knowledge and skills but rather to a society and economy that make it hard for parents, especially single mothers of color, to escape poverty. Just as most food banks don't require recipients to take nutrition classes because the problem is lack of resources, not lack of know-how when it comes to eating, mothers questioned the logic of requiring parenting lessons to receive diapers they already knew their children desperately needed.

Regardless of the source, seeking diaper support is often associated with embarrassment and hence efforts to hide the extent of diaper need, leading to social isolation and further deprivation. Many mothers shared stories of stigmatizing experiences trying to get diapers from family, friends, neighbors, or service organizations. Most never asked for help with diapers or diaper money from those sources ever again. Diaper assistance experienced as onerous—whether because it required parents to meet strict eligibility requirements or to subject themselves to intrusive questions or paternalistic activities—are counterproductive and make it more likely that parents will use diaper-stretching strategies that are potentially harmful to them and their children.

Of course, many mothers had positive experiences seeking diaper support from respectful and helpful staff. Some connected to case managers and valuable wraparound services after getting diapers from organizations that helped them access other sources of aid and support. But even the most courteous and respectful staff can reduce the indignity of seeking diaper support so much. Although diaper bankers often saw their work as giving down-on-their-luck families a "hand up," that didn't change mothers' reluctance to ask for a diaper "handout." It certainly helped when staff were friendly and nonjudgemental, but that didn't always prevent mothers' sense of needing to swallow their pride to use a diaper bank. Until our cultural norms of individual responsibility and parental accountability abate, any visit to a basic needs organization will likely lead to some embarrassment and shame. To meaningfully address diaper need, any policy or program must be designed to minimize and even counteract the stigma and inconvenience associated with seeking diapers. Ultimately diaper banks are a support, not a solution, but given the degree of diaper need, especially among those who don't qualify for other aid, public funding for diaper distribution programs is sorely needed.

3. Diaper Vouchers, Allowances, or Subsidies

The third most common recommendation from mothers was diaper vouchers or increases in the value of other means-tested public benefits to offset diaper costs. Diaper vouchers or allowances have several advantages. First, they allow parents to access diapers as part of their normal shopping trips during which they can choose the size, brand, and type of diapers best suited to their children's needs. Second, thirty collars—the cash value of the California diaper voucher as of 2025—will usually buy double, triple, or even quadruple the number of diapers parents were able to get at diaper giveaways. When combined with coupons, store sales, and other promotions mothers carefully tracked, that amount could meet nearly half of a child's monthly diaper needs. Third, cash diaper support affords parents more agency than having to access diapers through gatekeepers at diaper distribution organizations that may implicitly or explicitly question mothers' honesty, financial need, and parental fitness. Fourth, cash value for diapers circumvents many problems with requiring caregivers to be in a particular place, at a specific time, and with their children to receive diapers. Ultimately cash for diapers reduces the transportation and time costs of traveling to diaper distributions, while allowing parents to spend at their discretion and experience the sense of dignity that comes with meeting children's diaper needs.

But diaper vouchers have their own drawbacks and are unlikely to be enacted in many states. It took many years and much concerted advocacy in California, the first state to implement a diaper voucher program, to get a voucher system in place. Moreover, the voucher is available only to a limited number of California TANF recipients who have qualified work or education plans and don't earn income over a very low threshold. Recipients must meet strict requirements, including not having timed out on the sixty months of overall lifetime eligibility for cash aid. Although based off the California diaper voucher, the diaper subsidy program in the state of Washington, known as the Diaper Related Payment, took effect in 2023 and avoids many of these problems. For households with a child younger than three years that receive TANF or State Family Assistance, the subsidy increases the monthly cash benefit by $100 for diapers and supplies like wipes. As in California, the diaper payment is automatic for those who qualify and requires neither an additional application process nor proof of purchase. But Washington's diaper subsidy offers broader eligibility and isn't limited to welfare-to-work recipients. At more than triple the value of the California diaper voucher, the Washington subsidy covers the full cost of many families' diapering needs.

Other states will likely implement diaper vouchers eventually, but if they use the California model that offers vouchers only as a work support most families in need won't benefit. Welfare programs should support parents' efforts to work and earn enough to care for their children; mothers I interviewed shared these priorities. But in a system where full-time, low-wage work rarely earns enough to provide fully for a family's basic needs, justifying providing diapers only as a work support doesn't account for the deeply entrenched and intersecting class, race, and gender inequalities that create the need for welfare in the first place, especially among women of color trying to raise children in deep poverty. It also sends the message that children deserve adequate diapers only when their parents are engaged in money-making or educational activities that the government deems gainful employment or legitimate preparation for work—not because they are human beings with the same rights to resources and dignity as the children of parents who can easily afford diapers or afford a stay-at-home parent.

Ultimately, tying public diaper support directly to labor recognized as work reinforces many of the worse stereotypes of low-income parents and the most insidious ideologies of the US welfare system that seeks to promote "personal responsibility" and "self-sufficiency." Mothers who must or opt to stay out of school or the paid labor force because they need or want to focus on around-the-clock care for and bonding with their very young children—and in most cases after nearly a year of pregnancy, child labor and/or surgical delivery, and postpartum recovery and adjustment—are not considered to be working or learning and therefore do not qualify. This implicitly devalues care labor by refusing to recognize childcare as an integral form of work deserving of diaper assistance. Diaper subsidies that are broadly available as a care support, generous enough to cover most or all diaper costs, and don't require additional administrative burdens such as application or verification would have many benefits. Not only would they address diaper need and prevent harms it creates, but diaper subsidies would also strengthen the social safety net in a way that conveys trust of and valorizes the care labor of low-income parents.

It is especially important that diaper support is not contingent on employment or paying a certain amount into the tax system. However, as a taxpayer-supported service, publicly funded diaper banks make good financial and political sense, not only because all children deserve diapers regardless of their parents' jobs or abilities to pay but because diapers contribute to human capital in the strictest economic sense. As economist Nancy Folbre explained, the process of childrearing is a process not of consumption but rather production, in that caring for children is about producing our society's next generation of community members, workers, citizens, and voters.[9] This is one reason we have publicly funded schools. Yet children are a social investment whose costs are carried mostly by individuals. Parents, often mothers, bear the majority share of these costs, both in terms of money, such as paying for expensive diapers, as well as the time and energy childcare requires, including diaper work when they don't have enough.

As I've shown throughout this book, diapers are a significant part of the high price of early childrearing that can push families into poverty and keep them there. Taxpayer-supported diapers would be a significant step toward disrupting this cycle and living up to our social responsibility for the costs of childrearing. This is the collective logic on which other countries' more robust welfare states and safety nets, especially child allowances, are based. They send an important message to parents that their children—and their labor to care for them—have value, not only to individual families but also to the public. After all, the children who wear diapers today—and those who don't because their families can't afford them—are the future workers on which our economy will depend. We need them to have what they need during their earliest years.

4. Classifying Diapers as a Medical Necessity

Although providing cash assistance for diapers would most directly address families' diaper gaps, other promising policy approaches are likely more tenable in the US political environment, and they converge around classifying diapers as a medical necessity. The bill for the End Diaper Need Act of 2021 proposed providing federal funding to low-income families and adults through the Social Services Block Grant Program for diapers needed by infants, toddlers, medically complex children (those three years and older diagnosed with bowel or bladder incontinence), and low-income adults and those with disabilities who rely on incontinence products. The bill would have also permitted using state Medicaid funds to buy diapers for medically complex children and allowing the purchase of medically necessary diapers and supplies using money in health savings accounts and other tax-advantaged accounts for healthcare expenses.

A federal bill that officially designates diapers as "medically necessary" would have several benefits. First, it would lay the policy foundation for greater coverage of diaper expenses through income- and age-based programs like Medicaid and Medicare, superseding any state-level restrictions on using publicly funded healthcare programs to support diaper purchases. Discussions of diaper need tend to focus almost exclusively on infant diapers, but products used to manage adult incontinence can be just as or more costly and necessary for a longer period of the life course, creating an even larger economic burden for the millions of adults who rely on them daily.[10] One survey found that nearly three in four (72 percent) adult respondents struggled to buy incontinence products, while two in three (66 percent) reported having to choose between buying incontinence products and other basic needs such as food or electricity. Half of adult respondents reported stretching incontinence products, limiting fluid intake, and missing important events because they couldn't afford incontinence products.[11] Lack of access to sufficient incontinence supplies is associated with the same harms as infant diaper need, including health problems like urinary tract and skin infections as well as shame, stigma, and stress. Available at very few diaper banks and other basic needs organizations like food banks and not typically covered by Medicare, ongoing costs of these products add up very quicky, especially for adults with lower fixed incomes.

In envisioning supportive programs and policies to address diaper need, we must recognize that the need for diapers does not end with toilet training. For some, the need for diapers is lifelong from birth to old age.

For most of us, just as we begin our lives in diapers, we will end our lives in diapers too. Recognizing diapers as medically necessary would go a long way in carving out space in the social safety net for the incontinence management needs of those of all ages. It would also recognize that diapers are essential for maintaining health in its many forms—physical, mental, social, and emotional.

Second, officially designating diapers as medically necessary would be an important step toward removing remaining diaper taxes at the local, state, and federal levels. It is up to municipalities and states whether to tax diapers, and many still do by categorizing diapers as a discretionary paper product rather than a necessary healthcare item, clothing, or hygiene product, as they are classified in states without diapers taxes. As a qualified medical expense, diaper costs could potentially be deducted from income taxes. Families would save around five dollars or more each month on the typical diaper bill. California repealed its 7.25 percent state diaper tax—the highest in the nation at the time—in 2020 as I was doing research for this book. Before the repeal the typical family that purchased diapers spent well over $100 a year in diaper taxes alone. The change not only saved families sorely needed income, but it also chipped away at the stigma of diaper need. Most mothers I interviewed in 2019 were still buying diapers when the tax was repealed, and they represented the thousands of families in the state who saved five to ten dollars each month on their diaper bills. It was a seemingly small but significant step in gaining a greater sense that their state government wanted to recognize and reduce—rather than tax—their struggles as parents just trying to take care of their children. That half of states still tax diapers means that there is work yet to be done in reducing the economic burden of diapers resulting from governments generating revenue by essentially taxing parenting, childrearing, and carework.

Third, given what mothers shared with me about the symbolic importance of diapers, designating diapers as medically necessary would align political stances on diapers with parents' understandings of the centrality of diapers in their caregiving experiences. Diapers are a basic bodily need of early childhood, not a discretionary expense that families can somehow manage without. Deeming diapers as discretionary has fiscal repercussions that do more than increase the economic costs of diapering for poor families. They also increase the emotional costs of diaper need by invalidating parents' struggles and sacrifices to provide them.

5. Tax Credits, Child Welfare Laws, and Broader Policies for Real Diaper Need Change

Beyond policies targeting diapers specifically, there are several other policy arenas we could look to as we strategize how to reduce not only diaper need but also many of the negative ripple effects associated with it. The COVID-19 pandemic greatly exacerbated diaper need, as single mothers of color with young children were most likely to struggle with lost work and cut hours, while diaper prices significantly increased.[12] In the pandemic's wake, diaper banks received up to six times as many requests for diapers from families coping with job loss, reduced employment, and limited diaper supplies in stores. Amid these challenges short-term policy changes implemented during the early phases of COVID-19 taught us an important lesson about expanded child tax credits, a proven policy for addressing child poverty. During the latter half of 2021 the Child Tax Credit (CTC) program sent monthly payments of $250 to $300 per child to thirty-six million households with more than sixty-one million children, effectively cutting the child poverty rate in half.[13] More than nine out of ten families spent their credits on essentials, including food, utilities, housing, education, clothing, and yes, diapers.[14]

But when Congress failed to make the expanded CTC permanent for 2022, 3.7 million more children fell back into poverty.[15] Although we cannot be certain of the connection between cuts to the CTC and evidence of higher rates of diaper need immediately thereafter, there is likely a link. Permanently expanding the CTC as well as the Earned Income Tax Credit would offer an influx of funding to low- and moderate-income households with children. But many of the highest-need families do not receive these funds because they are dependent on tax filings and having income to which a tax refund can be applied. The poorest families are therefore not eligible. In addition, the more complicated a family's structure, the more difficult it is to prove eligibility, which can result in the benefit not reaching children living in the most fluid or complex family circumstances. Rethinking how we could increase and distribute tax credits to get more cash into the hands of more families so that they could buy basic needs would go a long way in reducing diaper need.

Even better, creating a universal, nonwork-based child allowance or guaranteed basic income would offer another set of resources for cash-strapped families, as research shows that families receiving monthly unconditional cash transfers spend much of the money on investments in children, including childcare, books, and diapers.[16] Allowing families access to unrestricted money to buy childcare basics based on their own assessments of their children's needs will help generate social trust and dismantle long-standing stigma about the morality and deservingness of poor and low-income families.

Child welfare laws are another policy area where we might find ways to reduce diaper need and assuage mothers' well-founded fears that their children could be taken from them for lacking adequate diapers. Most child maltreatment cases, including those deemed dangerous enough to warrant child removal, are not cases of abuse but rather neglect, which is closely linked to poverty.[17] In California, the state with the greatest number of children, not providing adequate housing, food, or other basic needs, even when parents are making every effort to do so, could lead to lost custody of children. Yet there is an important difference between whether a child has unmet needs due to family financial constraints and parents' inability to provide or because of parental unwillingness to care for their children. Most states don't make this key distinction; more than half do not exempt financial constraints that prevent meeting children's needs from state definitions of child maltreatment.[18] A child welfare system that connects parents with necessary resources, including diapers, rather than threatening family separation would be a system that truly promotes child welfare.

Ultimately any effort to broaden political conceptions of need and social safety nets to account for diapers and similar hygiene items necessary for health, cleanliness, autonomy, social participation, and dignity will be a significant step toward addressing the diaper despair that infuses the lives of so many families. If I learned anything from mothers and their policy recommendations, it's that a diaper is indeed more than a diaper. It's essential for recognizing what makes us human with bodies that leak and excrete, our shared hygiene norms and social connections, and our mutual responsibilities to provide and care for one another and the generations that follow.

. . . . .

On my desk sits a single diaper. Its tiny dimensions easily fit in the palm of my hand. Its pastel colors, whimsical cartoon character imprint, and lingering baby powder scent bring back memories of when my newborn daughter was small enough to wear it. It's the sole diaper I saved from the first pack of diapers I bought as I was preparing for her arrival. It sat on my desk as I conducted all the interviews for this book. More than a memento, it was a reminder of why I was doing this research. It has been my constant reminder not to take for granted the importance of a single diaper. One remaining clean diaper was all some mothers had when I spoke with them. After all, as mothers taught me, every diaper counts when you don't know where your baby's next diaper is coming from. It reminds me that every diaper represents a history of the long-standing inequalities that shaped diapering and the technological innovations and social trends that fundamentally changed it along the way.

That lone diaper represents many possible futures from which we can still choose. Will nearly all diapers of the future continue to live in landfills for centuries or pollute land and water, as used disposable diapers of the past and present do today? Or will we finally be able to create and use a low-cost diaper that leaves no environmental trace? The disposable diapers we and our parents used to diaper their babies will continue to decompose in landfills for the next twenty generations. But the diapers our children and grandchildren will use don't need to. Our babies—both the children we bear and those we have a collective responsibility for—were born into a world where it's likely that they will be the victims of diaper need, a likelihood that continues to grow.

The diaper on my desk signifies the privilege of being able to save even a single diaper for posterity's sake. But I like to think that it also symbolizes another possible future, one where no child or parent suffers diaper despair. We have the resources and power. Now we just need the collective commitment to a future where no one is forced to live diaper to diaper.

APPENDIX A   Methods

The seeds of this book were planted during interviews I conducted for a previous research project on poor fathers participating in a publicly funded program intended to promote marginalized men's economic opportunities and parental involvement.[1] I never intended to discuss diapers. Yet when I asked fathers what brought them to the program, most of them told me that part of the reason was because they got free diapers. As I analyzed my interview data and wrote about my findings, I tried to find citable published research on low-income families' struggles to afford diapers.

At that time, in 2015, there were only a handful of articles on what I would come to know as diaper need and few people studying its prevalence and impacts. Four in five states taxed diapers. It was rare for policymakers even to be aware of diaper need, much less trying to do something about it. Those who tried met quick defeat or disinterest among other public officials. Few family service organizations distributed diapers, pediatric healthcare providers rarely asked families if they had sufficient diapers, and parents would have been hard-pressed to find diaper resources in their communities. References to diaper need in the popular media were scant. Most scholars of low-income families and safety net policies, including me, failed to acknowledge diaper need as a fundamental part of raising young children among families in poverty. All the while, many of those families were silently struggling with a pervasive problem that far too few people in positions of power were working to fix.

I had found my next research project. Or rather, it had found me. I soon learned that there was a dedicated group of people who were very knowledgeable about diaper need and its larger repercussions and consequently working hard to address it. Since 2011 the National Diaper Bank Network has advocated for awareness of diaper need, promoted policies to address diaper need, educated and connected diaper bankers, and offered very low-cost diapers and bulk diaper purchasing programs for diaper banks. In the almost decade that I have studied diaper need, many things have changed. Both the research on diaper need and the availability of diaper resources have increased exponentially. Diaper legislation has been introduced in every state, fewer than half of states still tax diapers, and there is a multiyear, multimillion-dollar federal evaluation of diaper distribution. Every state has at least one official diaper bank, and most communities have numerous pantries available. I kept a running list of diaper resources in my own city of Fresno, California, where in 2015 only a small group of community organizations gave out free diapers to families in need. Now that list is so long and varied that I can't keep track. Not only has the number of diaper resources increased and diversified but so have their sources. Parents and caregivers can now access diapers through food banks, schools, colleges and universities, basic needs centers, doctors' offices, nursing facilities, hospitals, specialty clinics, pregnancy centers, prenatal and postpartum service organizations, childcare centers, and many other locations.

Nearly every major national media outlet—from the *New York Times* and *CNN* to the *Washington Post* and *TIME*—has covered diaper need and the growing national diaper bank movement. More children's hospitals and pediatricians are asking parents whether they have enough diapers on intake and discharge forms, just as they ask about food. This research has allowed me to be part of a crucial conversation with leaders of community benefit organizations, policymakers, pediatricians, nurses, educators, journalists, and community members wanting to know what they can do to help. Knowing that more than one in three families with young children struggle with diaper need and that one in four college students are parents or caregivers for minor children, I proposed creating a diaper pantry on my own campus called Diapers for Degrees as part of our university food cupboard. I'm delighted each time I see a student carrying a package of diapers they just received, knowing that those diapers are likely as crucial for their educational success as the books in their backpacks.

When Diapers for Degrees became a reality thanks to the commitment and hard work of administrators, staff, and colleagues who implemented the idea, in some small way I became a diaper banker myself. Though I have been inspired by so many people who study, write about, and advocate for supports and solutions to diaper need, here I want to highlight those two groups of individuals who inspired me most and whose diaper stories form the foundation of this book: mothers and diaper bankers. In what follows, I provide additional methodological detail about how I collected these stories and demographic characteristics of those who were gracious enough to share their stories with me. I conclude with an overview of how I systematically coded this data while maintaining focus on mothers' and diaper bankers' lived experience expertise as the empirical foundation of this book.

INTERVIEWING MOTHERS

I interviewed seventy parents experiencing diaper need from January 2018 to September 2019. These in-depth qualitative interviews took place over the phone. I recruited interviewees by distributing flyers to family and healthcare service providers, including WIC offices, hospitals, and postnatal support programs, and in social media groups for low-income parents. Anyone who self-identified as struggling to access diapers and who had primary responsibilities for a child in diapers, including people preparing to care for an unborn child, qualified for the study. I also utilized snowball sampling by encouraging interviewees to share my contact information with others who were eligible.

Recruitment materials did not specify any eligibility criteria related to race, income, or gender. I used gender-neutral language ("parents" and "caregivers") and images (a close-up picture of adult hands changing a child's diaper) on all recruitment materials. Despite this, only two men responded to interview requests during a nine-month period. During that same time more than seventy women contacted me to discuss their experiences with diaper need. To have more men represented in the sample, I next targeted fathering programs, diaper banks, and other social service organizations for recruitment using flyers specifically asking about fathers. This led to one additional respondent who identified as a man, and he asked his wife most of the questions during the interview.

Although initial recruitment efforts focused on service organizations serving mothers, which not surprisingly generated a sample of mostly women, subsequent unsuccessful efforts to recruit more fathers point to how diaper work is a form of care labor performed predominantly by women. That the sample was ultimately so skewed according to gender, despite targeted efforts to recruit men, is a finding itself about the highly gendered nature of diaper work. I ultimately chose to focus the analysis on women's performance of diaper work and did not include data from the three respondents who identified as men. Given that all caregiver interviewees included in the analysis identified as women and as primary parents/guardians, including two custodial grandmothers, I refer to respondents as "mothers" in line with language they used to describe their relationships to children for whom they struggled to access diapers.

Interviews with mothers lasted thirty to seventy minutes, with most lasting approximately one hour. I asked mothers about their family and financial situations (How would you describe your household's current money situation?); diapering practices (What kind of diapers do you use? How many per day?); experiences of diaper need (If you have ever run out of diapers, what did you do? Do you use any strategies to make diapers last longer?); strategies for accessing diapers (How do you get diapers or diaper money?); effects of diaper need on caregiving identities and experiences (How do diapers shape your experiences of parenting? How do diapers affect your relationship with your child(ren)? Does the diaper situation shape how you think about yourself as a parent?); and individual and family demographic and household data. Mothers each received $25 cash compensation from me via in-person delivery or mail to recognize the value of their time and to offset any costs associated with participation.

Most mothers (87 percent) were women of color living in poor households; 44 percent (31) of mothers identified as Latina/Hispanic, 24 percent (17) as African American/Black, 13 percent (9) as mixed race/multiracial, 13 percent (9) as white/Caucasian, and 6 percent (4) as Asian/Asian American. Mothers' mean age was twenty-nine years. In 2018 a two-person household, the smallest in the sample, was considered poor if they had an annual income of $16,460 or less.[2] The sample's mean annual income of $9,564 meant that almost all mothers and their children lived below the poverty line, and many near or under the threshold of deep poverty for a three-person household, which was $10,390 in 2018. The average monthly diaper bill for mothers who disclosed a specific amount was $66 (ranging from $22 to $175), or 8 percent of the mean household income. All mothers resided in California, most in urban or suburban areas.

A total of 26 (37 percent) mothers were single, 20 (29 percent) were dating or cohabiting, and 24 (34 percent) were married. A total of 12 (17 percent) mothers had less than a high school diploma, 21 (30 percent) had a diploma or GED, 30 (43 percent) had some college or vocational school, 6 (9 percent) had a college degree, and 1 (1 percent) had a graduate degree. Nearly two-thirds (66 percent) of mothers were unemployed, 24 percent (17) were part-time employed, and 10 percent (7) were employed full-time. Although I didn't ask about mothers' immigration or documentation status, ten mothers revealed that they were either born outside the United States and/or members of immigrant families.

Because telephone interviews do not allow for the collection of nonverbal and other contextual data and presumably compromise rapport and the ability to probe for clarification, such interviews are often deemed an inferior alternative to face-to-face interviews. However, evidence does not suggest that they produce less valid data, and phone interviews may allow for even greater rapport and respondent comfort, especially when interviewing marginalized women about sensitive topics.[3] Phone interviews seemed less intrusive and more convenient for mothers, most of whom were providing childcare, including diapering, during the interviews. This provided an in-the-moment opportunity for mothers to reflect on their thoughts and feelings about diaper need. Phone interviews also likely enabled a more diverse group of mothers to participate, including those who were geographically dispersed and those who were living in circumstances that would have made in-person interviews less feasible, including homelessness, cramped housing, and lack of transportation. Most mothers were in their homes during interviews, but many spoke to me from shelters, automobiles, healthcare facilities, and workplaces. Three in four mothers had children present during interviews. Phone interviews allowed for our conversations to be more embedded in the daily rhythms of mothers' lives, allowing for different, not necessarily less, contextual data than the kind I might have collected had we spoken in person.

Mothers had multiple demands on their time and attention during interviews, including their own children and my questions. To mitigate mothers' stress and allow for additional time to reflect on their answers, I offered mothers opportunities to pause the interviews for childcare and other needs. Knowing that they could call me right back at their convenience, rather than having me sit awkwardly in their personal spaces, helped us to maintain rapport while respecting all that mothers were managing in their daily lives. Ultimately, given the focus of this research and mothers' constrained circumstances, opting for phone interviews not only allowed for greater convenience but also, I believe, enabled me to collect better data about lived experiences of diaper need and the lives of those who experience it.

I was also mindful of how interviewer characteristics influenced the data I collected. As a white, highly educated, native-born, affluent woman asking questions of low-income mothers, most of whom were women of color, I carefully considered how social distance shaped interview encounters. Due to the contact information included on recruitment materials, mothers knew my professional affiliation, level of education, and job title prior to interviews. Because I deliberately chose to use audio recordings without videos for mothers' convenience and ease of access, neither mothers nor I had any visual data about one another to signal the other's gender, race, age, or other characteristics. Mothers never inquired about my race, but many were curious about my age, and most asked questions about whether I was a mother. Sharing with them that I had a child, especially one in the middle of toilet training, was a key source of rapport. Despite being mostly an outsider to their social worlds, I connected with respondents over having a shared insider status as mothers of young children.[4]

I tried to remain cognizant of how mothers' and my experiences of diapering radically diverged due to distinct racial and economic social positions, and how my multiple forms of privilege protected my diapering practices from stigma and scrutiny. I was also mindful of power dynamics and the likelihood that mothers would perceive my interests as aligned with public aid and child welfare systems. I emphasized the value of mothers' experiential expertise and that my goal was to understand their "diaper stories" and efforts to manage diaper need without judgment and with the intent to convey their perspectives accurately and respectfully while protecting their confidentiality.

INTERVIEWING DIAPER BANKERS

I interviewed forty individuals involved in diaper distribution and advocacy—those I call *diaper bankers* throughout the book—between August 2017 and December 2019. To capture the experiences and perspectives of those geographically dispersed across the United States, I opted for phone interviews for diaper bankers. Like mothers who were doing childcare and diapering during many of the interviews, phone interviews with diaper bankers allowed for in-the-moment opportunities for experiential reflection as they were directly engaged in diaper-banking activities, including wrapping diapers, moving or arranging diaper supplies, and traveling to collect or deliver diapers.

I recruited diaper bankers and advocates from twenty-five different states using the National Diaper Bank Network member registry, purposively selected to maximize geographical diversity across northern, eastern, southern, and western United States regions. Most were directors and/or founders of their respective diaper banks, which ranged in size from small pantries that distributed 300 diapers monthly to the nation's largest diaper banks that distributed more than 250,000 diapers weekly. Of those interviewed, 7 (18 percent) worked with banks that distributed cloth diapers, and one ran an exclusively cloth diaper bank. Interviews with diaper bankers lasted fifty to one hundred minutes, with an average length of seventy minutes. These interviews focused on views of diaper need (Why do you think parents struggle with diaper need? How does your organization address diaper need?); experiences with parents and partner organizations (How does your organization distribute diapers? What are your eligibility requirements?); and advocacy (Are you involved in political efforts to address diaper need? What do you say to potential donors or lawmakers?). I personally donated $20 to each interviewee's diaper bank as a token of my appreciation for their time and contributions to the research.

Most diaper bankers were white, middle-age, middle-class women, and hence my own positionality aligned more closely with diaper bankers' than with mothers'. Still, when asked, sharing that I had a child in diapers was a key source of rapport with diaper bankers, 80 percent of whom were parents. A total of 33 (83 percent) identified as white, 5 (15 percent) as African American or Black, 1 (2 percent) as Hispanic, and 1 (2 percent) as multiracial. Diaper bankers' average age was forty-eight years. Of the diaper bankers interviewed, 33 (83 percent) were women, 6 (15 percent) were men, and 1 (2 percent) was nonbinary. Among them, 33 diaper bankers were college graduates (83 percent; 14 of these also had graduate or professional degrees), 6 (15 percent) had some college, and 1 (2 percent) had a high diploma. Most (27) were involved in local, state, and/or national diaper advocacy activities, including lobbying and legislative testimony. Overall, diaper bankers were significantly more privileged than the families they served and the mothers I interviewed. Although it's worth noting that many diaper bankers became involved in diaper banking only after a period of significant upward mobility, as they themselves were inspired to become involved in diaper distribution due to their own experiences with diaper need.

That I recruited diaper bankers from among those banks listed on the National Diaper Bank Network (NDBN) member directory likely shaped my findings in several key ways that I should note. First, the NDBN has specific requirements for member diaper banks, including an application process that requires applicants to demonstrate "nonprofit best practices" and diaper program benchmarks related to governance, participation, fundraising, finance, and advocacy.[5] Thus representatives from NDBN member banks were likely those involved with relatively older, larger, and more established diaper banks, which may not have been representative of the full array of diaper-distribution organizations across the country.

Second, the NDBN, though explicitly nonpartisan, promotes liberal political perspectives of diapers as a basic necessity, diaper insecurity as rooted in systematic inequities and oppression, and diaper need as a social problem deserving of redress through broader policy intervention.[6] Drawing exclusively from the membership list likely led to recruitment of diaper bankers with relatively more collective versus individualistic understandings of the causes and consequences of and effective solutions to poverty and diaper insecurity.

Third, recruiting through the NDBN list meant that those I interviewed were directly involved in diaper distribution to organizations and/or families. This may have resulted in an oversampling of those who preferred giving families in-kind diaper aid through goods or services rather than or in addition to other kinds of direct cash support for diapers such as vouchers. Nevertheless, I was able to interview diaper bankers involved with banks and pantries of various sizes and operational and governing structures as well as those who expressed a range of views about root causes of diaper need and potential solutions. This suggests that there was some diversity of experiences and viewpoints among diaper bankers recruited from the same directory.

DATA ANALYSIS AND TRUSTWORTHINESS

I used an abductive analytical approach that relied on knowledge of previous literature to deductively shape the research questions and interview guides, while remaining open to inductive findings and explanations that emerged from the data.[7] With mothers' and diaper bankers' explicit permission and consent, all interviews were digitally recorded and fully transcribed. I took extensive notes during interviews and ethnographic observations and wrote thematic and methodological notes immediately after each interview and observation.

Using a combination of word-processing, spreadsheet, and concept-mapping software, I coded these notes, transcripts, and memos through a flexible coding process.[8] First, I coded for broad topics by applying index codes and a priori attributes to each paired transcript and memo, which allowed me to generate cross-case memos and a set of analytic codes. Second, I applied these analytic codes and generated new attributes by comparing respondents' references to these themes across the body of data. Finally, to ensure that accounts of the data met the threshold for theoretical validity and cross-case reliability, I reviewed the data for alternative explanations and negative cases that did not align with general trends.

I employed numerous strategies to ensure trustworthiness of the data.[9] For credibility I recruited respondents who experienced diaper need and those working to address it from a variety of diaper-distribution organizations. During interviews I positioned respondents as the experts of their own experiences and used probes, iterative questioning, and on-the-spot member checks to confirm data accuracy. To reveal the extent of transferability, I offer contextual information about respondents. For dependability and confirmability, I have provided methodological detail here. Opting for phone interviews meant forgoing opportunities for observations of participants' experiences and how their verbal accounts corresponded to their behaviors. Lack of visual and contextual data also meant that I had little opportunity to confirm mothers' descriptions of their living conditions and family situations and diaper bankers' activities. I was interested less in the veracity of mothers' narratives than their understandings of diaper insecurity and its impacts on their parenting identities and experiences.

For diaper bankers I was most interested in how they explained diaper need and justified and advocated for diaper distribution. Hence my analytic focus was more on what mothers and diapers bankers think and say, not necessarily what they do. Rather than allowing for claims of causality or verification of how much respondents' accounts aligned with what actually happened, this method captured the interpretive aspects of how they presented themselves as mothers managing diaper need and diaper bankers working to address it.[10] The next appendix provides details for how you can become involved in these efforts—ranging from small steps like donating unused diapers to more substantial ones like becoming a diaper banker yourself—should reading this book spark your own interest.

Getting Involved

WHAT YOU CAN DO IF YOU'RE INSPIRED TOO

If you are interested in promoting awareness of diaper need or getting involved in diaper distribution, this appendix provides information for how to begin, starting with quick talking points that you can share with others to convey what diaper need is, why it matters, and how it helps us understand strategies for addressing poverty and inequality. Most people have either diapered their own children or been close to a child in diapers. Consequently, in my experience speaking with students, professional groups, community leaders, and other stakeholders, I've found that there is something deeply impactful when they envision a baby without a diaper or a baby in an overworn wet or dirty diaper. It's a social problem people want to do something about and fix, and it can seem more tangible and surmountable than other deeply entrenched inequities.

As many diaper bankers shared with me, diaper need can be a profoundly personal way of talking about poverty and its myriad physical, economic, emotional, and social effects. A desire to address one tangible aspect of poverty is what inspired many to start diaper banking. It wasn't necessarily because they wanted to tackle diaper need specifically, but because they discovered that diapers touch on so many poverty-related problems, including food insecurity, housing instability, job loss, stress, shame, physical and mental health problems, and limited public acknowledgment and support for people's most basic needs.

I don't share mothers' diaper stories in this book just to highlight their hardships, evoke sympathy, or suggest that there are simple solutions to their struggles. I share these stories because they are a significant part of what shapes so many families' lived experiences of poverty, specifically in the United States where there is strong stigma attached to receiving public aid and having children if you're poor. I've also found that other common ways of talking about poverty—such as poverty threshold numbers, which groups are more likely to be poor, and distinctions between absolute and relative poverty—don't seem to resonate with audiences as much as stories of mothers breaking their older children's piggy bank to get change or selling their blood plasma to get desperately needed diaper money. Stories of mothers reusing soiled diapers or diapering their children in newspaper seem to convey a feeling of destitution and despair that definitions, demographics, and statistics about poverty don't.

There's also something unique about diapers that allow people to meaningfully grasp the other side of poverty, which is class privilege. I once organized an event to raise awareness of diaper need that included an activity with dolls and items mothers told me that they had to use in lieu of diapers. On the event table sat paper towels, duct tape, toilet paper, a pillowcase, a dish rag, rubber bands, and a T-shirt. As each person came to the table and read the activity instructions, which asked participants to choose what they would use to diaper their child if they couldn't afford diapers, you could see on their faces the realization of how struggles like diaper need force parents to make unbearable choices. The activity left a lasting lesson about the privilege of not living in diaper poverty, and how it's not just about having more of some things like money, possessions, and opportunities. It's also about having less of others—less worry, less stress, less constant vigilance about every cent spent, and making fewer impossible decisions that no parent should ever have to make, like *Should I diaper my child in toilet paper or a T-shirt?*

If you are ever in a position where you can increase awareness of diaper need, consider the following ten talking points:

1. *Diaper need* refers to when families don't have enough diapers to keep a baby dry, comfortable, and healthy.

2. One in three families in the United States struggle with diaper need.[1] Recent research suggests that the number could be closer to half of families with young children.[2]

3. Almost half of children younger than three in the United States live in low-income or poor families that may struggle to get enough diapers.[3]

4. Diaper need is connected to racial, ethnic, and educational inequalities. It is more common among Black, Latine, and immigrant families and families in which parents struggle with unemployment and do not have a high school diploma.[4]

5. Children without access to enough clean diapers get more infections and rashes and may be irritable and have difficulty sleeping, potentially leading to developmental delays like later crawling or walking.[5]

6. For parents and caregivers, diaper need can cause guilt and anxiety and feelings that they are not good parents. It can also make it harder to buy other essentials like food and medicine and cause parents to miss work or school, contributing to a cycle of poverty.[6]

7. Diaper need can predict postpartum depression among mothers better than housing instability or food insecurity.[7]

8. No government program available in all states provides or pays for diapers, and diapers are still taxed in many states.

9. The average monthly diaper bill is rising and for many families can cost around $100, which is almost half of the value of welfare cash assistance in many states.[8]

10. Cloth diapers are not a feasible solution to diaper need for most families. Most daycares require disposable diapers, and start-up and cleaning costs often make cloth diapering more expensive for poor families than using disposables.

These quick facts about diaper need could be shared as part of a class or community diaper drive project that raises awareness of the problem and collects diapers for those in need. The National Diaper Bank Network (NDBN) offers great resources on diaper drives, including an overview video and the NDBN Diaper Drive Toolkit how-to guide.[9] Produced in partnership with the NDBN, the brief "Individual Blame or Collective Responsibility?" by Elliot Marshall Cohen and colleagues of the FrameWorks think tank provides a helpful overview of common misperceptions and individualistic mind-sets about diaper need and systemic poverty, along with recommendations for how to talk effectively about causes, consequences, and potential solutions.[10]

If you want to make a personal diaper donation, there are likely many organizations in your local community that collect and distribute diapers, including diaper banks, food banks, supply banks, family service organizations, domestic violence support centers, housing programs, healthcare facilities, churches, high schools, colleges and universities, and childcare facilities that serve low-income families. Ask around in your local community to discover who and how they will accept diaper donations. Although in-kind donations of boxed or wrapped diapers are appreciated, most organizations will prefer monetary donations. Because many diaper distributors are part of bulk-purchasing programs or have other ways of buying significantly discounted diapers, a twenty-five dollar donation will buy three to ten times more diapers than a box you personally purchase at retail.

If you prefer to purchase and then donate diapers, it will be tempting to buy the smallest sizes because you get more diapers per dollar. However, infants wear small diaper sizes for only a short period of time, and diaper banks and pantries tend to have more smaller sizes on hand given the lower demand. Diaper bankers invariably told me that the greatest need is for diapers in larger sizes (sizes 3 and up) and disposable training pants for toddlers. In addition to allowing for the bulk purchasing of more diapers, monetary donations allow diaper distribution organizations to buy the sizes they need most given the populations they serve.

If you have leftover disposables, consider donating these to a local diaper bank or pantry. Most diaper banks will accept plastic-wrapped diaper sleeves already unpacked from boxes. Diaper banks may not be able to accept loose diapers given hygiene regulations, but you can ask staff if they know of other ways to utilize unwrapped diapers for families in need. If you have leftover diapers at a childcare facility, ask staff to add them to their emergency supplies closet they can use for families who run out.

If you have gently used cloth diapers you no longer need, consider passing these along to another family, as the environmental impacts of cloth diapers are significantly less when used on multiple children. Although not as common as banks that focus on distributing disposable diapers, some diaper banks specialize in cloth diapers and accept cloth diaper donations from across the United States. One is The Cloth Option, a social-justice cloth diaper collective that distributes cloth diaper sets to families in need and offers classes on cloth diapering.[11] The Cloth Option accepts cloth diaper donations of any size, style, and condition, including those in need of minor repairs. You can coordinate a drop-off with a local volunteer or email them to purchase a shipping label.

If you want to get more directly involved in diaper banking, there are many volunteer opportunities. Most diaper bankers I interviewed kept a waiting list for volunteers, some of which filled up months to nearly a year in advance. You can find out if there is an already established diaper bank in your area by consulting the National Diaper Bank Network's Member Directory.[12] Diaper banks are often in need of volunteers to collect donations, organize diaper drives, distribute diapers to families where they live, and assist with diaper wrapping. If you have an interest in starting your own diaper distribution organization, the National Diaper Bank Network also offers a how-to guide for getting started.

If you're interested in diaper advocacy, a good place to begin is reading the National Diaper Bank Network's advocacy toolkit.[13] The NDBN compiles and updates data by state and creates state-specific infographics on populations of children three years and younger, proportions of families who are poor and low-income and those who receive assistance through safety net programs such as WIC and TANF, and other demographic information relevant to diaper need.[14] There you can find out if your state currently taxes diapers and what other diaper-related policies have been proposed and/or passed in your state. The NDBN also hosts a Diaper Lobby Day each spring in Washington, DC. National Diaper Need Awareness Day is scheduled annually during the last week in September, and it can provide a good opportunity to connect with local lawmakers who might be willing to issue proclamations about the importance of public diaper support. You can get involved in local diaper politics by connecting with diaper bankers in your area, as many are connected to local lawmakers and have experience testifying on behalf of or even proposing diaper legislation. Contacting your government representatives when diaper legislation is on the docket and up for deliberation can be an effective way to promote awareness and advocate for diaper resources and solutions to diaper need, including public funding for diaper distribution and direct assistance for diaper purchases.

There are smaller, but still significant, ways to address diaper need in your profession and community. If you are a healthcare provider, please don't take a diaper without giving a diaper back. Numerous mothers I interviewed reported stress when an infant's still-clean diaper was removed and discarded by a nurse or doctor during a pediatric checkup. Don't assume that all families will have ample diaper supplies on hand to replace the diaper that was taken. It could very well be their last clean diaper. Many pediatricians' offices are now starting to stock and distribute diapers.[15] Ask about potential diaper need at intake and discharge, as many healthcare facilities already do about food insecurity and food resources. Better yet, offer a resource list of diaper support services and organizations available to families in your area.

If you need diapers, in addition to locating diaper banks and pantries in your community, ask about food banks, many of which are starting to collect and distribute diapers in response to frequent requests from families. In fact, many of the diaper bankers I interviewed for this book started diaper distribution organizations after volunteering at food banks that didn't have diaper supplies. If you attend, work at, or otherwise have access to a college or university, check to see if there are basic needs offices, centers, or support resources for parenting and caregiving students. If you are part of a prenatal or postnatal program or other programs that serve families in any capacity, ask if they offer diapers as part of program participation or know of other organizations that provide diapers. Ask any caseworkers with whom you connect, including those for welfare, food stamps, and WIC. Sometimes public aid programs will use additional funding for diaper support, and you may qualify based on your case plan and family and work circumstances.

Finally, please remember that you are not alone in your diaper struggle. With nearly half of US families with young children reporting some level of diaper insecurity, chances are that your friends, family members, neighbors, and coworkers have lived through or will experience the struggle themselves. Also remember that you are not a bad parent for doing what you must to get enough diapers for your child. Let's hope that one day no parent will need to make impossible choices or substantial sacrifices because they are living diaper to diaper.

Notes

CHAPTER 1

1. To protect confidentiality, throughout this book all names and other identifying details have been changed.

2. Belarmino, Malinowski, and Flynn (2021); Belarmino et al. (2022); Belarmino et al. (2024); Smith et al. (2013); Sobowale, Clayton, and Smith (2020).

3. Koball and Jiang (2018).

4. Massengale, Erausquin, and Old (2017b); Raver et al. (2010); Smith et al. (2013).

5. Adalat, Wall, and Goodyear (2007); Sugimura et al. (2009).

6. Shaffer et al. (2022a).

7. Smith et al. (2013).

8. Belarmino et al. (2024).

9. Belarmino et al. (2022); Belarmino et al. (2024); National Diaper Bank Network (2023).

10. Belarmino et al. (2024).

11. Ajmeri and Ajmeri (2016).

12. US Environmental Protection Agency (2020).

13. Salcito (2015).

14. United Kingdom Environment Agency (2008).

15. Schley (2018).

16. National Resource Center for Health and Safety in Child Care and Early Education (2022).

17. Paschall (2018).

18. US Department of Labor (2021).

19. Neuhaus (2013a; 2013b).

20. Thaman and Eichenfield (2014).

21. Dey et al. (2016).

22. National Center for Health Statistics (2022).

23. Austin and Smith (2017); Massengale et al. (2017b).

24. Crouch et al. (2020).

25. Porter and Steefel (2015); Raver et al. (2010); Smith et al. (2013).

26. Ghaedrahmati et al. (2017).

27. Daminger (2019); Silverstein and Sayre (2009); Yoshida (2012).

28. Economic Policy Institute (2020).

29. Tach and Edin (2017).

30. Massengale et al. (2017b).

31. Koball and Jiang (2018).

32. US Department of Agriculture (2021).

33. Bobel (2010).

34. Jervis (2001); Twigg (2000).

35. Hancock (2004:9).

36. Dusheck (2016).

37. Patel et al. (2022).

38. Shrivastava and Thompson (2022).

39. Safawi and Reyes (2021).

40. Center on Budget and Policy Priorities (2023).

41. Halpern-Meekin et al. (2015).

42. Ballon (2000).

43. Thompson, Azevedo-McCaffrey, and Carr (2023).

44. Thompson, Azevedo-McCaffrey, and Carr (2023).

45. Raver et al. (2010); Semega et al. (2020).

46. Azevedo-McCaffrey and Safawi (2022).

47. Bower et al. (2014).

48. Romero and Agénor (2009).

49. US Department of Agriculture (2025).

50. Massengale et al. (2017a).

51. Edin and Shaefer (2015).

52. National Diaper Bank Network (2020).

53. Diani (1992).

54. Massengale et al. (2019).

55. Denham (2021).

56. Wallace, Weir, and Smith (2017).

57. Roberts (2017); Ross and Solinger (2017).
58. Harrison (2022).
59. Collins (2009); Crenshaw (1991); Few-Demo and Allen (2020).

CHAPTER 2

1. Oswald (2012).
2. Grand View Research (2022).
3. Matchar (2018).
4. Thomas (1998).
5. Thaman and Eichenfield (2014).
6. Change-Diapers.org (2016).
7. Smith and Kiger (2004).
8. Cole, Lingeman, and Adolph (2012).
9. Krafchik (2016).
10. Brown (2011).
11. Cable (1972).
12. Cable (1972).
13. Larkin (1988).
14. Larkin (1988).
15. Brown (2011).
16. Hoy (1996:12).
17. Johnson (2006).
18. Johnson (2006).
19. Neuhaus (2011).
20. Lowe (2018).
21. Lowe (2018).
22. Brown (2011).
23. Hoy (1996:xiv).
24. Hoy (1996).
25. Cable (1972).
26. Hoy (1996).
27. Silvers (2011).
28. Smith and Kiger (2004).
29. Strasser (1999).
30. Decwikiel-Kane (1996).
31. Strasser (1999:200).
32. Zelizer (1985).
33. Apple (2006).
34. Conrad (2007).
35. Strasser (1982).

36. Hays (1996).

37. Neuhaus (2013b).

38. Neuhaus (2013b).

39. Neuhaus (2013a:np).

40. Neuhaus (2013b:np).

41. "P&G: Pampers Disposable Diapers, 1960s," Duke University Libraries, Repository Collection and Archives, https://repository.duke.edu/dc/adviews /dmbb12806, accessed March 28, 2023.

42. Neuhaus (2013b).

43. Neuhaus (2013a).

44. Neuhaus (2013b).

45. Neuhaus (2013b).

46. Hayghe (1986).

47. Hays (1996).

48. Williams (2000).

49. Hochschild (1989).

50. Cohn, Livingston, and Wang (2014).

51. Rosenfeld, Denice, and Laird (2016).

52. US Department of Labor (2021).

53. Dotti and Treas (2016).

54. Nobel (1981).

55. Neuhaus (2013b).

56. "Phylicia Rashad & Debbie Allen for Pampers. Doesn't Your Baby Deserve Pampers' Dryness," www.tiktok.com/@retro__dump/video /7279120226103397674, accessed August 26, 2025.

57. "Phylicia Rashad & Debbie Allen for Pampers. Doesn't Your Baby Deserve Pampers' Dryness."

58. Neuhaus (2013a; 2013b).

59. Cohn (2016).

60. Pew Research Center (2015).

61. Neuhaus (2013b).

62. "Pampers Keeps 'Em Drier in the End Zone," Pampers vintage television commercial, www.youtube.com/watch?v=Q7h5Tsnfq44, accessed March 28, 2023.

63. Thank you to Megan Carroll for collaboration on this paragraph, the original version of which appeared as part of Randles and Carroll (2019).

64. Dotti and Treas (2016).

65. Lafley (2013).

66. Neff (2006).

67. Deason (2018).

68. Frazier (2010).

69. Procter & Gamble (2012).

70. Ramachandran quoted in Frazier (2010).

71. "Welcome to the World, Baby," Huggies commercial aired during the Super Bowl, www.youtube.com/watch?v = aaC457-XO9M, accessed September 12, 2022.

72. Morse (2021).

73. Lemelson-MIT (2023).

74. Solarin et al. (2017).

75. Apple (2006).

76. Goode (1999).

77. Kaerts et al. (2012).

78. Horn et al. (2006).

79. Koc et al. (2008).

80. Goode (1999).

81. Centers for Disease Control and Prevention (2022).

82. Wolraich (2016).

83. WHO and UNICEF (2019).

84. Howard (2017).

85. Solarin et al. (2017).

86. Hooman et al. (2013).

87. Sundnes (2018).

88. Gottlieb (2004).

89. Gottlieb (2004).

90. Gottlieb (2017).

91. Binah-Pollak (2014); de Vries and de Vries (1977); Solarin et al. (2017).

92. de Vries and de Vries (1977).

93. Duong, Jansson, and Hellström (2012).

94. Bauer (2006); Schön and Silvén (2007).

95. Walker (2014).

96. Smith and Kiger (2004:157).

CHAPTER 3

1. Hays (1996).

2. Douglas (2002:2).

3. Hays (1996).

4. Collett (2005).

5. Whitson (2019). Other common and likely familiar examples of proprietary eponyms are Chapstick, Kleenex, Velcro, and Xerox.

6. Austin and Smith (2017); Belarmino et al. (2021); Belarmino et al. (2022); Belarmino et al. (2024); Shaffer et al. (2022b).

7. Shaffer et al. (2022a).

8. Lareau (2011).

9. Smith et al. (2013).

10. Austin and Smith (2017); Smith et al. (2013).

11. Smith et al. (2013).

12. Mullainathan and Shafir (2013).

13. Massengale et al. (2017b).

14. Tach and Greene (2014).

15. Kane, Nelson, and Edin (2015).

16. Edin and Nelson (2013); Halpern-Meekin and Talkington (2022); Randles (2020).

17. Massengale et al. (2017b).

18. Cashman (2015).

19. Mendoza (2011).

20. Carstensen and Gunther (2019).

21. Belarmino et al. (2022).

22. Ochoa, Shaefer, and Grogan-Kaylor (2021).

23. Massengale et al. (2022).

24. Annie E. Casey Foundation (2021).

25. Massengale et al. (2022).

26. Orhun and Palazzolo (2019).

27. Mendoza (2011).

28. Institute for Transportation & Development Policy (2019).

29. Dickens and Hughes-Cromwick (2019).

30. Massengale et al. (2022).

31. Massengale et al. (2022).

32. Roberts (2002).

33. Reich (2005); Roberts (2002, 2022).

34. Also see Elliott, Powell, and Brenton (2015).

35. Sarkisian and Gerstel (2004); Stack (1974).

36. Domínguez and Watkins (2003).

37. Collins (1994); Dow (2019).

38. Daminger (2019).

39. Hays (1996); Zelizer (1985).

40. Collett (2005).

41. Edin and Kefalas (2005); Roberts (2002).

42. Lan (2018).

43. Cohen (2017).

44. Randles et al. (2024).

45. Sobowale, Clayton, and Smith (2021).

46. Massengale et al. (2017b).

CHAPTER 4

1. Hinds (1988).
2. Nolte quoted in Hinds (1988).
3. Gilson and Butler (2008).
4. Latham (1999).
5. Okie (1990).
6. Hays (1997).
7. Rathje and Murphy (1992); Salcito (2015).
8. Notten, Gower, and Lewis (2021).
9. Lin et al. (2023).
10. Park et al. (2019).
11. US Consumer Product Safety Commission (2024).
12. Ferguson et al. (2020).
13. Paddison (2021).
14. Jewkes and Geller (2018).
15. Strasser (1999).
16. Mangizvo, Lumbe, and Sibanda (2024).
17. Vidal (2018).
18. Wynes and Nicholas (2017).
19. Hawkins (2006); Strasser (1999).
20. Denham (2021); Grose (2021).
21. Dunaway-Seale (2023).
22. Change-Diapers.org (2016).
23. Neuhaus (2013b).
24. Thaman and Eichenfield (2014).
25. Wels (2012).
26. Babylist Staff (2023).
27. Change-Diapers.org (2016).
28. Industry Research (2020); Odom (2013).
29. Livingston (2018).
30. Takeshita (2014).
31. Atkinson (2014).
32. Kennedy and Kmec (2018). About breastfeeding, see Blum (1999); about home-cooked meals, see Bowen, Brenton, and Elliott (2019).
33. MacKendrick (2014).
34. Braun and Traore (2015).
35. Fong (2023); Roberts (2022).
36. Renkert and Filippone (2023).
37. See "We Believe in a Good Cause," https://believebaby.com/pages/diaper-need, accessed August 28, 2025.
38. Littler (2008).

CHAPTER 5

1. Redd (2014).
2. Bitler and Karoly (2015).
3. Chaudry et al. (2016).
4. Parolin and Filauro (2023); Shrider (2024); Wimer et al. (2024).
5. Forgotten Harvest (2012).
6. Haveman et al. (2015).
7. Hardy, Samudra, and Davis (2019); Parolin (2021).
8. Azevedo-McCaffrey and Safawi (2022).
9. Meyer and Floyd (2020).
10. Shrivastava and Thompson (2022).
11. Purcell (2019).
12. Currie (2006).
13. Halpern-Meekin et al. (2015); Tach et al. (2019).
14. Meyer and Floyd (2020).
15. Smith (2022).
16. US Bureau of Labor Statistics (2023).
17. Wimer et al. (2024).
18. Wimer et al. (2024).
19. European Anti-Poverty Network (2024).
20. Eurostat (2014).
21. Cross-National Data Center (2024).
22. Haveman et al. (2015).
23. Lange et al. (2017).
24. UNICEF (2020).
25. Collyer, Harris, and Wimer (2019); Government of Canada (2024).
26. Parolin (2023).
27. Parolin and Filauro (2023).
28. Khan (2020).
29. Feeding America (2024).
30. Reese (2005).
31. Romero and Agénor (2009).
32. Hays (2003).
33. Kelly, Dreweke, and Gibson (2024).
34. Miller and Tate (2016).
35. Wallace, Weir, and Smith (2017).
36. Rodriguez-Franco (2024).
37. Belarmino et al. (2022).
38. Eifrig (2024).
39. Al-Abdulmunem et al. (2024).
40. Blair-Hamilton and Raphael (2023).

41. Gunja et al. (2024).

42. US Department of Health and Human Services (2024).

43. Guttmacher Institute (2024).

44. Klibanoff (2023).

45. Carrazana (2023).

46. Kruesi (2024).

47. See "Everylife: Our Mission," https://everylife.com/pages/our-mission, accessed August 28, 2025.

48. Author calculation based on Semega et al. (2020).

49. Swete and Lippold (2020).

50. Semega et al. (2020).

51. Urban Institute (2024).

52. Povich (2022).

53. Crawford and Spivack (2017).

CHAPTER 6

1. Massengale et al. (2019).

2. In 2020, the National Diaper Bank Network partnered with the Alliance for Period Supplies, and the annual conference was thereafter named the US Conference on Poverty and Basic Needs.

3. National Diaper Bank Network (2023).

4. National Diaper Bank Network (2023).

5. National Diaper Bank Network (2022a).

6. Poppendieck (1998).

7. Fisher (2017).

8. Fisher (2017).

9. Fisher (2017).

10. Fisher (2017); Martin (2021); Poppendieck (1998).

11. Martin (2021:22).

12. Goldblum (2016).

13. Sherman (2013).

14. Swales et al. (2020).

15. De Souza (2019).

16. De Souza (2019).

17. De Souza (2019); Middleton et al. (2018); Swales et al. (2020).

18. De Souza (2019).

19. Bowen, Brenton, and Elliott (2019).

20. Brucker, Stott, and Phillips (2021).

21. De Souza (2019).

22. Fothergill (2003).

23. Sherman (2021).
24. National Diaper Bank Network (2022b).
25. Raver et al. (2010).
26. National Diaper Bank Network (2022b).
27. Massengale et al. (2022).
28. Sadler et al. (2018).
29. Massengale et al. (2017b).
30. Public Profit (2021).
31. Tach and Edin (2017).
32. Massengale et al. (2017a); Public Profit (2021).
33. Berry and Blatt (2021); Public Profit (2021).
34. Thaman and Eichenfield (2014).
35. Sundnes (2018).
36. Fong (2023).
37. Gray (2002).
38. Poppendieck (1998).
39. Kimberly-Clark (2021).
40. Shah and Gennetian (2024).
41. Halpern-Meekin et al. (2024).
42. Blattman and Niehaus (2014).

CHAPTER 7

1. Calarco (2024).
2. Emam (2024); Porter (2021).
3. National Diaper Bank Network (2023).
4. Smith et al. (2013).
5. Carlson and Neuberger (2021).
6. Carlson, Greenstein, and Neuberger (2017).
7. Purdam, Garratt, and Esmail (2016).
8. Mullainathan and Shafir (2013).
9. Folbre (2008).
10. Coyne et al. (2014).
11. Aeroflow Urology (2023).
12. Kelly (2022); Kim et al. (2022).
13. Trisi (2024).
14. Zippel (2021).
15. Parolin et al. (2021).
16. Gennetian et al. (2024).
17. Sedlak et al. (2010).
18. Williams, Dalela, and Vandivere (2022).

APPENDIX A

1. Randles (2020).
2. US Department of Health and Human Services (2018).
3. Drabble et al. (2016); Novick (2008).
4. Dwyer and Buckle (2009).
5. See "Benefits of Membership," https://nationaldiaperbanknetwork.org/join-our-network/, accessed August 31, 2025.
6. Cohen et al. (2024).
7. Timmermans and Tavory (2012).
8. Deterding and Waters (2021).
9. Shenton (2004).
10. Holstein and Gubrium (1995).

APPENDIX B

1. Smith et al. (2013).
2. National Diaper Bank Network (2023).
3. Koball and Jiang (2018).
4. Raver et al. (2010).
5. Adalat, Wall, and Goodyear (2007); Shaffer et al. (2022a); Sugimura et al. (2009).
6. Porter and Steefel (2015); Randles (2021); Raver et al. (2010); Smith et al. (2013).
7. Smith et al. (2013).
8. Stanley, Floyd, and Hill (2016).
9. See "Host a Diaper Drive," https://nationaldiaperbanknetwork.org/host-a-diaper-drive/, accessed August 31, 2025.
10. Cohen et al. (2024).
11. See "The Cloth Option: A Cloth Diaper Advocacy Group," www.theclothoption.org/, accessed August 31, 2025.
12. See "Member Diaper Banks," https://nationaldiaperbanknetwork.org/member-directory/, accessed August 31, 2025.
13. See "Advocacy Toolkit," https://nationaldiaperbanknetwork.org/advocacy-toolkit/, accessed August 31, 2025.
14. See "State Diaper Statistics: Diaper Need in Your State," https://nationaldiaperbanknetwork.org/state-diaper-statistics/, accessed August 31, 2025.
15. Lee et al. (2025).

References

Adalat, Shazia, David Wall, and Helen Goodyear. 2007. "Diaper Dermatitis Frequency and Contributory Factors in Hospital Attending Children." *Pediatric Dermatology* 24(5):483–488.

Aeroflow Urology. 2023. "New Survey from Aeroflow Urology Reveals over 70% of Consumers Struggle to Afford Diapers for Adults and Children." www .prweb.com/releases/new-survey-from-aeroflow-urology-reveals-over-70-of -consumers-struggle-to-afford-diapers-for-adults-and-children-854958158. Accessed September 13, 2024.

Ajmeri, J. R., and C. J. Ajmeri. 2016. "Developments in the Use of Nonwovens for Disposable Diaper Hygiene Products." In *Advances in Technical Nonwovens*, edited by G. Kellie, 473–496. Sawston, UK: Woodhead.

Al-Abdulmunem, Monirah, Marneena Evans, Sarah Giordano, and Allison Hyra. 2024. "Diapers for Families in Need: An Overview of Federally Funded Approaches to Diaper Distribution [OPRE Report [2024-007]." Office of Planning, Research, and Evaluation, Administration for Children and Families, US Department of Health and Human Services. www.acf.hhs. gov/sites/default/files/ documents/opre/DDDRP-GrantOverviewBrief_ final---updated-September-2024-3.pdf. Accessed December 29, 2024.

Annie E. Casey Foundation. 2021. "Food Deserts in the United States." www .aecf.org/blog/exploring-americas-food-deserts. Accessed January 17, 2023.

Apple, Rima D. 2006. *Perfect Motherhood: Science and Childrearing in America*. New Brunswick, NJ: Rutgers University Press.

Atkinson, Lucy. 2014. "Green Moms: The Social Construction of a Green Mothering Identity via Environmental Advertising Appeals." *Consumption Markets & Culture* 17(6):553–572.

Austin, Anna E., and Megan V. Smith. 2017. "Examining Material Hardship in Mothers: Associations of Diaper Need and Food Insufficiency with Maternal Depressive Symptoms." *Health Equity* 1(1):127–133.

Azevedo-McCaffrey, Diana, and Ali Safawi. 2022. "To Promote Equity, States Should Invest More TANF Dollars in Basic Assistance." Center on Budget and Policy Priorities. www.cbpp.org/research/family-income-support/to-promote-equity-states-should-invest-more-tanf-dollars-in-basic. Accessed February 8, 2022.

Babylist Staff. 2023. "Cloth Diapering 101." Babylist.com. www.babylist.com/hello-baby/cloth-diapering-101. Accessed April 1, 2024.

Baden, Kelly, Joerg Dreweke, and Candace Gibson. 2024. "Clear and Growing Evidence That Dobbs Is Harming Reproductive Health and Freedom." Guttmacher Institute. www.guttmacher.org/2024/05/clear-and-growing-evidence-dobbs-harming-reproductive-health-and-freedom. Accessed August 28, 2025.

Ballon, Marc. 2000. "America Changes Diapers: From Cloth to Disposables." *Los Angeles Times*. www.latimes.com/archives/la-xpm-2000-mar-06-mn-5933-story.html. Accessed September 16, 2022.

Bauer, Ingrid. 2006. *Diaper Free: The Gentle Wisdom of Natural Infant Hygiene.* New York: Plume.

Belarmino, Emily H., Carollyne M. Conway, Jane Kolodinsky, Kaya M. Daylor, and Emma Spence. 2024. "Diaper Need in the United States: A Nationally Representative Study During the COVID-19 Pandemic." *Heliyon* 10(10):e31344.

Belarmino, Emily H., Amy Malinowski, and Karen Flynn. 2021. "Diaper Need Is Associated with Risk for Food Insecurity in a Statewide Sample of Participants in the Special Supplemental Nutrition Program for Women, Infants, and Children (WIC)." *Preventive Medicine Reports* 22:101332.

Belarmino, Emily H., Rachel M. Zack, Lauren A. Clay, and Nick W. Birk. 2022. "Diaper Need During the COVID-19 Pandemic Associated with Poverty, Food Insecurity, and Chronic Illness: An Analysis of a Representative State Sample of Caretakers with Young Children." *Health Equity* 6(1):150–158.

Berry, Winter S., and Steven D. Blatt. 2021. "Diaper Need? You Can Bank on It." *Academic Pediatrics* 21(1):188–189.

Binah-Pollak, Avital. 2014. "Discourses and Practices of Child-Rearing in China: The Bio-Power of Parenting in Beijing." *China Information* 28(1):27–45.

Bitler, Marianne P., and Lynn A. Karoly. 2015. "Intended and Unintended Effects of the War on Poverty: What Research Tells Us and Implications for Policy." *Journal of Policy Analysis and Management* 34(3):639–636.

Blair-Hamilton, Alexis, and Dennis Raphael. 2023. "A Critical Analysis of the Finnish Baby Box's Journey into the Liberal Welfare State: Implications for Progressive Public Policymaking." *Children and Youth Services Review* 149:106926.

Blattman, Christopher, and Paul Niehaus. 2014. "Show Them the Money: Why Giving Cash Helps Alleviate Poverty." *Foreign Affairs* 93(3):117–126.

Blum, Linda. 1999. *At the Breast: Ideologies of Breastfeeding and Motherhood in the Contemporary United States*. Boston: Beacon Press.

Bobel, Chris. 2010. *New Blood: Third-Wave Feminism and the Politics of Menstruation*. New Brunswick, NJ: Rutgers University Press.

Bowen, Sarah, Joslyn Brenton, and Sinikka Elliott. 2019. *Pressure Cooker: Why Home Cooking Won't Solve Our Problems and What We Can Do About It*. New York: Oxford University Press.

Bower, Kelly M., Roland J. Thorpe Jr., Charles Rohde, and Darrell J. Gaskin. 2014. "The Intersection of Neighborhood Racial Segregation, Poverty, and Urbanicity and Its Impact on Food Store Availability in the United States." *Preventive Medicine* 58(1):33–39.

Braun, Yvonne A., and Assitan Sylla Traore. 2015. "Plastic Bags, Pollution, and Identity: Women and the Gendering of Globalization and Environmental Responsibility in Mali." *Gender & Society* 29(6):863–887.

Brown, Kathleen M. 2011. *Foul Bodies: Cleanliness in Early America*. New Haven, CT: Yale University Press.

Brucker, Debra L., Grace Stott, and Kimberly G. Phillips. 2021. "Food Sufficiency and the Utilization of Free Food Resources for Working-Age Americans with Disabilities During the COVID-19 Pandemic." *Disability and Health Journal* 14(4):101153.

Cable, Mary. 1972. *Little Darlings: A History of Child Rearing in America*. New York: Scribner.

Calarco, Jessica. 2024. *Holding It Together: How Women Became America's Safety Net*. New York: Portfolio/Penguin Random House.

Carlson, Steven, Robert Greenstein, and Zoë Neuberger. 2017. "WIC's Competitive Bidding Process for Infant Formula Is Highly Cost-Effective." Center for Budget Policies and Priorities. www.cbpp.org/research/wics-competitive -bidding-process-for-infant-formula-is-highly-cost-effective. Accessed September 13, 2024.

Carlson, Steven, and Zoë Neuberger. 2021. "WIC Works: Addressing the Nutrition and Health Needs of Low-Income Families for More Than Four Decades." Center on Budget and Policy Priorities. www.cbpp.org/research /food-assistance/wic-works-addressing-the-nutrition-and-health-needs-of- low-income-families. Accessed September 13, 2024.

Carrazana, Chabeli. 2023. "For Years, Republican States Wouldn't Pass Diaper Laws. The End of Abortion Protections Changed That." *The 19th*.

https://19thnews.org/2023/07/state-legislatures-diaper-taxes-abortion
-rights/. Accessed July 18, 2024.

Carstensen, Fred, and Peter Gunther. 2019. "Better Health for Children
and Increased Opportunities for Families: The Social and Economic
Impacts of the Diaper Bank of Connecticut." https://nationaldiaper
banknetwork.org/wp-content/uploads/2019/02/The-Social-and-
Economic-Impacts-of-the-Diaper-Bank-of-Connecticut.pdf. Accessed
January 16, 2023.

Cashman, Kevin. 2015. "Policies Like the Hygiene Assistance for Families of
Infants and Toddlers Act Will Help the Poor Pay for Diapers." Center for
Economic and Policy Research. www.cepr.net/the-hygiene-assistance-for
-families-of-infants-and-toddlers-act-will-help-the-poor-pay-for-diapers/.
Accessed December 19, 2022.

Center on Budget and Policy Priorities. 2023. "Policy Basics: The Earned
Income Tax Credit." www.cbpp.org/research/policy-basics-the-earned
-income-tax-credit. Accessed December 11, 2024.

Centers for Disease Control and Prevention. 2022. "Clinical Growth Charts."
National Center for Health Statistics. www.cdc.gov/growthcharts/clinical
_charts.htm#Set1. Accessed September 9, 2022.

Change-Diapers.org. 2016. "Cloth Diaper User Demographics—The Survey
Results." https://change-diapers.com/cloth-diaper-user-demographics
-survey-results/. Accessed July 7, 2022.

Chaudry, Ajay, Christopher Wimer, Suzanne Macartney, Lauren Frohlich,
Colin Campbell, Kendall Swenson, Don Oellerich, and Susan Hauan.
2016. *Poverty in the United States: 50-Year Trends and Safety Net Impacts.*
Office of the Assistant Secretary for Planning and Evaluation, US Department of Health and Human Services. https://aspe.hhs.gov/sites/default/files
/private/pdf/154286/50YearTrends.pdf. Accessed July 18, 2024.

Cohen, Bernard. 2017. "Differential Diagnosis of Diaper Dermatitis." *Clinical
Pediatrics* 56(5):16S–22S.

Cohen, Elliot Marshall, Theresa Miller, Andrew Volmert, Rae Jereza, Nana
Baffoe, Charlotte Shaw, and Erin Lowe. 2024. *Individual Blame or Collec-
tive Responsibility?: Existing Mindsets about Diaper Need and Systemic
Poverty.* Washington, DC: FrameWorks Institute. www.frameworksinstitute
.org/resources/individual-blame-or-collective-responsibility/. Accessed
January 2, 2025.

Cohn, D'Vera. 2016. "It's Official: Minority Babies Are the Majority Among the
Nation's Infants, But Only Just." Pew Research Center. www.pewresearch
.org/short-reads/2016/06/23/its-official-minority-babies-are-the-majority
-among-the-nations-infants-but-only-just/. Accessed September 22, 2024.

Cohn, D'Vera, Gretchen Livingston, and Wendy Wang. 2014. "After Decades of
Decline, a Rise in Stay-at-Home Mothers." Pew Research Center. www

.pewresearch.org/social-trends/2014/04/08/after-decades-of-decline-a
-rise-in-stay-at-home-mothers/. Accessed August 30, 2022.

Cole, Whitney G., Jesse M. Lingeman, and Karen E. Adolph. 2012. "Go Naked: Diapers Affect Infant Walking." *Developmental Science* 15(6):783–790.

Collett, Jessica L. 2005. "What Kind of Mother Am I? Impression Management and the Social Construction of Motherhood." *Symbolic Interaction* 28(3):327–347.

Collins, Patricia Hill. 1994. "Shifting the Center: Race, Class, and Feminist Theorizing about Motherhood." In *Mothering: Ideology, Experience, and Agency*, edited by E. N. Glenn, G. Chang, and L. R. Forcey, 45–65. New York: Routledge.

Collins, Patricia Hill. 2009. *Black Feminist Thought: Knowledge, Consciousness, and the Politics of Empowerment*. Second edition. New York: Routledge.

Collyer, Sophie, David Harris, and Christopher Wimer. 2019. "Left Behind: The One-Third of Children in Families Who Earn Too Little To Get the Full Child Tax Credit." Center on Poverty & Social Policy, Columbia Population Research Center. Volume 3, no. 6.

Conrad, Peter. 2007. *The Medicalization of Society: On the Transformation of Human Conditions into Treatable Disorders*. Baltimore, MD: John Hopkins University Press.

Coyne, Karin S., Alan Wein, Sean Nicholson, Marion Kvasz, Chieh-I Chen, and Ian Milsom. 2014. "Economic Burden of Urgency Urinary Incontinence in the United States: A Systematic Review." *Journal of Managed Care Pharmacy* 20(2):130–140.

Crawford, Bridget J., and Carla Spivack. 2017. "Tampon Taxes, Discrimination, and Human Rights." *Wisconsin Law Review* 491:550.

Crenshaw, Kimberlé. 1991. "Mapping the Margins: Intersectionality, Identity Politics, and Violence Against Women of Color. *Stanford Law Review* 43(6):1241–1299.

Cross-National Data Center. 2024. "Inequality and Poverty Key Figures." www .lisdatacenter.org/lis-ikf-webapp/app/search-ikf-figures. Accessed July 19, 2024.

Crouch, Elizabeth, Jennifer Jones, Melissa Strompolis, and Melissa Merrick. 2020. "Examining the Association between ACEs, Childhood Poverty and Neglect, and Physical and Mental Health." *Children and Youth Services Review* 116(5):105–155.

Currie, Janet M. 2006. *The Invisible Safety Net: Protecting the Nation's Poor Children and Families*. Princeton, NJ: Princeton University Press.

Daminger, Allison. 2019. "The Cognitive Dimension of Household Labor." *American Sociological Review* 84(4):609–633.

De Souza, Rebecca T. 2019. *Feeding the Other: Whiteness, Privilege, and Neoliberal Stigma in Food Pantries*. Cambridge, MA: MIT Press.

de Vries, Marten, and M. Rachel de Vries. 1977. "Cultural Relativity of Toilet Training Readiness: A Perspective from East Africa." *Pediatrics* 60(2):170–177.

Deason, Rachel. 2018. "Why Do Chinese Babies Wear Split-Crotch Pants?" *The Culture Trip*. https://theculturetrip.com/asia/china/articles/why-do-chinese-babies-wear-split-crotch-pants. Accessed April 22, 2022.

Decwikiel-Kane, Dawn. 1996. "Oh, How Diapers Have Changed/The Disposable Changed Diapers for Babies." *Greensboro News & Record*. https://greensboro.com/oh-how-diapers-have-changed-the-disposable-changed-diapers-for-babies/article_a9dd948c-dbfb-5f22-bb22-aab335236d9d.html. Accessed August 15, 2022.

Denham, Hannah. 2021. "Millions Couldn't Afford Diapers Before the Pandemic. Now, Diaper Banks Can't Keep Up." *Washington Post*. www.washingtonpost.com/business/2021/03/01/diaper-banks-pandemic-poverty/. Accessed September 18, 2022.

Deterding, Nicole M., and Mary C. Waters. 2021. "Flexible Coding of In-Depth Interviews: A Twenty-First-Century Approach." *Sociological Methods & Research* 50(2):708–739.

Dey, Swatee, Mike Purdon, Taryn Kirsch, Hans Martin Helbich, Kenny Kerr, Lijuan Li, and Shaoying Zhou. 2016. "Exposure Factor Considerations for Safety Evaluation of Modern Disposable Diapers." *Regulatory Toxicology and Pharmacology* 81:183–193.

Diani, Mario. 1992. "The Concept of Social Movement." *Sociological Review* 40(1):1–25.

Dickens, Matthew, and McPherson Hughes-Cromwick. 2019. "Public Transportation Fare Database." American Public Transportation Association. www.apta.com/research-technical-resources/transit-statistics/fare-database/. Accessed January 17, 2023.

Domínguez, Silvia, and Celeste Watkins. 2003. "Creating Networks for Survival and Mobility: Social Capital Among African American and Latin-American Low-Income Mothers." *Social Problems* 50(1):111–135.

Dotti, Giulia M., and Sani Judith Treas. 2016. "Educational Gradients in Parents' Child-Care Time Across Countries, 1965–2012." *Journal of Marriage and Family* 78(4):1083–1096.

Douglas, Mary. 2002. *Purity and Danger: An Analysis of Concepts of Pollution and Taboo*. New York: Routledge.

Dow, Dawn Marie. 2019. *Mothering While Black: Boundaries and Burdens of Middle-Class Parenthood*. Oakland: University of California Press.

Drabble, Laurie, Karen F. Trocki, Brenda Salcedo, Patricia C. Walker, and Rachael A. Korcha. 2016. "Conducting Qualitative Interviews by Phone: Lessons Learned from a Study of Alcohol Use Among Sexual Minority and Heterosexual Women." *Qualitative Social Work: QSW Research and Practice* 15(1):118–133.

Dunaway-Seale, Jaime. 2023. "Home Prices Are Rising 2x Faster Than Income (New Data)." *Home Bay.* https://homebay.com/income-to-house-price -ratio-2023/. Accessed April 1, 2024.

Duong, Thi Hoa, Ulla-Britt Jansson, and Anna-Lena Hellström. 2012. "Vietnamese Mothers' Experiences with Potty Training Procedure for Children from Birth to 2 Years of Age." *Journal of Pediatric Urology* 9(6):808–814.

Dusheck, Jennie. 2016. "Overflowing Lives: How Urinary Incontinence Changes Us." *Stanford Medicine Magazine.* https://stanmed.stanford.edu /overflowing-lives/. Accessed September 1, 2024.

Dwyer, Sonya Corbin, and Jennifer L. Buckle. 2009. "The Space Between: On Being an Insider-Outsider in Qualitative Research." *International Journal of Qualitative Methods* 8(1):54–63.

Economic Policy Institute. 2020. "Child Care Costs in the United States." www .epi.org/child-care-costs-in-the-united-states/. Accessed September 14, 2022.

Edin, Kathryn, and Maria Kefalas. 2005. *Promises I Can Keep: Why Poor Women Put Motherhood before Marriage.* Berkeley: University of California Press.

Edin, Kathryn, and Timothy J. Nelson. 2013. *Doing the Best I Can: Fatherhood in the Inner City.* Berkeley: University of California Press.

Edin, Kathryn, and H. Luke Shaefer. 2015. *$2.00 a Day: Living on Almost Nothing in America.* Boston: Mariner.

Eifrig, David. 2024. "The Crisis Everyday Americans Are Facing." *Health & Wealth Bulletin.* Stansberry Research. https://stansberryresearch.com /articles/the-crisis-everyday-americans-are-facing. Accessed September 29, 2024.

Elliott, Sinikka, Rachel Powell, and Joslyn Brenton. 2015. "Being a Good Mom: Low-Income, Black Single Mothers Negotiate Intensive Mothering." *Journal of Family Issues* 36(3):351–370.

Emam, Hoda. 2024. "Diapers Are Unaffordable for Many Families. Now States Are Looking to Medicaid for Help." *NBC News.* www.nbcnews.com/health /health-care/rising-costs-make-diapers-unaffordable-many-families-can-medicaid-help-rcna161209. Accessed February 17, 2025.

European Anti-Poverty Network. 2024. "How Is Poverty Measured?" www .eapn.eu/what-is-poverty/how-is-poverty-measured. Accessed July 19, 2024.

Eurostat. 2014. "Europe 2020 Indicators: Poverty and Social Exclusion." https://ec.europa.eu/eurostat/statistics-explained. Accessed July 19, 2024.

Feeding America. 2024. "In Short Supply: Everyday Essentials." www .feedingamerica.org/research/poverty-and-unemployment/in-short-supply. Accessed July 19, 2024.

Ferguson, Lauren, Jonathon Taylor, Michael Davies, Clive Shrubsole, Phil Symonds, and Sani Dimitroulopoulou. 2020. "Exposure to Indoor Air

Pollution Across Socio-Economic Groups in High-Income Countries: A Scoping Review of the Literature and a Modelling Methodology." *Environment International* 143:105748.

Few-Demo, April L., and Katherine R. Allen. 2020. "Gender, Feminist, and Intersectional Perspectives on Families: A Decade in Review." *Journal of Marriage and Family* 82(1):326–345.

Fisher, Andrew. 2017. *Big Hunger: The Unholy Alliance Between Corporate America and Anti-Hunger Groups*. Cambridge, MA: MIT Press.

Folbre, Nancy. 2008. *Valuing Children: Rethinking the Economics of the Family*. Cambridge, MA: Harvard University Press.

Fong, Kelley. 2023. *Investigating Families: Motherhood in the Shadow of Child Protective Services*. Princeton, NJ: Princeton University Press.

Forgotten Harvest. 2012. "Data Driven Detroit: Southeast Michigan Poverty Report." https://datadrivendetroit.org/web_ftp/Presentations/Forgotten_Harvest_Final_Cover.pdf. Accessed July 18, 2024.

Fothergill, Alice. 2003. "The Stigma of Charity: Gender, Class, and Disaster Assistance." *Sociological Quarterly* 44(4):659–680.

Frazier, Mya. 2010. "How P&G Brought the Diaper Revolution to China." *Money Watch: CBS News*. www.cbsnews.com/news/how-pg-brought-the-diaper-revolution-to-china/. Accessed September 1, 2022.

Gennetian, Lisa A., Greg J. Duncan, Nathan A. Fox, Sarah Halpern-Meekin, Katherine Magnuson, Kimberly G. Noble, and Hirokazu Yoshikawa. 2024. "Effects of a Monthly Unconditional Cash Transfer Starting at Birth on Family Investments Among US Families with Low Income." *Nature Human Behavior* 8:1514–1529.

Ghaedrahmati, Maryam, Ashraf Kazemi, Gholamreza Kheirabadi, Amrollah Ebrahimi, and Masood Bahrami. 2017. "Postpartum Depression Risk Factors: A Narrative Review." *Journal of Education and Health Promotion* 6:1–7.

Gilson, Dave, and Kiera Butler. 2008. "A Brief History of the Disposable Diaper." *Mother Jones*. www.motherjones.com/environment/2008/04/brief-history-disposable-diaper/. Accessed March 25, 2018.

Goldblum, Joanne Samuel. 2016. "The Diaper Bank Concept." *Contemporary Pediatrics*. www.contemporarypediatrics.com/view/diaper-bank-concept. Accessed April 1, 2024.

Goode, Erica. 1999. "Two Experts Do Battle over Potty Training." *New York Times*. www.nytimes.com/1999/01/12/us/two-experts-do-battle-over-potty-training.html. Accessed September 1, 2022.

Gottlieb, Alma. 2004. *The Afterlife Is Where We Come From: The Culture of Infancy in West Africa*. Chicago: University of Chicago Press.

Gottlieb, Alma. 2017. "Toilet Training 101 for Parents Who Need To Relax." *Salon*. www.salon.com/2017/11/26/toilet-training-101-for-parents-who-need-to-relax/. Accessed September 1, 2022.

Government of Canada. 2024. "Canada Child Benefit." www.canada.ca/en /revenue-agency/services/child-family-benefits/canada-child-benefit-overview. html. Accessed July 19, 2024.

Grand View Research. 2022. "Baby Diapers Market Size, Share & Trends Analysis Report by Product, 2021–2028." www.grandviewresearch.com /industry-analysis/baby-diapers-market. Accessed July 6, 2022.

Gray, Alison, J. 2002. "Stigma in Psychiatry." *Journal of the Royal Society of Medicine* 95(2):72–76.

Grose, Jessica. 2021. "Living Paycheck to Paycheck, Living Diaper to Diaper." *New York Times*. www.nytimes.com/2021/03/17/parenting/diaper-bank-coronavirus.html. Accessed March 27, 2024.

Gunja, Munira Z., Evan D. Gumas, Relebohile Masitha, and Laurie C. Zephy-rin. 2024. *Insights into the U.S. Maternal Mortality Crisis: An International Comparison*. Commonwealth Fund. www.commonwealthfund.org/ publications/issue-briefs/2024/jun/insights-us-maternal-mortality-crisis-international-comparison. Accessed December 30, 2024.

Guttmacher Institute. 2024. "Interactive Map: US Abortion Policies and Access after Roe." https://states.guttmacher.org/policies/florida/abortion-policies. Accessed July 19, 2024.

Halpern-Meekin, Sarah, Kathryn Edin, Laura Tach, and Jennifer Sykes. 2015. *It's Not Like I'm Poor: How Working Families Make Ends Meet in a Post-Welfare World*. Oakland: University of California Press.

Halpern-Meekin, Sarah, Lisa A. Gennetian, Jill Hoiting, Laura Stilwell, and Lauren Meyer. 2024. "Monthly Unconditional Income Supplements Starting at Birth: Experiences Among Mothers of Young Children with Low Incomes in the U.S." *Journal of Policy Analysis and Management* 43:871–898.

Halpern-Meekin, Sarah, and Adam Talkington. 2022. "'Disconnected' Men: Understanding Men's Joint Roles as Workers and Romantic Partners." *RSF: The Russell Sage Foundation Journal of the Social Sciences* 8(5):98–119.

Hancock, Ange-Marie. 2004. *The Politics of Disgust: The Public Identity of the Welfare Queen*. New York: New York University Press.

Hardy, Bradley L., Rhucha Samudra, and Jourdan A. Davis 2019. "Cash Assistance in America: The Role of Race, Politics, and Poverty." *Review of Black Political Economy* 46(4):306–324.

Harrison, Laura. 2022. *Losing Sleep: Risk, Responsibility, and Infant Sleep Safety*. New York: New York University Press.

Haveman, Robert, Rebecca Blank, Robert Moffitt, Timothy Smeeding, and Geoffrey Wallace. 2015. "The War on Poverty: Measurement, Trends, and Policy." *Journal of Policy Analysis and Management* 34(3):593–638.

Hawkins, Gay. 2006. *The Ethics of Waste: How We Relate to Rubish*. New York: Rowman & Littlefield.

Hayghe, Howard. 1986. "Rise in Mothers' Labor Force Activity Includes Those with Infants." *Monthly Labor Review* 109(2):43–45.

Hays, Constance L. 1997. "In the Diaper Wars, Cloth Has Just About Folded." *New York Times.* www.nytimes.com/1997/02/09/weekinreview/in-the-diaper-wars-cloth-has-just-about-folded. Accessed March 25, 2024.

Hays, Sharon. 1996. *The Cultural Contradictions of Motherhood.* New Haven, CT: Yale University Press.

Hays, Sharon. 2003. *Flat Broke with Children: Women in the Age of Welfare Reform.* New York: Oxford University Press.

Hinds, Michael Decourcy. 1988. "Do Disposable Diapers Ever Go Away?" *New York Times.* www.nytimes.com/1988/12/10/style/consumer-s-world-do-disposable-diapers-ever-go-away.html. Accessed March 25, 2024.

Hochschild, Arlie Russell, with Anne Machung. 1989. *The Second Shift: Working Parents and the Revolution at Home.* London, UK: Penguin.

Holstein, James A., and Jaber F. Gubrium. 1995. *The Active Interview: Qualitative Research Methods.* Thousand Oaks, CA: Sage.

Hooman, Nakysa, Afshin Safaii, Ehsan Valavi, and Zahra Amini-Alavijeh. 2013. "Toilet Training in Iranian Children: A Cross-Sectional Study." *Iranian Journal of Pediatrics* 23(2):154–158.

Horn, Ivor, Ruth Brenner, Malla Roa, and Tina L. Cheng. 2006. "Beliefs About the Appropriate Age for Initiating Toilet Training: Are There Racial and Socioeconomic Differences?" *Journal of Pediatrics* 149(2):165–168.

Howard, Jacqueline. 2017. "How the World Potty Trains." *CNN Health.* www.cnn.com/2017/10/31/health/potty-training-parenting-without-borders-explainer/index.html. Accessed September 1, 2022.

Hoy, Suellen. 1996. *Chasing Dirt: The American Pursuit of Cleanliness.* New York: Oxford University Press.

Industry Research. 2020. "Global Cloth Diapers Market Report, History and Forecast, 2015–2026." www.industryresearch.co/global-cloth-diapers-market-16204022. Accessed July 16, 2022.

Institute for Transportation & Development Policy. 2019. "The High Cost of Transportation in the United States." www.itdp.org/2019/05/23/high-cost-transportation-united-states/. Accessed January 17, 2023.

Jervis, Lori L. 2001. "The Pollution of Incontinence and the Dirty Work of Caregiving in a US Nursing Home." *Medical Anthropology Quarterly* 15(1):84–99.

Jewkes, Stephen, and Martine Gellar. 2018. "Waste Not, Want Not: P&G Venture Aims to Squeeze New Life Out of Italy's Dirty Diapers." *Reuters.* www.reuters.com/article/us-italy-diapers/waste-not-want-not-pg-venture-aims-to-squeeze-new-life-out-of-italys-dirty-diapers-idUSKCN1MR26E/. Accessed March 27, 2024.

Johnson, Steven. 2006. *The Ghost Map: The Story of London's Most Terrifying Epidemic—and How It Changed Science, Cities, and the Modern World.* New York: Riverhead.

Kaerts, Nore, Guido Van Hal, Alexandra Vermandel, and Jean-Jacques Wyndaele. 2012. "Readiness Signs Used to Define the Proper Moment to Start Toilet Training: A Review of the Literature." *Neurourology and Urodynamics* 31:437–440.

Kane, Jennifer B., Timothy J. Nelson, and Kathryn Edin. 2015. "How Much In-Kind Support Do Low-Income Nonresident Fathers Provide? A Mixed-Method Analysis." *Journal of Marriage and Family* 77(3):591–611.

Kelly, Meghan B. 2022. "As Families Feel the Pinch of Inflation, Diaper Banks See Increased Need." www.wbur.org/news/2022/06/01/diaper-banks-inflation-parents-babies-expensive. Accessed September 13, 2024.

Kennedy, Emily Huddart, and Julie Kmec. 2018. "Reinterpreting the Gender Gap in Household Pro-Environmental Behavior." *Environmental Sociology* 4(3):299–310.

Khan, Mariam S. 2020. "Paid Family Leave and Children Health Outcomes in OECD Countries." *Children and Youth Services Review* 116:105259.

Kim, Andrew T., Matt Erickson, Yurong Zhang, and ChangHwan Kim. 2022. "Who Is the 'She' in the Pandemic 'SheCession'? Variation in COVID-19 Labor Market Outcomes by Gender and Family Status." *Population Research and Policy Review* 41(3):1325–1358.

Kimberly-Clark. 2021. "Annual Report." www.kimberly-clark.com/en-s/investors/annual-reports. Accessed November 4, 2023.

Klibanoff, Eleanor. 2023. "Texas House Votes To Repeal Sales Tax on Menstrual Products and Diapers." *Texas Tribune.* www.texastribune.org/2023/05/23/texas-legislature-diaper-tampon-tax. Accessed September 16, 2024.

Koball, Heather, and Yang Jiang. 2018. "Basic Facts About Low-Income Children." National Center for Children in Poverty. https://files.eric.ed.gov/fulltext/ED590425.pdf. Accessed September 8, 2022.

Koc, I., A. D. Camurdan, U. Beyazova, M. N. Ilhan, and F. Sahin. 2008. "Toilet Training in Turkey: The Factors That Affect Timing and Duration in Different Sociocultural Groups." *Child: Care, Health and Development* 34(4):475–481.

Krafchik, Bernice. 2016. "History of Diapers and Diapering." *International Journal of Dermatology* 55(S1):4–6.

Kruesi, Kimberlee. 2024. "Tennessee, Delaware To Become First States To Offer Free Diapers for Medicaid Families." *Associated Press.* https://apnews.com/article/tennessee-free-diapers-medicaid. Accessed July 18, 2024.

Lafley, A. G. 2013. "What P&G Learned from the Diaper Wars." *Fast Company.* www.fastcompany.com/3005640/what-pg-learned-diaper-wars. Accessed September 1, 2022.

Lan, Pei-Chia. 2018. *Raising Global Families: Parenting, Immigration, and Class in Taiwan and the US*. Redwood City, CA: Stanford University Press.

Lange, Brittany, Ana Luísa B. T. Dáu, Joanne Goldblum, Janet Alfano, and Megan V. Smith. 2017. "A Mixed Methods Investigation of the Experience of Poverty Among a Population of Low-Income Parenting Women." *Community Mental Health Journal* 53(7):832–841.

Lareau, Annette. 2011. *Unequal Childhoods: Class, Race, and Family Life*. Second edition. Berkeley: University of California Press.

Larkin, Jack. 1988. *The Reshaping of Everyday Life: 1790–1840*. New York: HarperPerennial.

Latham, Lisa Moricoli. 1999. "The Diaper Rush of 1999: Cloth Makes a Comeback on the Net." *New York Times*. www.nytimes.com/1999/09/19/business/business-the-diaper-rush-of-1999-cloth-makes-a-comeback-on-the-net.html. Accessed September 29, 2024.

Lee, Max, Janine S. Bruce, Shada Sinclair, Nicola Gerbino, Vanessa Baker-Simon, Elena Vinton, Samhita Kadiyala, Gaby Escobar, Lisa J. Chamberlain, and Baraka Floyd. 2025. "Diapers at the Doctor: Addressing Diaper Need in a Pediatric Clinic." *Journal of Health Care for the Poor and Underserved* 36(1):392–400.

Lemelson-MIT. 2023. "Jaime Lee Curtis: Diaper Pocket." *Consumer Devices Newsletter*. https://lemelson.mit.edu/resources/jamie-lee-curtis. Accessed July 10, 2024.

Lin, Nan, Ning Ding, Emily Meza-Wilson, Amila Manuradha Devasurendra, Christopher Godwin, Sung Kyun Park, and Stuart Batterman. 2023. "Volatile Organic Compounds in Disposable Diapers and Baby Wipes in the US: A Survey of Products and Health Risks." *Environmental Science & Technology* 57(37):13732–13743.

Littler, Jo. 2008. *Radical Consumption: Shopping for Change in Contemporary Culture*. New York: Open University Press.

Livingston, Gretchen. 2018. "Stay-at-Home Moms and Dads Account for About One in Five U.S. Parents." PEW Research Center. www.pewresearch.org/fact-tank/2018/09/24/stay-at-home-moms-and-dads-account-for-about-one-in-five-u-s-parents/.

Lowe, Lezlie. 2018. *No Place To Go: How Public Toilets Fail Our Private Needs*. Toronto, Canada: Coach House.

MacKendrick, Norah. 2014. "More Work for Mother: Chemical Body Burdens as a Maternal Responsibility." *Gender & Society* 28(5):705–728.

Mangizvo, Remigios V., Abigail Lumbe, and Alex Sibanda. 2024. "The Proposed Ban of Disposable Baby Diapers in Zimbabwe: Views from Old Senga Residents, in the City of Gweru, Zimbabwe." *International Journal of Research in Education Humanities and Commerce* 5(1):38–53.

Martin, Katie S. 2021. *Reinventing Food Banks and Pantries: New Tools to End Hunger*. Washington, DC: Island Press.

Massengale, Kelley E. C., Lynn H. Comer, Anna E. Austin, and Joanne S. Goldblum. 2019. "Diaper Need Met Among Low-Income US Children Younger Than 4 Years in 2016." *American Journal of Public Health* 110(1):106–108.

Massengale, Kelley E. C., Jennifer Toller Erausquin, and Michelle Old. 2017a. "Health, Social, and Economic Outcomes Experienced by Families as a Result of Receiving Assistance from a Community-Based Diaper Bank. *Maternal and Child Health Journal* 21(10):1985–1994.

Massengale, Kelley E. C., Jennifer Toller Erausquin, and Michelle Old. 2017b. "Organizational and Health Promotion Benefits of Diaper Bank and Community-Based Organization Partnerships." *Children and Youth Services Review* 76:112–117.

Massengale, Kelley E. C., Melissa A. Jones, Juncheng Liao, Christine Park, and Michelle Old. 2022. "Priority Areas for Child Diaper Access: Low-Income Neighborhoods with Limited Retail Access to the Basic Need of Diapers." *Health Equity* 6(1). http://online.liebertpub.com/doi/10.1089/heq.2021.0192.

Matchar, Emily. 2018. "Meet Marion Donovan, the Mother Who Invented a Precursor to the Disposable Diaper." *Smithsonian Magazine*. www.smithsonianmag.com/innovation/meet-marion-donovan-mother-who-invented-precursor-disposable-diaper-180972118/. Accessed July 6, 2022.

Mendoza, Ronald U. 2011. "Why Do the Poor Pay More? Exploring the Poverty Penalty Concept." *Journal of International Development* 23:1–28.

Meyer, Laura, and Ife Floyd. 2020. "Cash Assistance Should Reach Millions More Families to Lessen Hardship." Center on Budget Policies and Priorities. www.cbpp.org/research/family-income-support/cash-assistance-should-reach-millions-more-families-to-lessen. Accessed February 8, 2022.

Middleton, Georgia, Kaye Mehta, Darlene McNaughton, and Sue Booth. 2018. "The Experiences and Perceptions of Food Banks Amongst Users in High-Income Countries: An International Scoping Review." *Appetite* 120:698–708.

Miller, Joshua, and Luke Tate. 2016. "Innovative Approaches to Closing the Diaper Gap." The White House. https://obamawhitehouse.archives.gov/blog/2016/12/22/innovative-approaches-closing-diaper-gap. Accessed July 19, 2024.

Morse, Ann. 2021. "Fewer Babies Born in December and January but Number Started to Rise in March." United States Census Bureau. www.census.gov/library/stories/2021/09/united-states-births-declined-during-the-pandemic.html. Accessed September 1, 2022.

Mullainathan, Sendhil, and Eldar Shafir. 2013. Scarcity: *Why Having Too Little Means So Much*. New York: Times Publisher.

National Center for Health Statistics. 2022. "Birth Data." Centers for Disease Control and Prevention. www.cdc.gov/nchs/nvss/births.htm. Accessed September 13, 2022.

National Diaper Bank Network. 2020. "Member Survey." https://national diaperbanknetwork.org/wpcontent/uploads/2020/12/2019MemberSurvey .pdf. Accessed September 18, 2022.

National Diaper Bank Network. 2022a. "Annual Report 2021." https:// nationaldiaperbanknetwork.org/2021-annual-report/. Accessed October 31, 2023.

National Diaper Bank Network. 2022b. "2022 Member Survey." https:// nationaldiaperbanknetwork.org/ndbn-annual-member-survey/. Accessed September 13, 2022.

National Diaper Bank Network. 2023. "The NDBN Diaper Check 2023: Diaper Insecurity among U.S. Children and Families." https://national diaperbanknetwork.org/the-ndbn-diaper-check/. Accessed September 13, 2024.

National Resource Center for Health and Safety in Child Care and Early Education. 2022. "Health Promotion and Protection—Hygiene: Diapering and Changing Soiled Clothing." http://nrckids.org/CFOC/Database/3.2.1.1. Accessed September 13, 2022.

Neff, Jack. 2006. "The Battle for the Bottom Line." *AdAge*. https://adage.com /article/print-edition/battle-bottom-line/111523. Accessed September 1, 2022.

Neuhaus, Jessamyn. 2011. *Married to the Mop: Housework and Housewives in Modern American Advertising*. New York: Palgrave Macmillan.

Neuhaus, Jessamyn. 2013a. "Dad Test: Gender, Race, and 'Funny Fathers' in Disposable Diaper Advertising from the 1970s to 2012." *Advertising & Society Review* 14(2). https://doi.org/10.1353/asr.2013.0014. Accessed August 30, 2022.

Neuhaus, Jessamyn. 2013b. "'A Little Bit of Love You Can Wrap Your Baby In': Mothers, Fathers, Race and Representations of Nurturing in 1960s–1970s Pampers Advertising." *Advertising & Society Review* 14(3). https://doi .org/10.1353/asr.2013.0018. Accessed August 30, 2022.

Nobel, Kenneth B. 1981. "Johnson To Phase Out U.S. Diaper Business." *New York Times*. www.nytimes.com/1981/02/12/business/johnson-to-phase-out-us-diaper-business.html. Accessed August 30, 2022.

Notten, Philippa, Alexandra Gower, and Yvonne Lewis. 2021. *Single-Use Nappies and Their Alternatives: Recommendations from Life Cycle Assessment*. United Nations Environment Program. www.lifecycleinitiative.org/library/single -use-nappies-and-their-alternatives/. Accessed March 25, 2024.

Novick, Gina. 2008. "Is There a Bias Against Telephone Interviews in Qualitative Research?" *Research in Nursing & Health* 31(4):391–398.

Ochoa, Analidis, H. Luke Shaefer, and Andrew Grogan-Kaylor. 2021. "The Interlinkage Between Blood Plasma Donation and Poverty in the United States." *Journal of Sociology & Social Welfare* 48(2):56–71.

Odom, Erin. 2013. *Confessions of a Cloth Diaper Convert: A Simple, Comprehensive Guide to Using Cloth Diapers.* Self-published.

Okie, Susan. 1990. "The Disposable Society's 16-Billion Diaper Question." *Washington Post.* www.washingtonpost.com/archive/politics/1990/01/08 /the-disposable-societys-16-billion-diaper-question/. Accessed March 25, 2024.

Orhun, A. Yeşim, and Mike Palazzolo. 2019. "Frugality Is Hard to Afford." *Journal of Marketing Research* 56(1):1–17.

Oswald, Allison. 2012. "From the Archives: Daytime Talk and Invention." Lemelson Center for the Study of Invention and Innovation. https:// invention.si.edu/ archives-daytime-talk-and-invention. Accessed July 6, 2022.

Paddison, Laura. 2021. "Reuse? Compost? Dump? Solving the Eco-Conundrum of Nappies." *The Guardian.* www.theguardian.com/environment/2021 /nov/20/disposable-nappies-plastic-waste-diapers. Accessed March 25, 2024.

Park, Chan Jin, Radwa Barakat, Alexander Ulanov, Zhong Li, Po-Ching Lin, Karen Chiu, Sherry Zhou, Pablo Perez, Jungyeon Lee, Jodi Flaws, and CheMyong Jay Koa. 2019. "Sanitary Pads and Diapers Contain Higher Phthalate Contents Than Those in Common Commercial Plastic Products." *Reproductive Toxicology* 84:114–121.

Parolin, Zachary. 2021. "Temporary Assistance for Needy Families and the Black-White Child Poverty Gap in the United States." *Socio-Economic Review* 19(3):1005–1035.

Parolin, Zachary. 2023. *Poverty in the Pandemic: Policy Lessons from COVID-19.* New York: Russell Sage Foundation.

Parolin, Zachary, Sophie Collyer, Megan A. Curran, and Christopher Wimer. 2021. "The Potential Poverty Reduction Effect of the American Rescue Plan." New York: Center on Poverty and Social Policy at Columbia University. www .povertycenter.columbia.edu/news-internal/2021/presidential-policy /biden-economic-relief-proposal-poverty-impact. Accessed July 19, 2024.

Parolin, Zachary, and Stefano Filauro. 2023. "The United States' Record-Low Child Poverty Rate in International and Historical Perspective: A Research Note." *Demography* 60(6):1665–1673.

Paschall, Katherine. 2018. "Nearly 30 Percent of Infants and Toddlers Attend Home-Based Child Care as Their Primary Arrangement." *Child Trends.* www.childtrends.org/blog/nearly-30-percent-of-infants-and-toddlers- attend-home-based-child-care-as-their-primary-arrangement. Accessed September 13, 2022.

Patel, Ushma, Amy Godecker, Dobie Giles, and Heidi Brown. 2022. "Updated Prevalence of Urinary Incontinence in Women: 2015–2018 National Population-Based Survey Data." *Female Pelvic Medicine & Reconstructive Surgery* 28(4):181–187.

Pew Research Center. 2015. "The American Family Today." www.pewresearch .org/social-trends/2015/12/17/1-the-american-family-today/. Accessed September 22, 2024.

Poppendieck, Janet. 1998. *Sweet Charity?: Emergency Food and the End of Entitlement*. London: Penguin Press.

Porter, Gerald, Jr. 2021. "Diaper Inflation Wrecks Already-Strained Family Budgets in the U.S." *Bloomberg*. www.bloomberg.com/news/articles /2021-07-09/diaper-costs-crush-families-as-p-g-and-kimberly-clark-pass-along-inflation. Accessed February 17, 2025.

Porter, Sallie, and Lorraine Steefel. 2015. "Diaper Need: A Change for Better Health." *Pediatric Nursing* 41(3):141–144.

Povich, Elaine S. 2022. "As Prices Rise, the Push to End Diaper Taxes Grows." *Stateline*. https://stateline.org/2022/07/21/as-prices-rise-the-push-to-end-diaper-taxes-grows/. Accessed July 18, 2024.

Procter & Gamble. 2012. "Pampers: The Birth of P&G's First 10-Billion-Dollar-Brand." *P&G Blog*. https://us.pg.com/blogs/pampers-birth-pgs-first-10 -billion-dollar-brand. Accessed September 1, 2022.

Public Profit. 2021. "Help a Mother Out's Diaper Programs: Evaluation Brief, Alameda & San Francisco Counties." www.helpamotherout.org/impact. Accessed November 4, 2023.

Purcell, Patrick J. 2019. "Trends in Women's Wages, 1981–2015." *Social Security Bulletin* 79, no. 1. www.ssa.gov/policy/docs/ssb/v79n1/v79n1p17 .html#tableA2. Accessed December 29, 2024.

Purdam, Kinglsey, Elisabeth A. Garratt, and Aneez Esmail. 2016. "Hungry? Food Insecurity, Social Stigma and Embarrassment in the UK." *Sociology* 50(6):1072–1088.

Randles, Jennifer. 2020. *Essential Dads: The Inequalities and Politics of Fathering*. Oakland: California University Press.

Randles, Jennifer. 2021. "'Willing To Do Anything for My Kids': Inventive Mothering, Diapers, and the Invisible Inequalities of Carework." *American Sociological Review* 86(1):35–59.

Randles, Jennifer. 2022a. "Addressing Diaper Need as Racial Stratification Through Intersectional Family Justice." *Journal of Marriage and Family* 84(5):1408–1426.

Randles, Jennifer. 2022b. "Fixing a Leaky U.S. Social Safety Net: Diapers, Policy, and Low-Income Families." *Russell Sage Foundation Journal of the Social Sciences: Special Issue on Policy, Work, and Low-Income Families* 8(5):166–183.

Randles, Jennifer. 2022c. "'Why Don't They Just Use Cloth?': Gender Policy Vacuums and the Inequalities of Diapering." *Gender & Society* 36(2):214–238.

Randles, Jennifer, and Megan Carroll. 2019. "Dads and Diaper Ads: A Tough Gender Test." *Feminist Reflections/The Society Pages Blog.* https:// thesocietypages.org/ feminist/2019/02/20/dads-and-diaper-ads-a-tough -gender-test/. Accessed September 22, 2024.

Randles, Jennifer, and Jennifer Sherman. 2023. "Diaper Despair and Deflecting Inequalities." *Contexts* 22(1):12–17.

Randles, Jennifer, Justin van Zerber, Kristian Browning, Balaraman Rajan, and Benito Delgado-Olson. 2024. "Racial Disparities in Incidence of Diaper Dermatitis and Implications for Diaper Inequities." *Health Equity* 8(1):686–691.

Rathje, William L., and Cullen Murphy. 1992. *Rubbish!: The Archaeology of Garbage.* Tucson: University of Arizona Press.

Raver, Cybele, Nicole Letourneau, Jennifer Scott, and Heidi D'Agostino. 2010. "Every Little Bottom: Diaper Need in the U.S. and Canada." http:// nationaldiaperbank network.org/wp-content/uploads/2015/04/huggies-2010-every-little-bottom-study.pdf. Accessed September 9, 2022.

Redd, Zakia. 2014. "Children Still Left Behind 50 Years After War on Poverty." *Child Trends.* www.childtrends.org/publications/children-still-left-behind-50-years-after-war-on-poverty. Accessed July 18, 2024.

Reese, Ellen. 2005. *Backlash Against Welfare Mothers: Past and Present.* Berkeley: University of California Press.

Reich, Jennifer. 2005. *Fixing Families: Parents, Power, and the Child Welfare System.* New York: Routledge.

Renkert, Sarah R., and Richel Filippone. 2023. "The Carework of Cloth Diapering: Opportunities and Challenges for Mitigating Diaper Need." *Human Organization* 82(2):143–152.

Roberts, Dorothy E. 2002. *Shattered Bonds: The Color of Child Welfare.* New York: Civitas.

Roberts, Dorothy E. 2017. *Killing the Black Body: Race, Reproduction, and the Meaning of Liberty.* Second edition. New York: Pantheon.

Roberts, Dorothy E. 2022. *Torn Apart: How the Child Welfare System Destroys Black Families—and How Abolition Can Build a Safer World.* New York: Basic Books.

Rodriguez-Franco, Hiram. 2024. "California Has Helped Fund Diaper Banks for Years. Families Need that Support to Continue." *CalMatters.* https:// calmatters.org/commentary/2024/05/diaper-bank-california-funding-jeopardy/. Accessed July 19, 2024.

Romero, Diana, and Madina Agénor. 2009. "US Fertility Prevention as Poverty Prevention: An Empirical Question and Social Justice Issue." *Women's Health Issues* 19(6):355–364.

Rosenfeld, Jake, Patrick Denice, and Jennifer Laird. 2016. "Union Decline Lowers Wages of Nonunion Workers: The Overlooked Reasons Why Wages Are Stuck and Inequality Is Growing." Economic Policy Institute. www.epi .org/publication/union-decline-lowers-wages-of-nonunion-workers-the-overlooked-reason-why-wages-are-stuck-and-inequality-is-growing/. Accessed August 30, 2022.

Ross, Loretta J., and Rickie Solinger. 2017. *Reproductive Justice: An Introduction.* Oakland: University of California Press.

Sadler, Lois S., Eileen M. Condon, Shirley Z. Deng, Monica Roosa Ordway, Crista Marchesseault, Andrea Miller, Janet Stolfi Alfano, and Alison M. Weir. 2018. "A Diaper Bank and Home Visiting Partnership: Initial Exploration of Research and Policy Questions." *Public Health Nursing* 35(2):135–143.

Safawi, Ali, and Cindy Reyes. 2021. "States Must Continue Recent Momentum to Further Improve TANF Benefit Levels." Center on Budget and Policy Priorities. www.cbpp.org/research/family-income-support/states-must-continue-recent-momentum-to-further-improve-tanf-benefit. Accessed February 8, 2022.

Salcito, Kendyl. 2015. "Why Cloth Diapers Might Not Be the Greener Choice, After All." *Washington Post.* www.washingtonpost.com/opinions/why-cloth-diapers-might-not-be-the-greener-choice-after-all/2015/05/08/32b2d8dc-f43a-11e4-bcc4-e8141e5eb0c9_story.html. Accessed September 13, 2022.

Sarkisian, Natalia, and Naomi Gerstel. 2004. "Kin Support Among Blacks and Whites: Race and Family Organization." *American Sociological Review* 69(6):812–883.

Schley, Courtney. 2018. "The Best Diapers." *New York Times.* www.nytimes .com/wirecutter/reviews/best-diapers/#what-about-eco-friendly-diapers. Accessed September 9, 2022.

Schön, Regine A., and Maarit Silvén. 2007. "Natural Parenting: Back to Basics in Infant Care." *Evolutionary Psychology* 5(1):102–183.

Sedlak, Andrea, Jane Mettenburg, Monica Basena, Ian Petta, Karla McPherson, Angela Greene, and Spencer Li. 2010. *Fourth National Incidence Study of Child Abuse and Neglect (NIS-4): Report to Congress.* US Department of Health and Human Services, Administration for Children and Families.

Semega, Jessica, Melissa Kollar, Emily A. Shrider, and John Creamer. 2020. "Income and Poverty in the United States: 2019." US Census Bureau, Current Population Reports. P60-270. US Government Printing Office: Washington, DC. www.census.gov/content/dam/Census/library/publications /2020/demo/p60-270.pdf. Accessed September 13, 2022.

Shaffer, Emma, Sallie Porter, Eileen Condon, Peijia Zha, and Barbara Caldwell. 2022a. "Associations Between Diaper Need and Child Sleep in Under-

Resourced Families." *Journal of Developmental & Behavioral Pediatrics* 43(7):402–408.

Shaffer, Emma, Sallie Porter, Peijia Zha, and Eileen Condon. 2022b. "Diaper Need as a Measure of Material Hardship during COVID-19." *Nursing Research* 71(2):90–95.

Shah, Hema, and Lisa A. Gennetian. 2024. "Unconditional Cash Transfers for Families with Children in the U.S.: A Scoping Review." *Review of Economics of the Household* 22:415–450.

Shenton, Andrew K. 2004. "Strategies for Ensuring the Trustworthiness in Qualitative Research Projects." *Education for Information* 22(2):63–75.

Sherman, Jennifer. 2013. "Surviving the Great Recession: Growing Need and the Stigmatized Safety Net." *Social Problems* 60(4):409–432.

Sherman, Jennifer. 2021. *Dividing Paradise: Rural Inequality and the Diminishing American Dream.* Oakland: University of California Press.

Shrider, Emily A. 2024. "US Census Bureau, Current Population Reports, P60-283, Poverty in the United States: 2023." US Government Publishing Office, Washington, DC. www2.census.gov/library/publications/2024/demo/p60-283.pdf. Accessed December 18, 2024.

Shrivastava, Aditi, and Gina Azito Thompson. 2022. "TANF Cash Assistance Should Reach Millions More Families to Lessen Hardship: Access to TANF Hits Lowest Point Amid Precarious Economic Conditions." Center for Budget Policy and Priorities. www.cbpp.org/research/family-income-support/policy-brief-cash-assistance-should-reach-millions-more-families. Accessed September 15, 2024.

Silvers, Amy Rabideau. 2011. "Hellerman Kept Diapers Coming: He Ran Dy-Dee Wash for Decades." *Journal Sentinel.* https://archive.jsonline.com/news/obituaries/114252114.html/. Accessed August 2, 2022.

Silverstein, Michael J., and Kate Sayre. 2009. "The Female Economy." *Harvard Business Review.* https://hbr.org/2009/09/the-female-economy. Accessed May 14, 2023.

Smith, AshLee. 2022. "America Has More Children Living in Poverty Than Any Other Rich Nation. Can Guaranteed Income Help?" www.abtglobal.com/insights/perspectives-blog/america-has-more-children-living-in-poverty-than-any-other-rich-nation. Accessed July 19, 2024.

Smith, Martin J., and Patrick J. Kiger. 2004. *Poplorica: A Popular History of the Fads, Mavericks, Inventions, and Lore that Shaped Modern America.* New York: Harper.

Smith, Megan V., Anna Kruse, Alison Weir, and Joanne Goldblum. 2013. "Diaper Need and Its Impact on Child Health." *Pediatrics* 132(2): 253–259.

Sobowale, Kunmi, Ashley Clayton, and Megan V. Smith. 2021. "Diaper Need Is Associated with Pediatric Care Use: An Analysis of a Nationally

Representative Sample of Parents of Young Children." *Journal of Pediatrics* 230(2):146–151.

Solarin, A. U., O. A. Olutekunbi, A. D. Madise-Wobo, and I. Senbanjo. 2017. "Toilet Training Practices in Nigerian Children." *South African Journal of Child Health* 11(3):122–128.

Stack, Carol. 1974. *All Our Kin: Strategies for Survival in a Black Community.* New York: Basic Books.

Stanley, Megan, Ife Floyd, and Misha Hill. 2016. "TANF Cash Benefits Have Fallen by More Than 20 Percent in Most States and Continue To Erode." Center on Budget and Policy Priorities. www.cbpp.org/sites/default/files /atoms/files/10-30-14tanf.pdf. Accessed May 15, 2021.

Strasser, Susan. 1982. *Never Done: A History of American Housework.* New York: Pantheon Books.

Strasser, Susan. 1999. *Waste and Want: A Social History of Trash.* New York: Metropolitan.

Sugimura, Tetsu, Yoshifumi Tananari, Yukiko Ozaki, Yasuki Maeno, Seiji Tanaka, Shinichi Ito, Keiko Kawano, and Kumiko Masunaga. 2009. "Association Between the Frequency of Disposable Diaper Changing and Urinary Tract Infection in Infants." *Clinical Pediatrics* 48(1):18–20.

Sundnes, Anita. 2018. "Developing a Context-Sensitive Understanding of Infant Toilet Training: Cleanliness Regimes Adjusted for Everyday Life Considerations." *International Journal of Early Childhood* 50:279–296.

Swales, Stephanie, Christoper May, Mary Nuxoll, and Christy Tucker. 2020. "Neoliberalism, Guilt, Shame and Stigma: A Lacanian Discourse Analysis of Food Insecurity." *Journal of Community & Applied Social Psychology* 30:673–687.

Swete, Chelsea, and Kye Lippold. 2020. "The Distributional Impacts of Taxes on Health Products: Evidence from Diaper Sales Tax Exemptions." *Social Science Research Network*, University of Chicago. http://dx.doi.org/10.2139 /ssrn.3671021. Accessed July 18, 2024.

Tach, Laura, and Kathryn Edin. 2017. "The Social Safety Net After Welfare Reform: Recent Developments and Consequences for Household Dynamics." *Annual Review of Sociology* 43(1):541–561.

Tach, Laura, Sarah Halpern-Meekin, Kathryn Edin, and Mariana Amorim. 2019. "'As Good as Money in the Bank': Building a Personal Safety Net with the Earned Income Tax Credit." *Social Problems* 66(2):274–293.

Tach, Laura M., and Sara Sternberg Greene. 2014. "'Robbing Peter to Pay Paul': Economic and Cultural Explanations for How Lower-Income Families Manage Debt." *Social Problems* 61(1):1–21.

Takeshita, Chikako. 2014. "Eco-Diapers: The American Discourse of Sustainable Motherhood. In *Mothering in the Age of Neoliberalism*, edited by M. V. Giles, 117–132. Bradford, Ontario: Demeter.

Thaman, Lauren A., and Lawrence F. Eichenfield. 2014. "Diapering Habits: A Global Perspective." *Pediatric Dermatology* 31(S1):15–18.

Thomas, Robert, Jr. 1998. "Marion Donovan, 81, Solver of the Damp-Diaper Problem." *New York Times*. www.nytimes.com/1998/11/18/business /marion-donovan-81-solver-of-the-damp-diaper-problem.html. Accessed July 6, 2022.

Thompson, Gina Azito, Diana Azevedo-McCaffrey, and Da'Shon Carr. 2023. "Increases in TANF Cash Benefit Levels Are Critical To Help Families Meet Rising Costs." Center for Budget Policy and Priorities. www.cbpp.org /research/income-security/increases-in-tanf-cash-benefit-levels-are-critical-to-help-families-meet. Accessed September 15, 2024.

Timmermans, Stefan, and Iddo Tavory. 2012. "Theory Construction in Qualitative Research: From Grounded Theory to Abductive Analysis." *Sociological Theory* 30(3):167–186.

Trisi, Danilo. 2024. "Expiration of Pandemic Relief Led to Record Increases in Poverty and Child Poverty in 2022." Center on Budget Policy and Priorities. www.cbpp.org/research/poverty-and-inequality/expiration-of-pandemic-relief-led-to-record-increases-in-poverty. Accessed September 13, 2024.

Twigg, Julia. 2000. "Carework as a Form of Bodywork." *Ageing and Society* 20(4):389–412.

UNICEF. 2020. "Universal Child Benefits: Policy Issues and Options." www .unicef.org/media/70416/file/Universal-child-benefits-Briefing-2020.pdf. Accessed May 1, 2024.

United Kingdom Environment Agency. 2008. "An Updated Lifecycle Assessment Study for Disposable and Reusable Nappies." Science Report SC010018/SR2. www.gov.uk/government/publications/an-updated-lifecycle-assessment-for-disposable-and-reusable-nappies. Accessed September 13, 2022.

Urban Institute. 2024. "State Fiscal Brief: Michigan." www.urban.org/policy-centers/cross-center-initiatives/state-and-local-finance-initiative/projects /state-fiscal-briefs/michigan. Accessed July 18, 2024.

US Bureau of Labor Statistics. 2023. "Consumer Price Index." www.bls.gov /opub/hom/cpi/concepts. Accessed July 19, 2024.

US Consumer Product Safety Commission. 2024. "Baby Changing Products Business Guidance and Small Entity Compliance Guide." www.cpsc.gov /Business—Manufacturing/Business-Education/Business-Guidance/Baby-Changing-Products. Accessed September 28, 2024.

US Department of Agriculture. 2021. "What Can SNAP Buy?" www.fns.usda .gov/snap/eligible-food-items. Accessed September 19, 2022.

US Department of Agriculture. 2025. "WIC Program." USDA Economic Research Service. www.ers.usda.gov/topics/food-nutrition-assistance/wic-program. Accessed January 9, 2025.

US Department of Health and Human Services. 2018. "2018 Poverty Guidelines." Office of Planning and Evaluation. https://aspe.hhs.gov/2018-poverty-guidelines. Accessed November 16, 2019.

US Department of Health and Human Services. 2024. "Newborn Supply Kits Reduce Maternal Stress and Improve Trust in Government: Results of the 2023 Newborn Supply Kit Pilot Program." www.hhs.gov/sites/default/files/newborn-supply-kit-pilot-program.pdf. Accessed December 30, 2024.

US Department of Labor. 2021. "Mothers and Families." www.dol.gov/agencies/wb/data/mothers-and-families. Accessed August 30, 2022.

US Environmental Protection Agency. 2020. "Advancing Sustainable Materials Management: Facts and Figures Report." *Facts and Figures about Materials, Waste and Recycling.* www.epa.gov/facts-and-figures-about-materials-waste-and-recycling/advancing-sustainable-materials-management. Accessed September 13, 2022.

Vidal, John. 2018. "Baby Diapers Are Hiding Some Dirty, Dangerous Secrets." *HuffPost.* www.huffpost.com/entry/baby-diapers-ocean-plastic. Accessed May 1, 2021.

Walker, Madeline. 2014. "Intensive Mothering, Elimination Communication and the Call to Eden." In *Intensive Mothering: The Cultural Contradictions of Modern Motherhood*, edited by L. R. Ennis, 233–246. Ontario, Canada: Demeter Press.

Wallace, Lori R., Alison M. Weir, and Megan V. Smith. 2017. "Policy Impact of Research Findings on the Association of Diaper Need and Mental Health." *Women's Health Issues* 27-S1:S14–S21.

Wels, Kelly. 2012. *Changing Diapers: The Hip Mom's Guide to Modern Cloth Diapering.* Waterford, ME: Green Team Enterprises.

Whitson, Gordon. 2019. "How a Brand Name Becomes Generic." *New York Times.* www.nytimes.com/2019/06/24/smarter-living/how-a-brand-name-becomes-generic.html. Accessed January 16, 2023.

Williams, Joan. 2000. *Unbending Gender: Why Family and Work Conflict and What To Do About It.* Oxford, UK: Oxford University Press.

Williams, Sarah C., Reva Dalela, and Sharon Vandivere. 2022. "In Defining Maltreatment, Nearly Half of States Do Not Specifically Exempt Families' Financial Inability to Provide." *Child Trends.* www.childtrends.org/publications/in-defining-maltreatment-nearly-half-of-states-do-not-specifically-exempt-families-financial-inability-to-provide. Accessed September 14, 2024.

Wimer, Christopher, Ryan Vinh, Jiwan Lee, and Sophie Collyer. 2024. "2023 Poverty Rates in Historical Perspective." *Poverty and Social Policy Brief.* 8, no. 4 www.povertycenter.columbia.edu/publication/2023-poverty-rates-in-historical-perspective. Accessed December 18, 2024.

Wolraich, Mark. 2016. *The American Academy of Pediatrics Guide to Toilet Training*. Second edition. New York: Bantam.

World Health Organization (WHO) and United Nations Children's Fund (UNICEF). 2019. *Progress on Household Drinking Water, Sanitation and Hygiene 2000–2017: Special Focus on Inequalities*. https://apps.who.int/iris /handle/10665/329370. Accessed September 1, 2022.

Wynes, Seth, and Kimberly A. Nicholas. 2017. "The Climate Mitigation Gap: Education and Government Recommendations Miss the Most Effective Individual Actions." *Environmental Research Letters* 12(7). https:// iopscience.iop.org/article/10.1088/1748-9326/aa7541. Accessed March 27, 2024.

Yoshida, Akiko. 2012. "Dads Who Do Diapers: Factors Affecting Care of Young Children by Fathers." *Journal of Family Issues* 33(4):451–477.

Zelizer, Viviana A. 1985. *Pricing the Priceless Child: The Changing Social Value of Children*. Princeton, NJ: Princeton University Press.

Zippel, Claire. 2021. "9 in 10 Families with Low Incomes Are Using Child Tax Credits to Pay for Necessities, Education." Center on Budget and Policy Priorities. www.cbpp.org/blog/9-in-10-families-with-low-incomes-are -using-child-tax-credits-to-pay-for-necessities-education. Accessed September 13, 2024.

Index

abortion, 25, 154; and diaper policies, 165; industry of, 166

adult incontinence products, 17, 46, 182, 184. *See also* diapers

advertising, 36, 45, 70, 135; diversity of American families in, 56; gendered message for disposable diapers in, 48–58, 60, 70, 119–20; medical authority and expertise in, 52; Spanish-language used for Pampers, 55; Super Bowl used for disposable diapers, 61. *See also* disposable diapers

African Americans, 1–8, 16, 53–55, 63, 68, 74–75, 85, 88–90, 95, 99–102, 123, 127–30, 150, 155–58, 172–73, 180, 183, 186, 189–95, 198–99. *See also* mothers of color

Afro-Latina Americans, 83, 123

Aid to Families with Dependent Children (AFDC), 141–42

Allen, Debbie, 55

Amazon, 95

American Academy of Pediatrics, 37, 62

American Baby magazine, 107

American Dream, 129

American Rescue Plan Act (2021), 147

America's Second Harvest (Feeding America), 174

Apple, Rima, 47

Arizona, 173–74, 176

Asian Americans, 75, 79, 96, 101, 151–52, 155, 180, 198. *See also* mothers of color

Association of Women's Health, Obstetric and Neonatal Nurses, 166

Australia, 147

Babylist.com, 120

baby supply banks, 127, 158, 187–88. *See also* diaper banks

Baby2Baby (nonprofit organization), 136, 164

Believe Diapers, 136

birth control, 160

Bombeck, Erma, 106

Brazelton, Dr. T. Berry, 62–63

breastfeeding, 35, 94, 117, 121, 123, 164, 193. *See also* women

Brown, Kathleen, 43

budget: diaper need and household, 87, 89–92; precarity of household, 14–15, 53, 73–79, 92. *See also* families

Calarco, Jessica, 206

California, 7, 111–12, 151, 155–56; Medi-Cal in, 161; state diaper voucher program of, 161–62, 214–15. *See also* CalWORKS

www.ingramcontent.com/pod-product-compliance
Lightning Source LLC
Chambersburg PA
CBHW032345280326
41935CB00008B/457